COMPUTERS
in Management and Business Studies

COMPUTERS
in Management and Business Studies

HAROLD LUCAS

B.Com., B.Sc.(Econ.), A.C.I.S., M.I.S., A.M.B.I.M.
North East London Polytechnic

Second Edition

MACDONALD AND EVANS

MACDONALD & EVANS LTD.
Estover, Plymouth PL6 7PZ

First published 1973
Reprinted 1975
Reprinted 1976
Second edition 1979

©

MACDONALD & EVANS LTD.
1979

ISBN: 0 7121 0390 2

*Filmset in 'Monophoto' Times 10 on 11 pt. and
printed in Great Britain by
Richard Clay (The Chaucer Press), Ltd.
Bungay, Suffolk*

PREFACE TO THE FIRST EDITION

This book is primarily concerned with the uses of computers and other forms of data processing equipment in business. Its aim is to meet the needs of students reading for the following courses.

1. Institute of Cost and Management Accountants.

2. Institute of Chartered Accountants and Association of Certified Accountants and, also, Institute of Chartered Secretaries and Administrators, in so far as a knowledge of data processing is required under various syllabuses. The Joint Diploma in Management Accounting Services and the Certificate in Management Information (Design of Systems and Data Processing) have also been taken into account.

3. Institute of Work Study Practitioners, Institute of Administrative Management and O. and M. Society.

4. C.N.A.A. Degrees in the field of business and accounting, which are likely to have a computer content.

5. Diplomas in Management Studies, which may require easily assimilated reading on systems and computing related to the other subjects of study.

6. Higher National Diplomas and Certificates in Business Studies offering the syllabus in Business Data Processing.

7. Ordinary Diplomas and Certificates in Business Studies offering Elements of Computers. The emphasis of this syllabus is less directed to systems than is that for the Higher National, but students and teachers should find the coverage is satisfactory, while later being of use when studies are continued.

8. Non-examination courses attended by a large body of managers, business men, clerks and office machine operators, often at their firm's behest.

Readers should find that the manner of developing the subject is simple to follow and avoids unnecessary technicalities, the aim being to meet the needs of potential computer users. Some technical points, together with a brief historical review and an account of binary arithmetic, have been dealt with in the appendix. They are required by some syllabuses and may be regarded as providing a wider basis for the appreciation of computing, if somewhat ir-relevant to the immediate needs of computer users.

Approaches to teaching computing vary, often depending on the equipment, if any, available. A particular problem is that of pro-gramming. An appreciation of COBOL, as the chief commercial language, has been included. This is the language suggested for Ordinary National courses and in the Higher National guide syllabus.

Earlier in the book simple illustrations of programming in BASIC have been used. This may be of particular interest to in-stitutions equipped with terminal facilities, though the simplicity of the language may recommend it for introductory programming in other cases. It is likely that BASIC will be accepted as the language in which those who are not computer specialists will converse with computer systems in the future. Students with no previous know-ledge can produce results with it in about half an hour, and ex-perience shows that the insight obtained is not wasted when, if ever, more complex languages are tackled. It is widely available on com-puter time-sharing systems and the interactive techniques involved are of considerable value to students on the threshold of a world of real-time computing.

Managers and those employed in business, whether in a pro-fessional capacity or at more humble levels, are recognising the need to know something of the way computers will affect their jobs. The more forward-thinking may regard the development of sophisti-cated computer techniques as offering them opportunities for achieving better results, coupled with widened responsibilities and promotion.

The writer's experience in training such persons over several years is that the main wish is to see how computers can be put to practical use in business. This implies some knowledge of the physi-cal features of computers and their associated equipment, but, to a far greater extent, it involves an appreciation of how they fit into and affect business systems. We shall not be too much concerned with "taking the lid off the works", rather shall we consider how available apparatus can be made to achieve results.

The impact of computers is recognised as so far-reaching that it has been suggested that all students should have at least an ap-preciation of them built into their curriculum. With man-agement, professional and business students such a course might follow the lines of this book. It is also hoped that students of the technical and design aspects of computing and of computer operat-ing and programming may find the coverage helps in broadening their knowledge. Specialist examinations include those of the

British Computer Society, City and Guilds of London Institute, Institute of Data Processing, National Computing Centre, Royal Society of Arts, Scottish Council for Commercial, Administrative and Professional Education, as well as National and Higher National Diplomas and Certificates in Computer Studies.

At the end of each chapter will be found a selection of specimen examination questions.

Information on computer equipment, facilities and uses has been generously provided by the computer industry. Where use has been made of diagrams, print-outs and systems an acknowledgment is made in the text.

March 1973   H.L.

PREFACE TO THE SECOND EDITION

The silicon chip, or microprocessor, revolution, together with other advances in technology and systems, has made it desirable to produce this new edition. At the same time the title has been extended to reflect more clearly the content and purposes of the book, previously entitled *Computers in Business Studies*. With the trend towards the separation of Business, Commerce and Accounting on the one hand and Management (linked with the development of Regional Management Centres) on the other, in the organisation of education, it is felt that the suitability of the treatment for both types of studies should be stressed. This was the original intention and experience shows that the text has satisfactorily met the needs of a wide range of students and of more general readers.

The basic aim of the book remains that of providing a reliable, comprehensive and easily-digested account of business computing, data processing and management information systems for the use of students and of practising business men, managers, accountants, company secretaries, organisation and methods, management services and systems specialists and other professionals engaged in business systems.

In preparing the new text the opportunity has been taken to rearrange some of the material. In particular, the old first chapter on Management Information Systems has been placed later, linked with Systems Analysis and Organisation and Methods. What used to be the second chapter, concerned largely with the older forms of data processing, has been eliminated, except for a few pages still of interest which now appear in the Appendix.

The section on BASIC programming (Chapter 3) has been considerably strengthened and should serve as a simple programming manual for students with computing facilities, in particular those using terminals or minis or microcomputers. In cases where syllabuses do not demand programming experience this can still be a valuable adjunct to learning, especially if self-directed.

A new chapter (11) surveys some of the wider implications of computing for management and workers, examines the "electronic business office" concept and looks at the socially significant topic of computers and privacy.

Specimen questions at the end of each chapter are now based on typical and likely questions of the various examining bodies, not on reproductions of past questions. It is felt that this gives greater scope for grading questions, for covering a wide range of topics and for avoiding questions which soon become dated.

The author would like to express his thanks for the many helpful suggestions he has received from users of the book and from comments of reviewers. He hopes it will continue to serve the needs of teachers, students and more general readers.

July, 1979   H.L.

CONTENTS

LIST OF ILLUSTRATIONS

Chapter 1

COMPUTERS

INTRODUCTION TO COMPUTER SYSTEMS

Office systems are largely concerned with processing information, which is the very thing computers were invented to do. We shall go into much more detail as to how they do it in the following chapters. For the moment we may regard a computer as equipment which is capable of being programmed to handle many different types of information to match the needs of particular situations. Computers have been likened to brains which can be trained to cope with specific problems. They store some information in their memories but can also draw on other sources from input devices (in the same way as a clerk might refer to a ledger or set of tables). They can perform calculations and assemble information in particular ways (as a clerk could put names in alphabetical order) and also compare data and use the comparison to determine their next action. Finally, they can make relevant results available through output devices to their human masters (equivalent to jotting down a total or typing a report). They can do no more than follow strictly the instructions (programs) fed into them, which must provide for any contingencies before they occur, whereas an experienced clerk dealing with the same problems might be able to cope with them by using his discretion. Computers, if they are justified at all in being likened to human brains, must be regarded as very low down the intelligence scale. Their virtues arise from their speed of handling information, once it has been input to them, and the reliability with which they can repeatedly process information without error. The saying "garbage in, garbage out" helps to sum up the situation that computer results depend on the accuracy of the data and programs with which we feed them. The human brain, sometimes called the "wet computer", is limited and fallible in handling large calculations and masses of data but it can think and speedily adapt its thought processes, of which the workings are not fully understood.

Computers may be conveniently divided into three categories.

1. Large, mainframe computers.
2. Minicomputers, including visible record computers.
3. Microcomputers, including pocket and desk calculators.

1

However clear may have been the dividing lines in the early and middle 1970s, they have been eroded by rapid technological advances. Large computers incorporate microtechnology, of which some details are given in the Appendix. Microsystems may reproduce some or all of the characteristics of certain large computers. Minis acquire increasingly sophisticated programming facilities and larger memories. This implies that there are problems in classifying certain equipment.

Mainframe computers

These were the first computers, now improved almost out of all recognition. They are capable of handling masses of data and long programs. Generally associated with a centralised computing service which undertakes the data processing of functional divisions of a business, such as accounting, production planning and research, they may also be the heart of more dispersed processing, such as through time-sharing terminals (*see* Chapter 4). Mainframe computers come in a wide range of sizes and capabilities. Designs vary between manufacturers who themselves usually offer a range of models. An unfortunate feature of the multiplicity of manufacturers and designs in the early stages of computing, later to be somewhat ameliorated by amalgamations, was the incompatibility of the ranges of different manufacturers. The programming aspects of this were softened by the development of high level languages, such as COBOL and FORTRAN (*see* page 14). By the mid 1970s mainframes were being developed which have no special characteristics until these are inserted using an appropriate microcode (*see* page 21).

Mainframe computers tend to be expensive in capital outlay and the development of appropriate systems. Their introduction requires long and often costly planning and preparation. Managers may be tempted to try to hurry things along, possibly with disastrous consequences. On the bright side, large computers can effectively and speedily deal with large scale processing and can handle a number of applications concurrently. Effectiveness is, however, not built into the computer; it depends on the skill with which it is used, which is bound up with the effectiveness of its programs and the speeds at which associated equipment, known as peripherals, can operate.

Minicomputers

During the early 1970s minicomputers became significant in business use. They appealed both to some users of mainframe computers, generally larger organisations wishing to disperse some aspects of their computing, and also to smaller businesses whose scale of operations did not justify acquiring a mainframe system. Minis have not been precisely defined but they are made up of compact apparatus which can be used under normal office conditions and are cheap compared with mainframe systems. They are usually designed to perform a defined set of applications using limited memory and processing facilities. Accounting is an obvious example but minis have been used in manufacturing, an example being the numerical control of machine tools. Flexibility can be achieved by a variety of input and output devices, linked to the processing units, and also by the possibility of having a number of minis in a large organisation. These can be grouped in various ways to cope with batches of work and switched from one job to another. They may be linked with mainframe computers, sometimes being used as intelligent terminals, to relieve the load on a main computer by a process known as "front ending". Another approach is to produce summarised tapes as a by-product of their processing. These can later be input to a main computer, perhaps for management control purposes.

Developing sales of minis have destroyed the dominance of mainframe computers. Not only have minis mopped up the smaller end of the market but larger minis threaten to supplant mainframes for larger applications. Mini facilities are available which enable systems to be expanded so that several minis act as one computer. Mainframe manufacturers, once reluctant to produce minis, now generally offer a range from small minis to large mainframe systems. They are still subject to effective competition from specialist producers of minis.

Visible Record Computers

On the margin between older types of accounting machines and minis is the visible record computer (V.R.C.) which uses a ledger card on which limited information can be encoded in one or more vertical stripes of magnetisable material deposited on the card. These details are also printed on the account card so that they can be read by the user. Account numbers of customers, action levels for stock and the balance to date are examples of what can be recorded on the stripe. When such a card is used this information is read from the stripe by the equipment and avoids the possibility of errors, such as when an operator types in the previous balance at the start of a conventional machine-ledger posting operation. The data on the stripe is recorded at low density so that the card may be handled and subjected to normal atmospheric risks of dust, etc., without fear of the record deteriorating. The cards are fed into a magnetic ledger console or card processor by a top feed system, or some variation, such as horizontally from the desk top. When processed they are disposed of by stacking or returned to the operator.

Microcomputers

These ultra-small computers result from the development of silicon chip technology. Some technical aspects are considered in the Appendix. The significance for businessmen is that the essentials of a computer can be compressed into incredibly small circuitry etched into tiny chips of silicon only a few millimetres square. Such chips have to be provided with electrical contacts to form micro-processors which can then be incorporated in computers and other systems. Chips performing separate functions may be coupled but a single chip can incorporate a processing unit, preprogrammed memory and variable memory for data. With mass production such computers can be sold very cheaply. They are light and easily portable and can offer high technical reliability although input and output devices are still needed which are not easily reduced in size, since keyboards, print units and display screens have to be on a scale compatible with human operators. Such devices can also be expensive. However, a television receiver, primarily used for other purposes, may act as a visual display unit (V.D.U.). From the mid-1970s many homes acquired sophisticated television games which depended on microcomputer techniques and personal computers became a reality.

The comparatively small memories of early microcomputers call for supplementary storage by means of discs and tapes but developments in chip memory technology are providing microcomputers with memories to rival the larger mainframe computers of the past.

Microprocessors have not only a use as components of microcomputers but may be incoporated in all sorts of mechanisms and systems to perform control functions. They may provide the key to a revolution in automation. Incorporated in computer terminals they can convert the latter into intelligent terminals having features of small scale computers. This theme is further developed in Chapter 11.

Calculators

A minor revolution was effected in the 1970s by the spread of small electronic calculators, both desk models and the ubiquitous pocket type. Costs decreased rapidly, as did size and weight, while the calculations offered became increasingly sophisticated. Essentially these devices are small computers using silicon chips programmed to perform calculations by pressing the appropriate keys. Facilities for storing data tend to be very limited and such data is usually lost when the calculator is switched off, though it is technically possible to produce calculators which retain data when power is disconnected. Some calculators can be programmed to perform a limited number of operations in sequence. The programs may be keyed in and not retained when the device is switched off or, alternatively, recorded, in some instances on plastic strips which can be fed in when required. A limited form of print-out is available on some models, thus reproducing a feature much valued on some of the older mechanical calculators. Equipment to handle special types of calculation, such as occur in statistics and financial mathematics, has been developed. Calculators have been incorporated in wrist watches; they can play games and contain educational programs. Alphabetic information is accepted by some and can be retained, so that the calculator acts as a memo pad. A pocket language translator for common words is available. ✓

HARDWARE AND SOFTWARE

Computer systems involve the use of hardware and software.

Hardware consists of the equipment from which users make a selection to be linked together to meet their particular processing needs. The resulting hardware system of any user is often called a computer configuration. It comprises the computer proper, generally called the central processing unit (C.P.U.), together with devices joined or interfaced with it for data input and output and for external storage purposes, which are known as peripherals. A greatly simplified schematic arrangement is shown in Fig. 1. It must be emphasised that almost any number of combinations of peripherals may be linked to a computer. Such apparatus is said to be on-line when it is directly under the control of the central processor, such as when a card-reading device is used for data input, or a line printer for output. It is said to be off-line when it operates independently of the computer, such as when a card punch is used to prepare cards for subsequent computer input. Different configurations may be suited to entirely different requirements for processing, taking into account factors such as the volume of data to be processed, whether it is chiefly commercial or scientific, whether the processing is to be centralised or dispersed, and whether the data can be handled in batches, where a particular type of processing is done once a week or month, or has to be dealt with urgently as it arises.

Software is the name given to the programs which determine

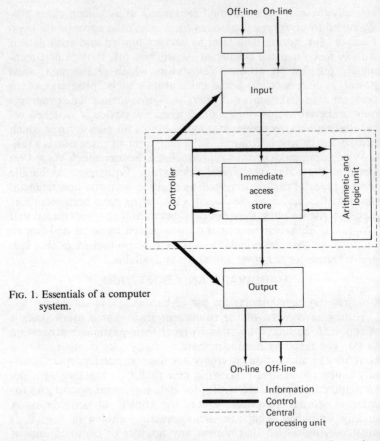

FIG. 1. Essentials of a computer
     system.

how data is handled by the hardware to achieve desired results.
Programs consist of sequences of instructions which control with
strict logic the items of data to be dealt with at a particular time,
what arithmetic and other processes are performed on them, and
which of the peripherals are being used for input and output at
particular stages of the processing. Computer manufacturers have
to provide at least basic software, permanently kept in store and
generally not accessible to users. These are referred to as operating
systems (O.S.) or executive programs. They enable the computer to
carry out basic manipulation of data and its input and output, and
also enable other programs to run, including systems such as multiprogramming, under which several programs operate apparently
simultaneously. There are also utility programs applicable to peripheral units, controlling the way they handle data. Beyond this,

software consists of programs which control computers to achieve particular objectives for their users, including special programs called compilers which are essential if programming is to be simplified by being done in a standardised programming language. We shall later consider aspects of this type of programming in some detail. At the moment we may note that hardware is useless without appropriate software, which may be costly and time-consuming to produce to meet the needs of a particular user and has to be paid for even when of the general purpose type available from the computer manufacturer.

CENTRAL PROCESSING UNITS

The central processing unit (C.P.U.) of a computer configuration has three main elements—a control system, an arithmetic and logic unit (A.L.U.) and a memory or store.

Control

The basic operation of a computer depends on rapidly recurring electrical pulses which permeate and activate the whole central processing unit. A distinction is made between synchronous working, in which a clock is used to generate equally spaced signals which control the timing of all operations, and asynchronous working, in which an operation is initiated by the completion of the previous operation. This difference is important also in connection with the transmission of data over telephone and other lines (*see* Chapter 4). Computer control is not a single process but the user takes this and related technical matters for granted, being chiefly interested in the program controller. This interprets and implements the instructions supplied by the programs residing in the computer memory at any time and also by the switches on the control panel on the computer console, together with the control keyboard on which certain commands may be typed.

Arithmetic and logic unit

This is the unit which performs calculations and can also distinguish between the truth or falseness of statements relating to the data, such as arise from comparisons as to whether, say, one number is bigger than another. The unit works at very high speed using binary arithmetic in which each number can be represented electronically by a series of "on" or "off" states, generally employing minute transistors in small chips of silicon. This is explained more fully in the Appendix. Computer users do not usually need to concern themselves with the binary system of calculation since computers normally accept decimal (denary) datum, which is converted internally to binary form for calculation and storage, after which the results are output in denary form. Human beings are much happier at recognising and performing calculations with numbers composed of the numerals from 0 to 9. It is much easier to design reliable computers, however, if all their data can be built up from just two digits, 0 and 1. This is the reason for the name "digital computer" because it first breaks down all its information into this basic digital form, in which it can be subsequently processed electronically at fantastic speeds. An appreciation of computers is considerably enhanced by an understanding of the binary approach, to which we shall briefly return in the present chapter in connection with computer memory.

Memory or Immediate Access Store

The memory or immediate access store (I.A.S.) of a computer contains information which is rapidly available to the rest of the central processing unit. It is the combination of such a store with fast calculating facilities that places the computer in a class apart from the rest of data processing equipment.

The store is normally split into two sections—a main memory and a buffer memory (sometimes called a register, accumulator or scratch pad). The buffer is used to hold data on which operations are being currently performed. It has to work at high speed and in ·practice governs the rate at which the whole computer can operate. It tends to be a more expensive form of storage than the main memory which has a vastly greater capacity and has to be produced using a technology giving a cheaper storage cost for each item of data, though this implies a slower response. The size of the memory is very significant in determining the ways in which the computer can be made to handle data, with implications for the time processes will take. For example, sorting is much more efficient and speedy if all the data can be accommodated at once in the memory instead of requiring four magnetic tape units to juggle with the data as with external sorting.

How is this storage achieved? The first need is a simple way of coding data such as is afforded by the binary system. All numbers are built up from just two symbols—1, indicating the presence of a digit, and 0, showing its absence. On the decimal system we have units, tens, hundreds etc. as we move successively from right to left. The binary system doubles the value as we make similar progress from the extreme right hand units column, so that, if we have five positions, they are respectively equal to 16, 8, 4, 2 and 1. The number 25 would be indicated in binary notation as 11001, which is the equivalent of $16 + 8 + (no\ 4) + (no\ 2) + 1 = 25$. The essential point is that data expressed as 11001 can be stored by any method that can indicate the presence or the absence of the digit in any position.

Each position or component of a binary number is known as a bit (binary digit) and our example is of a 5-bit number. We may also note that in computer work it is convenient to regard a sequence of such bits as a unit for computer operation, referred to as a byte. A byte may represent one or more numeric characters or alphabetic characters. It is obvious that four adjacent bits, representing 8, 4, 2 and 1 are sufficient to cope with any numeric character from 0 to 9, while more will be required for alphabetic characters. A byte consisting of eight bits might cope with two numeric or one alpha character. A computer may operate on a word rather than a character basis. This is a unit of data for purposes of computer handling and may be of variable length or of a fixed number of bits, from 12 to 64. When computer storage capacity is being quoted it is important to distinguish between these units. The capacity may be quoted in terms of characters, bytes or words, with the letter K and a number. The K (kilo) implies a thousand, and a 16K byte store would actually hold 16,384 bytes, since powers of two are used. Such a store (2^{14}) would hold twice the information of an 8K store, of which the capacity would be one step down on the binary scale at 2^{13} or 8,192.

Having translated our data into an "on or off" type of code the next requirement for storage is that equipment should be devised capable of holding large quantities of such coded data in a readily located manner. Immediate access storage achieves this by using a large number of devices which can be switched on or off, each indicating the presence or absence of a bit and all assembled into a matrix of rows and columns, as shown in Fig. 2.

From the early 1970s silicon chip technology became dominant, of which further details are given in the Appendix. One method is to represent bits by minute capacitors which may be charged or not. Transistors act as current switches, enabling appropriate cells to be selected by activating the row and column having the cell at their intersection. The charges on the capacitors have to be regenerated at short intervals and after information has been read from memory. The previous form of technology had made use of ferrite cores, small rings of material, up to a millimetre diameter, which could be magnetised (or flipped) when sufficient current was passed through two wires at right angles which passed through the centre of each core. These wires formed the rows and columns of the memory matrix, having a core at each intersection, which could

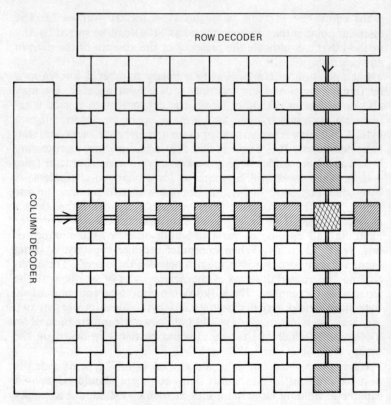

FIG: 2. A 64-bit memory matrix, consisting of eight rows and eight columns. The shaded cell has been selected by activating the appropriate row and column lines. In the older type of core store each cell would be a small (say 1 mm diam.) ring or core of ferrite threaded by horizontal and vertical wires. With silicon chip integrated storage a complete store of several thousand bits could be compressed into the area of one such core. Switching would be by tiny transistors and each cell could be a minute capacitor. A selected cell may be regarded as binary 1, and combinations of cells enable binary information to be stored.

be selected and flipped by passing current through the appropriate row and column wires.

Some memory systems are volatile, that is they retain their contents only while the electric current is on. Such is the case of silicon chip memories as just described. Other forms may be non-volatile or static, retaining the information even when the power is off, requiring action to destroy their contents or to replace or overwrite them with new material. Ferrite cores and bubble memories (*see* later) are non-volatile as are, necessarily, most forms of backing store, such as magnetic tape and magnetic disc stores, together with physical means of recording data, such as by punching holes in paper tape or card.

Computer store or memory serves two main purposes. First, it holds the data that the computer will need to use in its arithmetic and logic operations, together with strings of text used in print-out. Second, there are sets of instructions, known as programs, which control the operations to be carried out on this data and their sequence. Both data and programs have also to be fed into the computer memory as input, while the processing would be of little value if some results were not made available as output. The program will take charge of this, informing the computer of the appropriate peripherals to be used as it progresses.

Read-only Memory

We have noted that the success of the first real computers depended on their ability to store programs, of infinite variety, which could be fed into the memory and used by the computer as required. Additionally, certain basic processes could be programmed by permanent circuitry. A development associated particularly with minicomputers and micro-processors is the read-only memory (ROM) which is a memory preprogrammed to control specified operations and which the user cannot change. Such memories are especially suited to programs which are used repeatedly without alteration, a situation for which the term read-most memory has been coined. Pocket calculators have used this type of program for standard, keyed operations, as have many business and accounting processors. These memories have been designed and manufactured for specific purposes or may be based on standard circuitry containing fusible links which can be blown according to a pattern which will provide the appropriate program. The latter version is usually called programmable read-only memory (PROM), but it is only programmable once. More versatile is the optically erasable read-only memory (EROM) which can be restored to a blank state by an ultra-violet device preparatory to reprogramming the whole memory, since it is not practical to select parts of the program for alteration. Such selectivity is available with electrically alterable read-only memory (EAROM). These devices are collectively referred to as erasable programmable read-only memory (EPROM). The term firmware may be used to denote programs originating as software which are incorporated permanently or semipermanently in hardware circuits. Programs are sometimes said to be burnt in to chips.

Random Access Memory and Serial Devices

Read-only memories are non-volatile, the program being established by the transistor linkage pattern in the silicon chips which contain them, unlike the silicon chip programmable immediate access store which is volatile. Both are examples of random access memory (RAM) which implies that any part of the memory is almost immediately accessible. Some forms of memory offer serial access, implying that the memory bits have to be read in sequence. This is the case of many peripheral devices, such as magnetic tape units. These are examined in the following chapter. In our present context we may note charge coupled devices (C.C.D.) in which the bits circulate through a sequence of storage locations. They are volatile but require less space than random access devices for the same amount of information. Magnetic bubble memories are non-volatile, consisting of magnetic domains which move about in chips, generally of garnet, offering a very compact approach to storing information. Cost is a major consideration. It is a major reason for the division of memory between immediate access store (which is highly effective and speedy for processing, but costly) and backing store (which is relatively slow and has to be linked with the computer, but tends to be cheap). Data which is used infrequently tends to be located on backing store, for cheapness, until required for processing.

Virtual Systems

At the risk of bewildering those who are meeting computers for the first time we may note that it has become common to make available to users a sort of combined hardware and software known as a virtual system and incorporating a virtual memory. Such a system simulates the physical resources of an actual or desirable computer. The concept is useful for a number of reasons. It facilitates effective operation of multiprogramming and time-sharing (*see* Chapter 4), by which several users can have access to the computer concurrently. It solves some of the problems related to the running of large programs which tend to overload the memory. Also, it simplifies programming, since users of different equipment may treat it as though they have the same system. The user programs the virtual system as though it actually exists in hardware form. These benefits may be somewhat offset by reduced speed of processing. When a computer is programmed by hardware to act like another computer the process is described as emulation. It is a feature of modern computer systems using microcode or flexiware.

SOFTWARE

Programming Languages

Fundamentally the only way of "talking" to a computer is by writing a program in what is known as machine code, in which binary digits provide the basic instructions. Manufacturers of computers must have staff who can write such instructions in order to provide the other language facilities described below, but the average user will not wish to program his computer at this level. Such programming guides the computer in the precise storage location and processing of each unit of data. Writing such a program is a lengthy process and the program is incomprehensible to the nonspecialist. The programming instructions tend to be peculiar to a particular model of computer, though some of the basic skill of programming will help the programmer who moves to new equipment. Programs written directly in machine code tend to be efficient in running, so that standard packages of programs to cope with frequently arising problems may be provided in such code by the computer manufacturer.

About the mid-1950s a simplification referred to as autocoding began to be used. This employs letters and combinations of letters as mnemonics to assist the programmer and to provide a much more readily-understood program. Such autocodes have first to be converted into machine code within the computer, a facility provided by the computer manufacturer. Assembly languages or assemblers follow this mnemonic system. Sometimes economy of instructions is achieved by grouping selected combinations of machine code instructions into routines, each represented by a combination of letters. This may be referred to as a macro system. Such systems are designed for use with a particular make of computer, as are autocodes. These programming languages are referred to as low level languages.

High level languages are of much more interest to users, especially to managers who do not wish to become involved in the intricacies of programming. They have the characteristics of being usable on different makes and models of equipment, so that programming skill is not lost with a change of job or the introduction of a new computer; they are often easy to understand by people who may not be skilled enough to program in them; they permit program amendments to be made relatively easily; they change little over the years; and improvements generally do not invalidate earlier versions of the language when run on newer computers. As for ease of learning this varies; the reader should compare the programming in BASIC in Chapter 3 with the outline of COBOL in

Chapter 7. Such languages can only be used with a particular computer if the manufacturer has provided an appropriate compiler. This is a computer program to convert the written program into machine code. Compilers are expensive to produce and not all of the best-established high level languages will necessarily be available to a user. Disadvantages of such languages are the comparatively large storage required for the compiler, which occupies store like any other program, and the loss of efficiency in running.

The original version of the program, written in the high level language, is called the source program. When this has been converted by the computer into machine code, under the instructions of the compiler, we have the object program.

In the load-and-go method of operating the compiler will be read into store, followed by the source program, followed by the data to be handled by the program. An alternative method is to read in the compiler and source program and to output the object program, which may be stored for future use. This enables the compiler to be cleared from the store, releasing the space it previously occupied. The object program can be input when required (often along with a small routines program related to the compiler) and followed by the data.

The following are the chief high level programming languages.

1. COBOL (**CO**mmon **B**usiness **O**riented **L**anguage) which is probably the chief language used for business data processing (*see* Chapter 7).

2. PL1 (**P**rogramming **L**anguage **1**), devised more recently than COBOL and intended to provide facilities both for business data processing and for scientific programming.

3. FORTRAN (**FOR**mula **TRAN**slation) which is probably the best-established scientific language, especially in the U.S.A.

4. ALGOL (**ALG**orithmic **O**riented **L**anguage), also used for scientific programming. An algorithm is a sequence of steps in the solution of a mathematical problem.

5. BASIC (**B**eginners **A**ll purpose **S**ymbolic **I**nstruction **C**ode), a language of more recent date, developed especially for use with computer terminals operating on an interactive basis, that is where a conversation is held between the person at the terminal keyboard and the computer (*see* Chapter 4), and later offered on most micros.

The BASIC language has the great merit of simplicity and is intended primarily for managers and others who may wish to come to grips with computing, and have programming at their fingertips, without devoting much time to it. It is widely available and used. Further details are given in Chapter 3.

These high level languages are oriented towards the procedures required by the programmers rather than to the particular computer being used. Other programming approaches are available related primarily to specific problems, such as the generation of reports (R.P.G.—Report Program Generator—is an example). Interpreters offer a cheaper alternative to compilers. They convert the high level language into machine code, line by line as the program runs.

Flow Charts

Before writing a computer program it is normal to indicate the steps to be followed in a flow chart. The symbols needed for the simpler forms of chart are shown in Fig. 3 while more specialised symbols are shown in Fig. 42.

The terminal symbol is used at the beginning or end of a program or where the program is halted, delayed or interrupted. In the

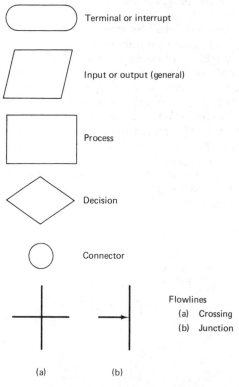

Terminal or interrupt

Input or output (general)

Process

Decision

Connector

Flowlines
(a) Crossing
(b) Junction

(a)   (b)

FIG. 3. Flow chart symbols (1).

simplest cases there will be just two of these symbols in a flow chart, clearly indicating the start and finish.

The input or output symbol is used where these functions are being considered in general terms. Where a configuration affords several possible choices of equipment, the special symbols (*see* Fig. 42(*a*)) for card reader, magnetic tape deck and the like should be used.

The rectangle indicates a process to be performed by the computer. Examples are calculation (where a selected variable will be made to equal the outcome of some mathematical process), movement of data within the memory of the computer and changes in the form of data (such as conversion of a number containing decimals into an integer).

The diamond shape signifies that a decision must be made, so that one of two alternative routes through the program will be followed. In some programs more complicated switching to one of several parts of the program may depend on a condition tested by the computer.

These symbols are linked by straight lines in the order in which they are to occur. Such flow lines may be arrowed where the direction of flow might be in doubt. The standard direction of flow is from left to right or from top to bottom and, in these cases, arrows are not strictly necessary. With complicated charts flow lines may cross but this is to be avoided, if possible, perhaps by rearranging the layout. The connector circle is used to link parts of the chart that are inconveniently placed for joining. A number (or letter) is placed in the circle at the end of the exit line (perhaps to the edge or bottom of a page) and the same circled number shows the entry point from that line somewhere else in the diagram.

A simple flow chart is given in Fig. 4. This shows the steps arising in performing the type of calculation involved in invoice ex-

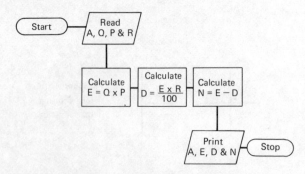

FIG. 4. A simple flow chart.

tensions. Input first must be the code number (A) of an article, the quantity (Q) and the price (P) and the discount rate (R) applicable to the transaction. The calculation that follows has been broken down into three stages.

1. Calculation of the extension (E), which is the product of quantity and price.
2. Calculation of the discount (D).
3. Subtraction of discount from extension to give the net amount (N).

The final stage is to print out the code number, extension, discount and net amount. Such a procedure is intended to act as an introduction to programming rather than to give a fully satisfactory approach to handling this kind of data.

A slightly more complex situation is shown in Fig. 5 which in-

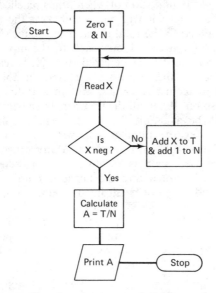

FIG. 5. Flow chart for average of positive numbers.

volves the use of the decision symbol. The problem is to print out the average of any number of positive numbers. Analysis of the problem shows that this involves:

1. reading the numbers;
2. totalling the numbers;
3. counting the numbers;

4. deciding when the last number has been reached;
5. dividing the total by the count;
6. printing out the result.

The first process, after the start, is shown as "zero T and N". These letters have been chosen to represent total and count (or number) respectively. Their value in store is made zero to start with because they are to be used to accumulate totals and anything in the store from a previous program would otherwise be added in. On some time-sharing systems (*see* Chapter 4) the store may be automatically cleared, but we shall ignore this.

Next is the input of the data, referred to as X. A number will be read and will be checked to see whether it is one of the set of numbers involved in the calculation or is an end marker. In this case a dummy number with a minus sign is used to show the end of the run of positive numbers. Such a marker is needed as the computer requires some indication of when it has reached the end of its data. In the flow chart it will be seen that, if the number is not negative, it is added to the total (T) and the count (N) is increased by one. The program then loops back to the input symbol. The next number, now in its turn referred to as X, is read and stored, overwriting the number previously stored in the part of the memory used to record X values, and then tested to see if it is negative, and so on. When all the numbers have been read the total and count will be available for the average calculation and the presence of the negative number will switch the program into the average calculation and print sections. Many other forms of end marker may be used, such as an alphabetic character instead of a numeral. It will be noted that the negative number is not added into the total and does not result in the count being increased.

Simple Programming

A detailed study of programming in BASIC is postponed until Chapter 3. For the moment the reader may care to look at Fig. 6

```
10    REMARK FIRST DEMONSTRATION PROGRAM
20    READ A,Q,P,R
30    LET E=Q*P
40    LET D=E*R/100
50    LET N=E-D
60    PRINT A,E,D,N
70    DATA 21, 8, 5.25, 10
80    END
```

```
21      42      4.2      37.8
```

FIG. 6. Simple BASIC program with data and output.

which is a BASIC program for the invoice extension calculation described in Fig. 4. There should be no difficulty in relating the lines of the program to the stages in the flow chart. We shall commence our study of BASIC in the later chapter with a full analysis of this program.

Debugging programs

Few programs run successfully the first time and errors have to be traced and eliminated. For the moment we may consider errors to arise from three causes.

1. Logical errors, so that the program does not produce the required result. Test data to which the answers are known can be used to find such errors. They may be due to faulty flow charting or incorrect interpretation of the flow chart by the program.

2. Data errors, where the data does not occur as specified in the program. If the end marker is omitted the computer will seek additional input and signal this to the operator. The precise format of data is very important with some program languages but little trouble should arise with BASIC.

3. Syntactic errors, where the rules of the programming language have not been obeyed. Most compilers have built-in checks for these errors and will indicate by a print-out where the errors occur in the program and what mistakes seem to have been made. Some compilers give very full print-outs to cover this. Others may rely on a numbered error list published by the manufacturer. The line identification and the error number are then printed out when the program is being compiled, and the user refers to the numbered list to establish the precise nature of the error.

Operating Systems and Multiprogramming

An essential element of software, normally provided by the computer manufacturer and outside the scope of the user, is the operating system that goes with a particular computer configuration.

This set of software will have routines that supervise input and output, for example, opening and closing data files, program compilation and debugging and, possibly, the automatic logging of work done on the computer. In the case of multiprogram computers it will control the running of several programs stored in the computer at one time and, with time-sharing computers (*see* Chapter 4), it switches control to programs in sequence. Such a set of routines is often referred to as an executive or monitor system.

Input–output control systems, usually abbreviated to I.O.C.S. take from the user programmer much of the hard work involved when peripherals have to be controlled in conjunction with the computer. The organisation and storage and naming and retrieval of data will be systematised, taking account of the characteristics of the peripheral device.

Operating systems are also concerned with control of overlapped and multi-programmed systems. The comparative slowness of peripherals compared with the speed of operation of the central processing unit has led to the overlapping of input and output with the internal computing to give higher utilisation of the central processor and to reduce throughput time for programs. This is achieved by using a buffer, a temporary storage device for input and output data, having the effect of isolating the central processor when convenient, from both input and output peripherals. The buffer area may be filled from a slow reading device and the whole of its contents released to the central processing unit to be effectively processed. Conversely, the central processor may output the results of its calculations into the buffer, without impeding its own speed of operation, and, from the buffer, these results will be released at a speed suited to the output peripheral. A print-out can take place while further data is being read into the computer.

Even with overlapping the processing of one complete program at a time generally results in a very low proportion of C.P.U. time to operating time. Multiprogramming represents a further advance in the direction of efficient utilisation of computers. Basically the idea is that more than one program shares the computer memory at one time, and these programs are overlapped, so that the central processor is used more effectively. Programs may be given a priority ranking, perhaps varying from low priority for run-of-the-mill processing to rapid response for real-time peripherals (*see* Chapter 8). The state of the peripherals will be taken into account by the operating system and a program will be automatically suspended when it tries to address an occupied peripheral unit. When a peripheral transfer has ended the operating system will take over and pass control to the highest priority program that is in a state to proceed. This is sometimes referred to as an interrupt, though this term is also used, generally, to cover the temporary interruption of a procedure when a fault requiring operator intervention has been automatically detected, for example an output device may have been wrongly switched off-line. A good operating system can relieve human operators of much of the physical and mental work that might otherwise be involved in supervising data input and output.

When random access devices are used in real-time computing (*see* Chapter 8), very sophisticated supervisory programs may enable access to various items to be overlapped so that several transactions can be processed in parallel, each being only partially completed at one time. This is referred to as multi-threading, distinct from single-threading, where a message is completely processed before a different message is dealt with.

An alternative to the use of software for multiprogramming is to partition the core storage into fixed areas, to each of which is assigned a program. This is called fixed-partition multiprogramming and is established on installation by means of plugboards. This, coupled with hardware control of the operating system, may be more suited to the smaller user than software-controlled systems.

When a peripheral unit can operate at its own speed and is not subject to delays caused by the inability of the central processor to cope with it, the term autonomous operation is sometimes used.

Microprogramming and Microcoding

The term microprogramming implies the software for achieving simple basic processes in the computer, for example multiplication. Such programs are generally provided in read-only memory (ROM) and cannot be changed by the user, though different basic microprograms may be used with the same hardware to give greater efficiency for specialist uses. Computers with differing hardware may have the same inbuilt comprehensive instruction set by the use of microprogramming. The effects of microcoding are sometimes called "flexiware".

Packages, Software Houses and User Pools

It is not always necessary or desirable for a computer user to devise all or any of the programs used. To do so may involve high costs for systems and programming staff. It has, however, the merits that the user has greater control over the systems employed, which may also be more tailor-made for the special requirements of the user firm. In addition staff employed by a user will be helpful for systems development and amendment.

If data processing requirement can be standardised the use of "packages" supplied by the computer manufacturer or by a software specialist may be suitable. Such packages have been developed in connection with statistical and operational research calculations (including critical path analysis) and also for standard routine business applications. A package is more satisfactory if it permits flexibility of approach by the user who may, perhaps, control its operation by an interactive technique. The availability of a library of programs or routines is an important factor in deciding on a computer system.

Software houses, as the name implies, may offer ready-made programs and also will take on assignments to provide programs for clients. This work may be charged either on a fixed price basis, perhaps with penalty clauses, or on an open-ended basis, where the client pays the actual cost of the work done. "Turnkey" operations relieve the user of all systems analysis and programming worries.

Users with systems analysis and programming facilities will build up a stock of programs, some of which, if not too revealing of the firm's business methods, may be made available to other users. There are user pools, membership of which is generally based on the make of computer used by the firms. In such pools programs of general interest are made available, sometimes freely, but usually on a payment basis, perhaps with a percentage to the computer manufacturer if he organises the pool.

SPECIMEN EXAMINATION QUESTIONS

1. Draw a block diagram to show the basic functions performed by a central processing unit and make brief notes on the nature of these functions and how they are related.

2. Computers are often divided into rough categories according to their size. List these categories and comment on their relevance to business users.

3. Distinguish clearly between hardware and software and explain how they are related.

4. Write brief notes on the following, distinguishing clearly between them: (a) random access memory, (b) read only memory, (c) virtual memory.

5. Explain the growth in popularity of high level programming languages, distinguishing clearly between these and machine codes and assemblers.

6. "The development of programming languages such as BASIC opens the door to the full use of computers by managers." Discuss.

7. (a) What is meant by the size of immediate access store in a computer? (b) Why is this so important in considering the suitability of a computer for different purposes?

8. Explain the uses of computer flow charts and programs, clearly indicating how they differ.

9. Write explanatory notes on operating systems and multiprogramming, indicating their importance to computer users.

10. (*a*) Distinguish between source programs and object programs showing how they are related. (*b*) Briefly explain the different types of errors which may arise in programs.

11. Explain the differences between on-line and off-line operation and discuss the advantages of each method.

Chapter 2

INPUT, OUTPUT AND
STORAGE DEVICES

PERIPHERALS

The previous chapter has been devoted primarily to the heart of the computer system, the central processing unit. To enable this to function it has to be linked with the business system by means of input and output devices, generally known as peripherals.

Some of these devices are concerned with data collection or what is sometimes called the capture of data to bring it into the computer system. Examples occur when cards have to be punched and passed through a card reader, or when data is encoded on to magnetic tape or disc to be used as a computer file. Other devices present select aspects of what is in the computer system to the clerk or manager, or perhaps to a customer with a monthly statement of his account. The most obvious way is to print this information, but there are many alternatives, such as to display it on the screen of a video unit or to photograph it on microfilm.

Closely associated with input and output is the problem of backing store, that is external storage facilities not forming part of the computer's immediate access storage. Such stored information has to be input to the immediate access store before the computer can use it, and the processed information, obviously, has to be output to the backing store if it is to be retained other than in the immediate access store.

Storage may be off-line, as with reels of magnetic tape or decks of punched cards, while they are kept in the computer department library. When mounted in the appropriate devices for reading, such information becomes on-line. Off-line methods give practically unlimited storage capacity, with the drawbacks of difficulty and slowness of access, compared with information that is always on-line, which in its turn takes longer to access than information stored within the computer's immediate access store.

Speed of access is generally related to equipment costs and these must be considered in the light of the true needs of different runs of work to be done on the computer. Real-time systems place emphasis on rapid access and depend heavily on on-line random access storage devices, such as discs, while batch processing systems accumulate the work to be processed by various programs until an economic run can be performed, relying on off-line storage.

Different peripheral devices are associated with their own advantages or drawbacks, relating to the way in which data using them has to be organised. Information on tape must generally be processed in the order in which it appears on the tape, while information on discs is much more readily available. Similar considerations apply to all forms of storage and access and the following terms may be noted.

1. *Sequential*, where the records are stored and accessed in some logical order.

2. *Serial*, where this order relates to the physical position of the storage, as on tape, with the records in adjacent positions.

3. *Random* (often synonymous with "direct", though this latter term is also used as equivalent to "immediate access storage", or the "working store" of the computer) implying that one record may be accessed as readily as any other, in the sequence in which they happen to be required. A record must be kept of the key of each record and its location. In this context a key is the identification code or number of each record stored.

4. *Indexed sequential*, where particular records in the file are indexed and access involves finding the nearest index location to the record required and then searching beyond this to find the precise record. This access technique is known as selective sequential access.

The time taken to reach an individual record and transfer it into the immediate access store is known as the access time. The transfer rate refers to the speed of transfer from an on-line device to the computer store, which is not the same as the rate at which individual items of data may be accessed for processing. A complete tape may be read into store more efficiently than when it has to start and stop for each record it contains.

A practical consideration in determining the most appropriate equipment is the file activity, that is the percentage of all the items on a file that have to be updated at any time. If the activity is high then serial techniques may be economic. With low activity a great waste of time may be involved by sequential methods because of the need to go from record to record in order. This would generally be the case with real-time computing where random access is desirable.

Towards the end of the 1970s the concept of content addressable memory (CAM) began to be realised enabling users to address specific items without knowing their location in store. The Post Office experimented with Content Addressable File Store (CAFS) to index directory entries.

Consoles and keyboards

Control over the working of the computer is exercised through a console, with switches, keys, display lights and, perhaps, some audible device. For some time the trend in design has been to reduce the number of these and to achieve much of the control through a keyboard. Coded instructions are typed in and the computer's needs appear in typewritten form.

Typical of the basic communications between the operator and the computer are "switch on", "stand by", "switch off", "reset", "initial instructions", "make input and output devices available", "input programs and data", "reload paper tape punch" and "awaiting data". Each program may in addition incorporate its own messages.

The tendency to control by typed instructions is epitomised by the use of time-sharing terminals, where control over a large computer configuration is exercised remotely, perhaps over long distances. Control is further facilitated by the incorporation of visual display units in terminals and consoles.

PUNCHED CARDS

Before the advent of computers punched card systems represented the most advanced form of data processing suited to business use. Punched cards are still used extensively for computer input and output.

The basic principle of the system is that each data record has a special card, usually containing eighty columns, the value in each column being indicated by a hole punched in the appropriate vertical position. Columns are grouped into fields sufficient to cope with the highest numbers or combinations of letters likely to be encountered. Thus for numbers up to 999 we should need a field of three columns. Each field represents, say, a code number, a person's name, a price, a stock balance, etc. Because each record usually occupies its own card the term unit record processing is sometimes used to describe this system.

A specimen card is shown in Fig. 7. The punching for the numeric values is easy to follow; there is simply one hole in the required vertical position. As well as these numeric rows it will be seen that two further rows (eleven and twelve) are provided at the

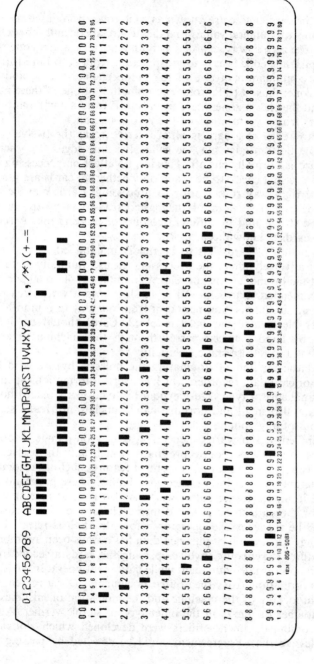

FIG. 7. 80-column punched card.

top of the card. These are known as zone rows, being used in combination with numeric values to indicate alphabetic and other characters. The zero row is regarded as both a numeric and a zone row. The alphabetic code is easy to grasp; letters from A to I are formed from a combination of one of the numbers one to nine and the twelve zone; those J to R from a combination of one of these numbers and the eleven zone; these from S to Z from a combination of numbers from two to nine and the zero zone punch.

The top edge of a card is often referred to as the twelve edge, while the bottom edge may be called the nine edge. A corner of each card is normally cut off. This has no effect on processing but enables a visual check to be made on whether all cards are assembled the right way round prior to processing. Cards may be distinguished by the colour of the basic card stock, by the use of coloured stripes and by different colours of printing ink. A set of related cards is known as a deck or file.

The quality of cards has to be rigidly maintained so that they will not adversely affect the processing. In use, humidity is an important factor and a constant relative humidity of 40 to 60 per cent is recommended. Cards moved from store into a work area may require an acclimatisation period of from one day to a month if a considerable change has been involved. Cards should be lightly fanned by hand between passes through the machine to assist alignment and release static electricity.

The basic method of originating the holes is by use of a key punch, or card data recorder, which converts information typed on the normal sort of typewriter keyboard into correctly placed holes. There are also small and portable hand punches, not really suited to output of any volume.

Equipment design varies, depending largely on its age. Modern punches usually incorporate programs (which may themselves be fed in using up to six cards) to control features such as automatic skipping and duplication of selected columns. These programs are located in an electronic buffer which is also used as a temporary store for the data to be punched into each card, enabling corrections to be made by the operator before the data is released for punching. Verification of punched data has always been an important feature. It generally involves passing the cards a second time through appropriate equipment while a different operator types the same information from the source documents. Disagreement resulted in locking of the machine and the indication of mistakes by error notches or marks in the older type of simple verifier. Automatic combined punch/verifiers were developed which elongated the holes, so that disagreement could be detected by passing the cards at high speed through an automatic card verifier, which deposited a signal card behind each wrong card in the stacker. Modern equipment of the punch/verifier type uses the program control to facilitate verification. If printing punches are used, which print at the top of each card the letters, etc., represented by

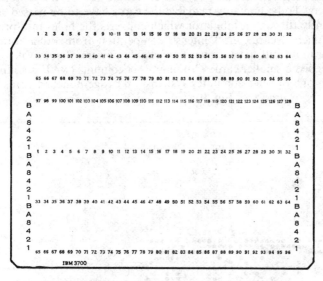

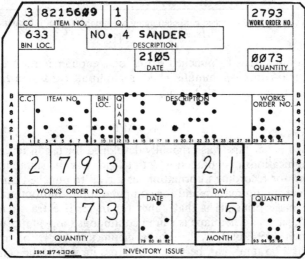

FIG. 8. I.B.M. 96-column binary-punched cards (8·3 cm × 6·7 cm approx.).

the holes, it is possible to make a visual verification, but this would be liable to human error under the pressures of large volumes of work. It is often used by students and others to check on the lines of programs they are developing or altering. After punching cards are passed through a card reader to form computer input. Automatic card punches may be used as on-line output devices for computers. To be humanly readable the cards have to be passed subsequently through a tabulator which converts the holes into print.

Punched cards meet intense competition from other forms of data input but have shown remarkable powers of survival. I.B.M. designed a smaller card, with ninety-six columns (*see* Fig. 8) for use with one of their computer systems, and edge-punched cards have also been used (*see* Fig. 9).

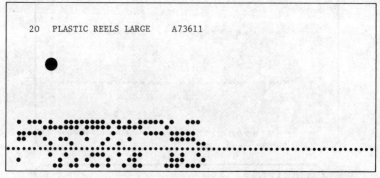

20   PLASTIC REELS LARGE   A73611

FIG. 9. An edge-punched card containing a standard item of information
(18 cm × 7·5 cm approx.).

Reading speeds of punched cards for computer input are up to about 900 cards per minute while, for output, cards can be punched at about 300 cards per minute.

PAPER TAPE

Punched paper tape was originally developed for use in telegraphic communications in conjunction with teleprinters. Its suitability as a medium for recording information, as a rival to punched cards, led to its use in automation and for computer input and output.

The basic principle is that paper (or mylar if extra strength is needed, such as when tape is run in continuous loops) tape, usually one inch (25·4 mm) wide (but sometimes $\frac{7}{8}$ or $\frac{11}{16}$ of an inch (22·2 or 17·5 mm)) can be punched across its width, the combinations of holes representing characters and instructions, such as "carriage return" and "line feed". Various codes are available; five-track used to be very popular but eight-track code on one-inch tape has tended to replace it (*see* Fig. 10). One track usually provides for a parity check, each character being made up to an even number of holes and this being tested on reading to detect mis-punching. Alternatively an odd number system may be used. For details see Chapter 9—Control of Inputs.

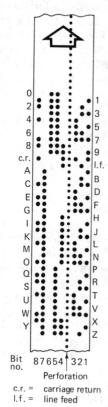

Fig. 10. Eight-bit paper tape code (even parity). This is the same as the I.S.O. seven-bit code (International Alphabet No. 5) with the addition of an eighth parity bit. The numerals are represented by binary code in the first four bits.

Bit no. 8 7 6 5 4 ↑ 3 2 1

Perforation

c.r. = carriage return
l.f. = line feed

Punching and verifying of paper tape is very similar to that of punched cards. Data is recorded serially on the tape and it is impossible, directly, to do the equivalent of inserting extra cards in a deck of punched cards or of changing some of the information by substituting new cards. This may be an advantage in that cards may be lost or become out of order. Mistakes noticed during punching may be corrected by back-spacing and deleting the characters, by punching out all the holes in each row from the mistake, and then punching the correct information. The punch is, of course, under the control of a typewriter keyboard, so there is no need for the operator to be acquainted with the particular code being used.

Punching is usually done on perforating typewriters or on the teletypewriters used as part of terminal equipment. These produce a hard-copy version (typescript) of what has been punched, useful for immediate visual checking by the operator and for subsequent verification. Mistakes can be corrected by reading the tape into the machine and generating a copy tape. Simple editing is done by stopping the tape at the error, pulling it through so that a character (or number of characters) is not copied, and then typing the correct version, which will appear on the copy tape. A more satisfactory method may be to read the tape into a computer and edit it, through the keyboard or by an edit tape, under the control of an edit program. The revised tape is punched as output. There are also keyboard perforators, not having hard-copy and units incorporating an internal memory which provide a visual display of what has been typed, this being punched by pressing a button when it has been visually checked.

Paper tape can be punched as the by-product of some machines, such as a cash register or visible record computer. Such tape may be used for subsequent computer input.

A major use of paper tape is to provide a verified version of programs and data to be transmitted through time-sharing terminals (see Chapter 4). The tape can be prepared off-line with the terminal set to "local" mode, thus saving a waste of computer and telephone facilities while the information is slowly typed for transmission and errors are corrected.

Reading speeds for computer input vary from a few hundred up to about 1,500 characters per second, reading generally being done photo-electrically. As a form of computer output, tape may be punched automatically at up to 100 or 200 characters per second. Such tape must be fed subsequently through a print device for its information to be meaningful to human readers. When tape is used for transmission through a terminal the speed is limited to what the system can handle (see details of Datel services in Chapter 4). Comparisons with card input and output depend, to an extent, on the number of characters actually punched on each card. When this is considerably below the maximum of eighty, time as well as space is wasted, compared with paper tape where blank columns do not have to be left. The equivalent of a new card is signalled by "carriage return, line feed" at the end of each line.

MAGNETIC TAPE

This has long been a major medium for encoding and storage of computer information. Originally reel-to-reel equipment was available but this is now supplemented by cassettes and cartridges, which are small, easy to handle, dust resistant and particularly suited to smaller installations.

The operation of magnetic reel-to-reel decks is similar to that of tape recorders (*see* Fig. 11). A reel of tape, generally half an inch (12·7 mm) wide (but sizes up to one inch (25·4 mm) have been used) moves from a feed or file reel to a take-up or machine reel. Be-

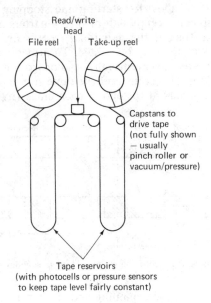

FIG. 11. Principle of operation of typical magnetic tape drive.

tween these reels are read/write heads (and sometimes an erase head). To prevent tape breakages due to frequent starting and stopping of the tape drive mechanism, a reservoir of slack tape hangs down between the reels and this mechanism. This also allows even tape movement past the heads and prevents the tape stretching.

The traditional design of deck has the reels operating vertically side by side, as shown in the sketch, but reels may be one above the other or horizontal.

The width of the tape is divided into as many tracks (generally seven or nine) as are required by the recording code that is being used. As many as forty tracks are technically possible. Bits can be recorded on these tracks (somewhat like holes on paper tape) by controlling the direction of flow of current in the appropriate write coils. Writing blanks out anything previously on the tape but reading does not affect its contents.

Reading or writing takes place as the tape moves past the read/ write head at the appropriate speed. Rewind facilities are obviously needed and some tape units provide for reading the tape backwards, which can considerably speed up sorting. If data is being read intermittently a gap must be allowed between each separately read set of data to allow for starting and stopping the tape. This inter-record gap may occupy half or three-quarters of an inch (12·7 or 19·1 mm) so that, if the individual records are short, a large proportion of the tape may be wasted. To provide more economic recording several records are usually read or written at a time. This is termed blocking of records and the same size gaps, called inter-block gaps, occur only at the end of each block (*see* Fig. 12).

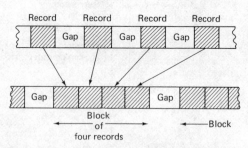

FIG. 12. Blocking records on magnetic tape to economise its use.

Sections of tape at the beginning and end must be left blank for threading, and the recording is between a load point marker and an end of tape marker. Header and trailer labels will probably be used, for identification and continuity purposes, relating to the files of data recorded on the tapes.

An end of file marker (sometimes an extra long gap) may be recorded on the tape to indicate the last of a set of records considered together as a file. The term segment may be used for a group of records treated as a subfile and identified by a segment marker.

The record density (or packing or data density) which is the number of characters for each inch length of the tape or the number of bytes or bits per inch (25·4 mm), is important for deciding how much information may be held on each tape. Sometimes it may be controlled manually or by the program. A 10½ inch (266·7 mm) diameter 2,400 ft (732 m) reel, at a density of 800 characters to the inch (31 to the mm), will hold the equivalent of from 30,000 to about 250,000 eighty column punched cards, depending on the blocking of the data.

The record density combined with the speed at which the tape passes the read/write head (but ignoring inter-record gaps) gives the character rate, which is the maximum rate for reading or writing characters. This may go up to over 300,000 characters per second with high speeds and high densities.

Access time may be quoted as the time taken to reach a record from the immediately preceding one on the tape. If it is regarded as the time taken to reach any particular record then it will vary depending on how much of the tape has to be searched to find it. On magnetic tape data is normally recorded serially, in the order in which it is to be processed, so that the time from one record to the next is relevant.

Insertion of extra records (or deletion of existing records) as well as any alterations involves copying all the records, with appropriate amendments, on to another tape.

The popularity of magnetic tape as a storage medium is readily accounted for when the volume of data a reel will hold, the speed at which it can be processed, the fact that it can be used over and over again and the comparative cheapness of the tape are considered. Serial organisation of data has its drawbacks, but the systems flow can be related to this, being batch processed.

Protection against accidentally overwriting live data can be secured by physical means or by program and other controls (see Chapter 9). One physical method is by a plastic ring fitted into a groove in the reel. When in position reading or writing can take place; when removed only reading is possible. Another system uses a slide on the cartridge.

Because of the speed of magnetic tape reading punched card data are often converted into magnetic tape form before a computer run, special apparatus being available. The tendency is to eliminate the punched card stage and to code the data directly on to magnetic tape ("key-to-tape", as is explained later).

Practical work may call for several tape decks (for example tape sorting normally requires four). Tape units are often specified to include, say, two, four or six decks together with control circuits for the group.

MAGNETIC CARDS

The use of magnetic ledger cards with the equivalent of a length of magnetic tape in one or more vertical bands has already been noted in Chapter 1. Magnetic cards are used in connection with word processing (*see* Chapter 10). Special magnetic card keyboard machines are available, together with readers and printers, which to some extent have taken the place of punched card equipment.

MAGNETIC DISCS

The introduction of magnetic discs, offering random access to the information stored on their surfaces, made an important contribution to computing. The original discs and disc packs have been augmented by floppy discs and diskettes which can play a valuable role in smaller systems and distributed programming.

Disc storage (*see* Fig. 13) has affinities with recording on gramophone records. Information is recorded magnetically on both surfaces of a disc, on concentric rings known as tracks, which may be grouped into bands for recording a number of bits in parallel.

Bands, which are complete circles, are divided into sectors or

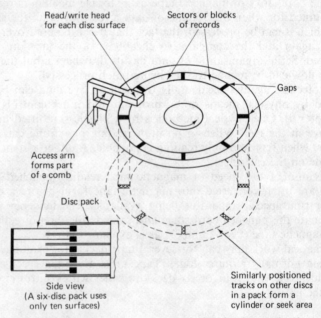

Fig. 13. Schematic diagram of magnetic disc showing one band.

blocks, one or more of which, termed a bucket, is transferred into the computer's immediate access store, on reading (or from this store, on writing). The bucket size can usually be varied by the user, up to a maximum number of blocks.

Read/write heads cover each surface, being moved over the appropriate band. The disc is revolving constantly. Access time involves the time required to move the read/write head into position over the required band (which will be zero if each band has its own head) plus the time needed for the disc to revolve into the appropriate position (referred to as latency time), averaging the time for half a revolution. At 1,000 revolutions per minute the latency is 0·03 s (or thirty milliseconds). Considerably higher speeds are available.

Single disc units or drives are available and also drives with disc packs containing several discs on a single vertical spindle. These single discs and packs are generally interchangeable. There are units incorporating permanent and interchangeable discs. Several million characters may be stored on each disc, and a disc drive unit may have sixteen of these. These drives may be further grouped, say in fours, under a control unit. The total storage available can exceed a billion bytes.

With more than one disc surface we can imagine similarly placed tracks on different surfaces as forming cylinders from which information can be accessed by one positioning of the read/write heads. The bands on each surface forming this "cylinder" may be accessed in turn, without further head movement. This can be important in reducing access time. These cylinders of information are often referred to as seek areas and files of information will be located on them, rather than adjacently on one disc.

Records stored within buckets may be of fixed or variable length. With fixed length records, stored sequentially, the address of a record may be calculated from its key if the number of the lowest bucket is known. It is necessary for the keys to run in sequence, without gaps where data is non-existent, which may be wasteful. Suppose a file consists of 1,000 records, with keys (that is code numbers) running from 1 to 1,000 and each bucket holds ten records, starting at bucket number 500. The location of the record with key thirty-three involves first locating the number of buckets from the start in which the key will occur ($\frac{33}{10} = 3$, remainder 2). The actual bucket is then the first bucket number added to this quotient ($500 + 3 = 503$). The location within this bucket will be the remainder plus 1, giving $2 + 1$, i.e. the third record within bucket 503 (*see* Fig. 14). This method is known as self-indexing or self-addressing.

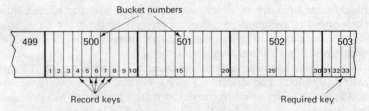

FIG. 14. Location of record in sequential storage on disc, using fixed length records. Part of one band is shown, straightened out.

A modification, which can also be used with variable length records and where blank records are omitted, is known as partial addressing, where the bucket number is first calculated from the key and the records in the bucket are then searched to find the required key. With variable length records, implying varying numbers of records per bucket, the average spread of keys per bucket is used to calculate the bucket number.

It is much more usual, instead of calculating as above, to maintain an index of the highest key in each bucket. This index will be either permanently in the immediate access store or read into it from a bucket on the disc, when required. After locating the appropriate bucket from the index the appropriate key is found by searching within this bucket. This system is referred to as partial indexing and is related to indexed sequential storage, mentioned earlier in this chapter. With large files several seek areas may be involved of which the lowest and highest keys will be shown in a seek area index. Setting up and searching indexes will generally be done using software of the computer manufacturers.

A more complex relationship between the record key and the storage location may be used for random files. The key is treated by an address generation algorithm. An algorithm is some standard calculating process, such as squaring the key and extracting two digits from the result, to indicate the bucket number.

As with all storage media the packing or data density is important. As much data as possible is crammed within a given space. The number of keys to each bucket may be underestimated by making too high an allowance for keys that are not used. This may result in overflow. A simple way of providing for this is by allocating overflow buckets to store such data, at some cost in access time.

An important use of discs is to provide computers with programs that can be rapidly read into the immediate access store. The disc storage may be divided into different areas, some of which are not accessible to the user. A typical arrangement would be areas as follows.

1. An area fixed by the computer manufacturer, and including the compilers and library routines.

2. A user area in which user programs, etc., can be stored for future use.

3. A working storage area for current operations.

The boundary of the first area would be fixed but that between 2 and 3 might be variable, the area devoted to 2 tending to increase with time. A single disc with a capacity of, say, half a million sixteen-bit words would be a useful adjunct to a small computer.

Floppy (or flexy) discs, of flexible material sealed into a protective envelope (*see* Fig. 15), have an understandable popularity. A

FIG. 15. A floppy disc. The "record" is permanently sealed in its protective envelope which is loaded into a control unit. Read/write access is through the slot. Other slots and holes in the envelope are for indexing and protection against overwriting.

user can easily slot the appropriate program or data disc into equipment which is often readily portable and relatively cheap. Floppy discs capable of recording on both sides have been developed, though originally one side only was used. Dual disc systems are available in which, typically, one disc contains systems and application programs and the second is used for data and text. One such disc can hold a hundred or more pages of A4 text.

KEY-TO-TAPE AND KEY-TO-DISC SYSTEMS

To avoid the time and costs associated with card punching, verifying and subsequent conversion to magnetic form for computer input, systems have been developed to enable data to be encoded directly on to magnetic tape and discs.

Single unit models enable an operator to record via a keyboard. The data first enters a core memory in the unit before being recorded permanently, so that errors can be corrected, if necessary, after checking with a data display.

Multi-station systems enable a number of operators to key in data from separate keyboards. These are connected, through a multiplexor, which is a device for linking various circuits, to a control computer, with its own supervisory console. Format is controlled by the computer. Verification can be by re-keying from any of the stations, an error indication resulting from a mismatch with what has previously been keyed, or may be by a visual check on a data display.

Key-to-tape apparatus may have facilities in addition to the basic one of writing on magnetic tape. Searching a tape for specified records and producing a print-out, consolidating several tapes into one (known as "pooling") while including extra data through the keyboard (or omitting data) and also acting as terminals to transmit data over telephone circuits, are examples.

Claims made for multi-station systems are that data preparation is more streamlined and controllable, that accuracy is improved, that the throughput time to the computer is reduced and that equipment and personnel costs are lower. Operators are said to work more quickly, partly because of the speed of operation of the equipment and also because of its silence. Experienced punched card operators can be retrained in a few days.

In addition to their conventional use for data capture, methods have been developed where the equipment can be regarded as part of a distributed processing system. Relatively cheap small processors, often dedicated to particular tasks, may be linked to share and amend a common data base, in a very flexible system which may be an alternative to a mainframe computer system or may be linked with it or relieve it of some of its load.

LASER DISCS

Developments in Laser Accessed Memory (L.A.M.) have enabled discs to be produced into the surfaces of which information can be burnt by lasers, which are also used for reading from them. These discs are of high capacity and are claimed to be rugged and relatively cheap. The discs have a spiral groove, which aids positioning. A disadvantage is that they can record once only.

DRUMS

Magnetic drums (*see* Fig. 16) provided the chief internal storage of many earlier computers. Their later use has been mainly as backing store for random access systems.

The principle of operation is to record on to parallel tracks

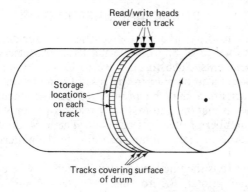

Fig. 16. Principles of magnetic drum storage.

going round the outer magnetisable surface of a revolving drum. Read/write heads are located over these tracks and access involves selecting the appropriate head and then waiting for the drum to revolve into the position where the desired part of a track is available. With one head for each track the access time and the latency (the time to rotate into position) are the same, an average figure being the time for half a rotation. The drum speed is of the same order as that of disc systems. For example, at 1,800 revolutions per minute the average access time would be seventeen milliseconds. Capacities vary greatly from 100,000 up to several millions. Drums may be linked.

MAGNETIC INK CHARACTER RECOGNITION (M.I.C.R.)

M.I.C.R. uses stylised characters printed in an ink that can be magnetised and detected by appropriate equipment. The single line of such characters has been a familiar feature on cheques. These are pre-encoded with the cheque number, the bank number and the customer's account number in magnetic ink (and also with the customer's name in ordinary print). When a cheque has been drawn, postencoding of the transaction details is done by passing the cheque through a special keyboard machine. Sorting equipment is available, similar to that used with punched cards.

Optical character recognition may well supersede magnetic systems, though the latter have the advantage of being able to cope with dirty and crumpled paper. There are two main founts. The E13B fount, of U.S. origin, has been used by British banks, while the C.M.C.7 fount has been favoured in Europe and by the Post Office.

OPTICAL MARK READING

Optical mark reading involves the sensing of information by the presence or absence of appropriate marks in predetermined positions on documents. Such forms have to be strictly designed and attention should also be paid to the ease of completion by clerks.

Some information may be pre-printed on the document in a form in which it may be automatically read. An example would be an account number printed in a bar code. The bars can occupy five vertical positions in each column according to the pattern shown in Fig. 17.

An alternative is the one code system, which may be output on a computer line printer, where ones represent binary values, as shown in Fig. 18.

Humanly readable perforated characters may also be used as shown in Fig. 19. The readable reverse characters can be perforated through other information printed on a form, without obscur-

BAR CODE VALUES

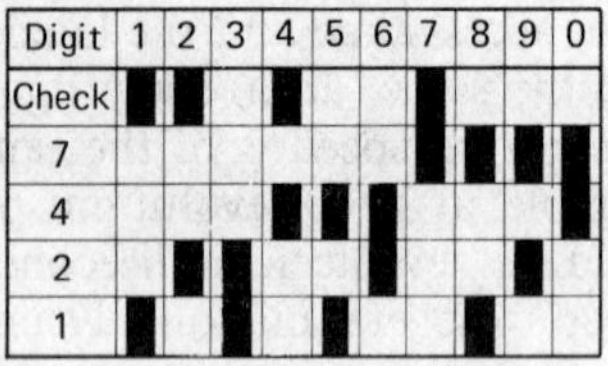

Digit	1	2	3	4	5	6	7	8	9	0
Check										
7										
4										
2										
1										

FIG. 17. Bar code.

ONE CODE VALUES

Digit	1	2	3	4	5	6	7	8	9	0
1	1		1		1		1		1	
2		1	1			1	1			1
4				1	1	1	1			
8								1	1	1
Check	1	1		1			1	1		

Courtesy Automatic Input Systems Ltd.

FIG. 18. Five-level B.C.D. "one code".

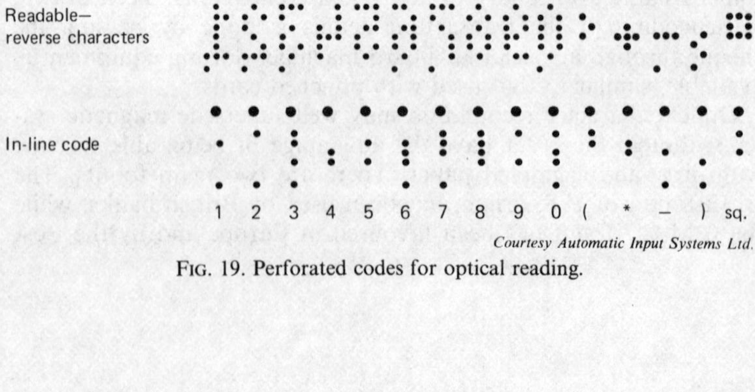

FIG. 19. Perforated codes for optical reading.

Courtesy Automatic Input Systems Ltd.

ing it, thus saving space. The condensed (in-line) version that is not humanly readable is used for information such as client numbers, printed on all documents sent to the client but of no interest to him. In the case of a simple choice between alternatives a form may provide boxes in which a mark is recorded for each choice, as in Fig. 20.

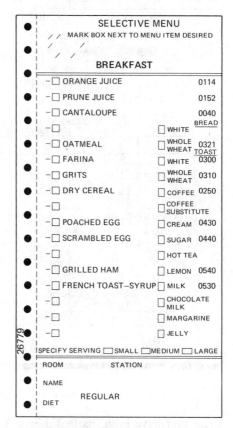

Courtesy Automatic Input Systems Ltd.

FIG. 20. Document for selective marking involving multiple choices without quantities.

Quantitative information may be overmarked in pencil on a pre-printed pattern, using a coloured printing ink that is ignored by the scanner. The mark is made either vertically or at an angle, between two guide dots over the appropriate number. Figure 21 gives an example of such a document.

Special forms of bar codes have been developed for use on merchandise tags, shop assistants' identification badges and customers' credit cards. These consist of black and white lines or may also introduce colours. Such tags are produced by encoder/imprinters normally, or by hand-operated imprinters for special work, such as

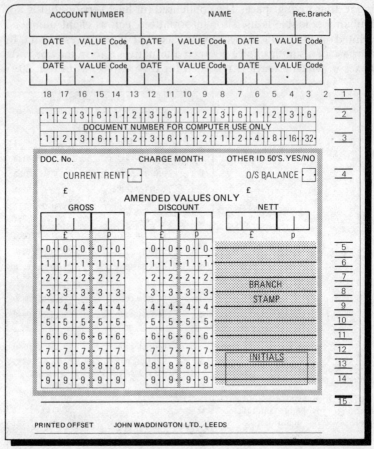

Courtesy John Waddington Ltd.

FIG. 21. Form for overmarking quantitative information.

prices that have been marked down. A light pen employing fibre optic techniques is used to scan the tags, which may be done without removing them from the articles to which they are attached. This apparatus is used in connection with point-of-sale (P.O.S.) data collection systems in retailing (*see* Chapter 10).

OPTICAL CHARACTER RECOGNITION (O.C.R.)

A major problem with most versions of computer input is that they are not suited to human reading, so that conversion of written records is involved when the computer is used. This results in a split in the data system between the clerical functions and those of computing.

Optical character recognition attempts a solution of this problem. Characters may be scanned, using a photo-electric cell, and the amount of light reflected from each causes current variations, which can be recognised by the electronic circuitry. Sophisticated equipment may be used to break up the character image into hundreds of elements to assist recognition.

O.C.R. equipment varies enormously with regard to price, design of characters (the fount or font) that may be read, size of document, number of lines that can be handled, specifications as to quality, thickness, contrast of letters with background, etc., of documents handled and speed and reliability.

Costs of the most sophisticated equipment, which really constitutes a small computer system itself, are such that only large businesses can consider its adoption. Such equipment might feature in a bureau service for the use of smaller companies.

Some of the fonts acceptable for machine reading (such as OCRA) are highly stylised and of low compatibility for human reading. More natural typeface, such as OCR-B (or ECMA-B, after the European Computer Manufacturers' Association) has a higher compatibility, while the inclusion of lower-case letters, as well as the usual upper-case (or capitals) gives very high compatibility. *See* Fig. 22.

Multi-font readers are available and also readers that will accept fonts only resembling specific machine fonts. Standard typewriter fonts (pica at ten characters per 25 mm and elite at twelve char-

OCR-A

IS AVAILABLE IN UPPER CASE AND WITH COMPATIBLE LOWER CASE AND SHOULD BE USED IN APPLICATIONS THAT ARE PRIMARILY HUMAN FACTORS INSENSITIVE.

The compatible lower case extends the available character set.

OCR-B

With lower case provides good human compatability with some compromise for ease of machine reading. It is recommended for applications that are human factors sensitive.

ELITE

When maximum interchange with humans is a requirement, an elite face can be utilized with utmost efficiency, for the total man/machine system.

Courtesy Interscan Data Systems (U.K.) Ltd.

FIG. 22. Fonts (or founts) for optical character recognition.

acters per 25 mm), typeset fonts and computer print-out fonts can be used with some equipment. Facilities may be available for accepting handwritten characters (*see* Fig. 23). Characters may be printed in dropout colour (generally red) so that the machine will not read them.

Low-cost equipment is available for handling documents of about the size of a standard eighty-column punched card, on each of which one line of O.C.R. characters can be placed, as well as other printed or written matter. In many ways this is similar to punched card equipment, having sorting facilities. Such documents are suited to "turn-around" processing, as occurs with slips for billing customers, requesting payment of subscriptions, stocktaking and consumer market research. Other forms of equipment are especially suited to reading information printed on to cash register rolls and are generally referred to as journal-roll readers.

At the other end of the scale, page readers will accept a great variety and size of documents, with or without pre-printed field blocks, at instantaneous reading rates of a few hundred to several thousand characters a second. Documents move at a constant speed through the reader, in which a scanning device inspects a band at right angles to the paper movement, and, under the control of a built-in computer, interprets what it finds. In some systems scanning control can be used to extract information in specific parts of the document by using an imaginary system of X and Y co-ordinates.

The requirements as to paper quality, thickness, opacity, etc., may be very stringent, but the more sophisticated devices allow for a wide range in these respects.

Reading reliability and capability of correction is important. Substitution of the wrong character can occur, giving rise to a read error, while some characters may not be recognised, perhaps due to faulty printing. It has been claimed that accuracy is much higher than with punched cards. A keyboard may be used to cope with characters that are not recognised, these being flashed on a monitor screen, together with surrounding text, so that the operator can override the doubtful character by depressing the appropriate key. O.C.R. equipment may sometimes be on-line to the computer but more usually the information is output on to magnetic tape for use as computer input.

PRINTING DEVICES

Printing is by far the most important of the forms of computer output and techniques have been devised and are still being de-

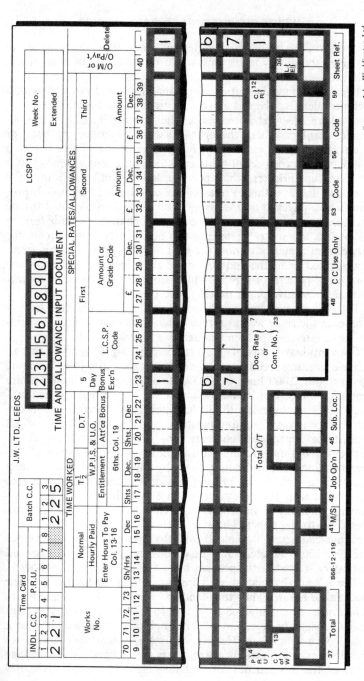

Fig. 23. Document for hand-written O.C.R. (Actual form is printed in green and black.) *Courtesy John Waddington Ltd.*

veloped to cope with a wide variety of needs, from the print out of massive tabulations to the tiny width of the paper of a small calculator.

Users are more concerned with capabilities and costs than with technical details. There is a broad distinction between impact printers, where the type impinges on the printing surface, and non-impact printers, where the characters are generated by heat, or electrostatically, or chemically, or by a jet of ink. There is also a distinction between serial printers, which print one character at a time, and line printers, which print (or have the effect of printing) a complete line at a time. Printers have also been developed to produce whole pages at a time, using laser technology. As for the type itself, there are devices in which each print character is fully formed (as with a typewriter or teleprinter) and others which create the shape from a matrix of dots (as with a stylus printer, using a pattern formed from the ends of wires, or a thermal printer, which may use a pattern of ceramic chips sequentially heated in contact with heat-sensitive paper moving over them).

The console typewriter and the teleprinter print one character at a time, in the same way as a typewriter. This results in slow operation at a rate of about ten characters a second.

Conventional forms of line printer use various mechanisms to achieve printing speeds varying from less than 100 lines a minute up to about 2,000 lines (or 3,000 if only numeric characters are required). These include barrel, chain and bar printers. A continuously revolving barrel, with all characters reproduced round its circumference in each printing position, may have the paper pressed against the appropriate characters by means of hammers. Alternatively, a continuous chain, with all the letters, may move parallel to the print line, the paper being struck by a hammer when the correct character arrives in each printing position. Another approach is to have bars, with all the characters in each printing position, each moving vertically to the appropriate character, which is then hammered on to the paper. The size of the character set available (64 separate characters is typical) and the number of characters per line (96, 120, 160, etc.) must be considered. Continuous interfold stationery is used, with sprocket holes that may later be removed.

The potential speed of such impact printers is limited by their mechanical nature, while they tend to be bulky items of equipment. When properly maintained they can produce a high quality of print against a clean background, which is not always the case with some rival systems. Specially treated stationery, which may sometimes discolour even with the heat from a person's hand, is required by some of the modern devices, but it is claimed that this is partly offset by not having to buy inked ribbons. In some applications more than a single copy of the print-out may be required. This is easily achieved by carbon-interleaved stationery or by non-carbon-copy forms on impact printers, but may be impossible or expensive with some other kinds of printer. Ink-jet printers, for example, are restricted to one copy at a time because of the nature of the process, but speeds of 100 characters a second are possible. Xerographic printing is again a single copy process but offering high speed and the facility to generate form layout and headings as part of the print process. Professional printing, using different fonts and sizes, can now be set up by equipment similar to that used for word processing (*see* Chapter 10). Speeds as high as 18,000 lines per minute are claimed with page printers, which also perforate, punch, collate, stack and address.

Business men and managers must pay regard to their real needs when considering the purchase of printing equipment. Certain prints, such as statements, have to be generated regularly and sent to customers; others are required for internal control, but these are useful only in so far as they can be read and their contents used as the basis of action. It is pointless generating a library of printed material every month if it just remains on the shelves awaiting its destruction date. The "exception" approach, in which only information of significance for decision-making according to some established criterion is printed, may be examined with profit. Much information may be retained in the computer storage as part of a data base, until called for, while techniques such as using microfilm can reduce the bulk of humanly readable output.

MICROFILM

Microfilm consists of small transparencies developed originally to save storage space, since whole pages and documents can be photographed at great reduction. Savings of over 99 per cent of original storage space may be possible. Retrieval of the information involves enlarging the appropriate frame of film in a viewer. Hard-copy reproductions can also be made.

Various versions and sizes are available, generally based on eight, sixteen or thirty-five millimetre film, which may be in rolls, cartridges, aperture cards or microfiche. The latter, which is very popular, is a rectangular sheet of mounted film, often 6 in. × 4 in. (approx. 15 cm × 10 cm), on which can be stored for example, sixty images, in five rows and twelve columns, as well as a title strip. Much higher packing densities, up to several thousands per fiche, can be attained, using suitable apparatus and grain-free film.

Microfiche viewers have an indexing device enabling the required image to be selected and projected, after the appropriate microfiche has been automatically withdrawn from a storage carousel, in more sophisticated systems.

Use of microfilm for retaining computer output goes back to the late 1950s but great advances in commercial applications took place towards the end of the 1960s. The term COM (Computer Output Microfilm) is used.

The rate of printing (for example 30,000 lines a minute) is much higher than achieved by normal impact printing methods. Equipment costs are high compared with costs of impact printers but film costs may be much less than the costs of stationery.

Microfilm units may operate off line from magnetic tape produced by the computer or may be on-line to the computer. Some equipment has facilities for producing hard copy, in the form of enlarged prints on paper, either as required, at the touch of a button, or automatically, through a high-speed printer.

Large organisations, with correspondingly large files of customers, stock items, etc., are the chief users of COM equipment. Bureaux services are available for smaller firms and those wishing to experiment with the system.

COM offers opportunities for retrieval of information from a data base without using print facilities. In this respect it may be seen as a rival to the video unit, with the advantage of permanency and potential for displaying more information. The computer may be used to reassemble data which may then be printed on to microfiche and indexed. Typical applications would be stock records and customers' accounts.

TERMINALS AND VISUAL DISPLAY UNITS

A terminal is an input and/or output device, normally on-line to a computer, but possibly linked over a communication line with some other peripheral device. The term thus includes the conventional sort of teleprinter terminal, the visual display terminal and special shop-floor terminals. The conventional telephone is a form of terminal and may be used in conjunction with time-sharing systems and Prestel (*see* Chapter 4).

The most usual form of terminal is the teleprinter, having a keyboard like a normal typewriter, with some extra keys for control functions, rub out, etc. Information and instructions are typed on the keyboard and transmitted to the computer. A speedier and more reliable way of transmitting is to punch a paper tape on the equipment first and then, after this has been checked, to feed this into the read device. The teleprinter can receive as well as transmit information, though speeds are very low compared with, say, line printers. Teleprinters normally print one character at a time through a ribbon, after the fashion of a typewriter, but variations such as heat printing and printing on pressure-sensitive paper are available.

Special keyboards may be designed for particular purposes. A numeric keyboard with the digits in three rows and columns, for ease of operation with one hand, is an example.

A visual display unit (V.D.U.), also termed a video unit, consists basically of a television-type screen on which output of characters, graphs and diagrams and facsimiles of documents and records may be displayed. An input keyboard, generally with a typewriter layout, is often incorporated for the transmission of data. Portable units of brief-case size are available with plug-in facilities. Hardcopy, that is print-out, from V.D.U.s may be obtained by attaching a print unit in the circuit, perhaps of the impactless printer type. An alternative is to obtain a photo-copy of the end of the screen, which is useful for retaining diagrams (*see* Fig. 39).

Visual display units proliferated in the 1970s, becoming an accepted and even dominant feature of the computer scene. They helped to speed the process of data retrieval, were associated with the control of data input and word processing, and were very helpful in the editing of data and the creation of computer files. A typical V.D.U. offers twenty-four lines of eighty characters width. Character sets include both upper and lower case characters ("capitals" and "small letters"). There are special facilities for drawing lines and diagrams. Colour systems are available, with a choice of eight colours from which bar charts, graphs and diagrams can be drawn. Such V.D.U.s are likely to be "intelligent", with built-in microprocessors to facilitate achieving the desired images with the minimum of software, together with random access memory, supplemented, in some cases, by floppy discs. Bubble memory technology enables information to be retained in store when a terminal is switched off. There are facilities for displaying preformed lines and columns to assist in data layout.

A light pen, a hand-held device similar to a pen and connected by a flexible light guide to a light-sensitive circuit, is useful in design (*see* Chapter 10). With appropriate programs it can be used to "draw" on the screen (really inputting new positions) and also to "point" to visible parts of a picture to enable action to be taken.

Programmable terminals have been developed, with their own small processors, to perform off-line functions as well as to communicate with main computers.

GRAPH PLOTTERS

We have noted the use of visual display units in connection with graphical displays, including the use of colour. Another approach of long standing is to use graph plotting devices.

A simple mechanical system uses a computer controlled pen positioned over a flat bed or drum, on which a variety of types of paper may be mounted. Such digital incremental plotters control the movement of the pen along each axis by a separate motor receiving digital commands from the computer which cause movement in predetermined increments. One method is for the pen to be moved laterally across the paper while the paper drum turns back and forth at right angles to this movement. Commands are also incorporated to raise and lower the pen. High speed plotting of straight lines and smooth curves is possible using a zip mode, where input commands represent velocity increments, causing changes in speed relative to the axes. Sophisticated systems are available which control colour pens and also enable the user to select speeds and styles of characters and lines.

Electrostatic machines mark specially treated paper electronically, so that carbon particles will adhere, the image being automatically "toned" in the machine to give a dry copy. These machines generally have a dual row of stylus printers across the printing width, any one or combination of which can be activated to produce a shape (including alpha characters) in any position as the paper is drawn from its roll. Speeds of about 2,000 lines per minute can be obtained.

An alternative to pen plotting is electronic digital plotting where plots on the surface of a cathode ray tube are recorded on paper or microfilm.

It is possible to produce graphical output without special graph-plotting equipment. A teleprinter or line-printer can be programmed to print out, say, Xs, line by line, to form the pattern required by the graph. Users can write their own programs or may avail themselves of packages provided by manufacturers and bureaux (*see* Fig. 38).

ADD-ON MEMORIES

The idea of extending the memory of a computer by additional units is an old one. Core stores became available for enhancing mainframe computers. Minis could be enlarged by add-on units, at some risk of destroying their initial cost advantage over larger systems. If such additions are integrated with the main memory, as distinct from acting as backing store as is the usual case with tape and discs, they may be used to expand a system up to its theoretical addressing capacity. Beyond this they may be used as protected parts of store, say for machine language programs or for display storage. Such memories may be designed for direct interfacing with particular computers and are increasingly based on silicon chip random access memory. The term add-in memory may be used when they are small enough to locate within the computer frame.

OTHER EQUIPMENT

Among the many items of specialised equipment the following may be mentioned.

1. Devices which check the identity of a person who may wish to use a terminal. Identification cards or badges, generally in plastic, are chiefly used. Special equipment is required to produce these. Security may be assisted by requiring the user to key into the terminal some identification code which he has committed to memory. More sophisticated systems will compare signatures with an established pattern or use voice analysis.

2. Devices which respond to spoken commands and those with a spoken form of output. The latter presents special problems. It is not just a matter of recording standard messages as with a speaking clock or telephone answering device. The ultimate aim is to string words into sentences appropriate to the information being output in a way that pays attention to the subtleties of human speech.

3. Special forms of terminal, such as for the automatic collection of technical data (telemetering) perhaps from a remote site or where it is inconvenient or impossible to use a human inspector. Simple terminals have also been devised to cope with the collection of data from the shop floor in connection with, say, production control and time recording as a basis of wage payment and of job timing and costing.

4. Off-line equipment involved making print-out presentable. Separating continuous stationery (bursting), separating copies (decollating) and removing sprocket holes by edge-cutting are examples.

5. The advent of programmable read-only memory silicon chip devices (*see* Chapter 1) has caused equipment such as ultra-violet erasers and PROM programmers to become available. The latter can be linked with a variety of input/output peripherals.

6. Devices which interpret letters and figures which are being written on forms placed over them.

7. Unromantic furnishings, such as tape racks and floppy disc filing systems, used to back up the computer facility.

SPECIMEN EXAMINATION QUESTIONS

1. Explain the functions of peripherals in a computing system, mentioning at least five specific examples.

2. How do you account for the survival of punched cards for computer input in the face of so many rival methods?

3. Discuss the uses of punched paper tape in connection with computers.

4. Compare magnetic tapes and magnetic discs as computer storage media and explain why both are frequently used in the same configuration.

5. Explain what is meant by backing store, discussing its importance in practice and giving examples of suitable equipment.

6. Account for the popularity of magnetic cassettes and floppy discs in modern office systems.

7. Write explanatory notes on: (a) access time, (b) packing density, (c) blocking of records and (d) buckets, in connection with magnetic storage devices.

8. Briefly describe four modern peripheral devices that you consider may have a significant impact on present office methods. Give reasons.

9. Distinguish between optical mark reading and optical character recognition in connection with computer input and discuss their likely applicability to office work.

10. List and briefly explain the method of operation of the different forms of printing devices available for computer output.

11. "In selecting a printing device attention has to be paid to many factors other than speed of operation." Discuss.

12. A large organisation is experiencing problems with its cumbersome and ever-expanding conventional filing system. Write a brief report to the office manager explaining how the use of microfilm may help and how this may be linked with a computer system.

13. "The new business office will be controlled through computer terminals and visual display units." Comment on this statement.

14. Explain three of the following: (a) key-to-disc, (b) point-of-sale data collection, (c) light pen, (d) ultra violet eraser, (e) telemetering.

Chapter 3

BASIC PROGRAMMING

SOME FUNDAMENTALS

The aim of the present chapter is to introduce the reader to basic concepts of programming using the high level language BASIC. This language is both simple to learn and valuable in practice, especially when terminals are being used. Versions are also available for running on smaller computers and for batch use on large systems.

We shall refer again to Fig. 6 (*see* p. 18) explaining the simple program line by line.

First notice that each line is given a number by the programmer. With BASIC programs the computer will follow the order of these numbers. This will generally be the sequence in which the lines occur, but BASIC, as developed for use with computer terminals, has the feature of allowing lines to be inserted by typing an appropriate line number later in the program. This is the reason for spacing the line numbers in steps of 10. If we wish to insert, say, two lines between lines 20 and 30 we can type lines numbered, say, 25 and 26 at the end of the program and they will fall automatically into place. A line can be altered by typing the same line number below, followed by the correct version. The sequence rule for most program languages, e.g. COBOL, is that the lines are obeyed in the order in which they are written, unless a particular instruction in the program breaks this sequence.

Line 10 is a "REMARK" that will be ignored by the computer. Such lines may be inserted in the program to explain what is happening to a human reader. The programmer may insert them to remind himself of the purpose of particular program lines.

Line 20 tells the computer to "READ" the four numbers at the read device and to allocate these to storage spaces that will be referred to by the programmer subsequently as A, Q, P and R. This allocation is taken care of automatically and the programmer is not concerned with the precise location of such data in the memory, as he would be with machine-code programming. Notice that the variables are separated by commas.

Variables can take on different values according to the data on which the program is working. The rules in BASIC are that we

55

may use any single letter of the alphabet or any letter followed by a single number, for example Al, E3, etc. Combinations of letters, such as TOT, AV, STOCK, etc., are not allowed.

Lines 30, 40 and 50 are examples of assignment statements. Line 30 tells the computer to multiply the number it finds in the storage location called Q by that found in location P and to make the storage location called E equal to the product. Notice that all such statements must begin with LET and that the normal mathematical operation signs plus (+) and minus (−) are used, while a star (*) is used for multiplication and a slash (/) is used for division. Raising to powers, or exponentiation, is done with two stars (**) or by a vertical arrow (↑). Brackets may be used to control the order of the calculation. For example LET A = P(1 + R / 100)↑N is the statement to calculate the amount (A) of a principal (P) invested for N years at R per cent compound interest. It will be noted that a separate line is used for each assignment statement.

Line 60 is an instruction to PRINT the data required. The variables are separated by commas. Simple BASIC allows for up to five numbers to be printed on each line in what are called zones, each fifteen characters wide. If we wish to print, say, Q on the line below we should have an instruction

65 PRINT Q

The Q could be caused to print as the fifth number of the first line by placing a comma after the N of the print statement of line 60.

Skipping of print lines can be achieved by a PRINT statement containing no print instructions for each blank line required.

The data on which the program is to operate is shown on lines each starting with the word DATA. Such data will be interpreted according to the READ statements in the program. The order must be that indicated in such instructions. For example the first number will be interpreted as A, the second as Q, the third as P and the fourth as R, according to the READ statement of line 20.

The end of a program is indicated by END on a line bearing the highest line number. Different terminal systems vary with regard to this. In some cases the program end is shown by a STOP statement, after which DATA lines may be included.

The use of variables such as Q and P enables the same program to be used for similar calculations for any number of different values of data. Special one-off programs may be written where all the data occurs in the program, with statements such as 10 LET E = 8 * 5·25. Such programs are more likely to occur with complex scientific calculations rather than in business. The result of a single calculation can be printed out by a simple statement, e.g. 10 PRINT 8 * 5·25.

The program may be typed in through a terminal keyboard or pre-punched on paper tape and read in automatically. The requirements of the computer or time-sharing system being used must also be obeyed by typing the appropriate command instructions, for instance RUN, to cause the program to operate. This is dealt with in Chapter 4.

CORRECTING ERRORS IN PROGRAMS

In Fig. 24 we see some of the errors which could arise on typing the first program at a computer terminal and how they could be corrected. The interactive compiler vets the program lines for syntactic errors—mistakes in using the BASIC language—and draws attention to these with an upward arrow, followed by a brief explanation on the line below. Most compilers have some such facility but, unless they are interactive, we have to wait until the complete program is compiled before it is vetted for errors.

Line 10 has been typed without a proper indication that it is a REMARK. This gives rise to the print-out STATEMENT NOT RECOGNISED. The operator traces the mistake and types the complete line correctly. Note that REM is an acceptable abbreviation for REMARK.

Line 20 should have a comma between variables Q and P, giving rise to the INCORRECT FORMAT print-out.

Line 30 tries to use X as the multiplication operator instead of *.

Line 40 shows the use of brackets to add clarity to a formula. Unfortunately the final right-hand bracket has been omitted.

Line 50, Syntactically there is nothing wrong with this line, but the variable F has been used in mistake for E. Since F is never given a value by the included data or formulae the computer cannot perform the calculation as indicated in this line when the program is run. The mistake is latent until this stage (see lower down, after RUN) when it results in the computer print-out UNDEFINED VARIABLE F. Some languages require that all variable be "declared" at a stage before they are used. A declaration list is usually found near the start of such programs. We shall later see that certain more complicated variables in BASIC require declaration (as by DIMENSION or MATRIX statements).

Line 60 requires no amendment.

Line 70 shows the effect of waiting too long to input data. The second attempt succeeds but is not recognised by the computer

```
-10   RE FIRST DEMONSTRATION PROGRAM
      |
STATEMENT NOT RECOGNISED
-10   REM FIRST DEMONSTRATION PROGRAM
-20   READ A,QP,R
      |
INCORRECT FORMAT
-20   READ A,Q,P,R
-30   LET E=QXP
      |
OPERATOR NOT RECOGNISED
-30   LET E=Q*P
-40   LET D=E*(R/100

BRACKETS MISMATCHED
-40     LET D=E*(R/100)
-50     LET N=F-D
-60     PRINT A,E,D,N
-70     21,8,5,  WAITING
-70     21,8,5,25,10
        |
STATEMENT NOT RECOGNISED
-70     DATA 21,8,5,25,10
-80     END
-LIST
  10    REM FIRST DEMONSTRATION PROGRAM
  20    READ A,Q,P,R
  30    LET E=Q*P
  40    LET D=E*(R/100)
  50    LET N=F-D
  60    PRINT A,E,D,N
  70    DATA 21,8,5,25,10
  80    END

OK
-RUN

UNDEFINED VARIABLE F
HALTED AT LINE  50
-50  LET N=E-D
-RUN
21              42                    4.2              37.8
STOPPED AT LINE 80
-70 DATA 25,10,6,75,20
-RUN
25              67.5                  13.5             54
STOPPED AT LINE 80
  SAVE AS DEMO
OK
-BYE
OK
12.05.12-LOGOUT
CONNECTED FOR      17 MINS
MILL TIME USED      6 SECS
```

FIG. 24. Interactive detection and correction of program errors. (University of Southampton BASIC Mark 9S run on multi-access system.)

since the figures do not commence with DATA. The line is typed again commencing correctly.

The revised version of the program is now printed by the computer, following the typing of instruction LIST. The print OK shows that this version obeys the rules of BASIC. The instruction RUN is typed, causing the error discussed at line 50 above to be revealed. A revised line 50 is typed and the program is again run, resulting in the print-out of the four numbers.

A fresh set of data has been included by typing a new line 70 and the program has again been run to give the new print-out.

TRANSFERS AND LOOPS

A program for calculating the average of an unspecified number of positive numbers is shown in Fig. 25. It is based on the flow chart of Fig. 5.

```
10   REMARK AVERAGE CALCULATION POSITIVE NUMBERS
20   LET T=0
30   LET N=0
40   READ X
50   IF X<0 THEN 90
60   LET T=T+X
70   LET N=N+1
80   GO TO 40
90   LET A=T/N
100  PRINT "AVERAGE = ",A
110  DATA 3,5,12,9,25,2,-1
120  END


AVERAGE =        6.25
```

Fig. 25. Program, data and output for average calculation.

The principle is to read the numbers one at a time (line 40) until the end of the series is indicated by an end marker, in this case a negative number deliberately added to the data. Both T (the total of numbers) and N (the count of the numbers) are set a zero initially (lines 20 and 30) to prevent anything previously in the memory from being accumulated. Time-sharing systems generally present the user with a blank memory, so this may strictly be unnecessary.

After each number is read it is checked for being negative by the comparison in line 50, where IF $X < 0$ (if X is less than zero) implies a test for a negative value of X. Other signs that may be used are:

$>$ is greater than
$=$ is equal to

$>$ = is greater than or equal to
$<$ = is less than or equal to
$<$ $>$ is not equal to.

The whole statement of line 50 is what is termed a conditional transfer with an IF/THEN command. If the condition applies then the program is diverted to the line number indicated, otherwise it will continue at the next line.

Line 60 shows the way to accumulate a total. The value just read in is added to the previous total. Such statements must be interpreted as meaning that the variable on the left of the assignment statement becomes what it was previously plus the new number; they cannot be regarded as algebraic expressions where = implies equality. The method of counting is shown in line 70. One is added to the previous count each time a number is processed.

An unconditional transfer occurs in line 80. The computer is told to GO TO line 40. This provides the necessary loop to keep reading in numbers until the end marker is reached. When this occurs the program omits lines 60 to 80 and jumps to line 90, where the calculation of the average occurs.

The print-out is slightly more ambitious than in the previous example. Any characters or blanks enclosed in quotes will be printed out in that form, followed by any variables indicated. Such a string of characters is sometimes termed a literal constant or label, though the latter term is more generally used to signify the address of an instruction in machine code.

It is possible to include calculations as part of the print instruction instead of dealing with them in separate statements. Thus we could omit line 90, as it stands, and have print line:

100 PRINT "AVERAGE =", T/N

This is satisfactory in such a simple case but is not advisable where calculations are interdependent because of the complexity of the print statement.

LISTS AND TABLES

We have seen that BASIC permits the use of any letter to represent a variable in a program, and the program for the calculation of the average allowed X to take on successively the values of the numbers read in. At any time the storage location assigned to X would contain the latest value of X read in, the previous value being overwritten.

Frequently it is useful to read into memory, at one time, a series of numbers representing, say, different values of X. These may be regarded as a list or column of figures from a table headed "X values". The position in the column can be indicated by placing a number in brackets after the variable. Thus, X(1), X(3), Y(5) refer, respectively to the first X value, the third X value and the fifth Y value. Such variables are referred to as subscripted variables. In programming it is of great help to be able to refer to a position in general terms, such as X(N), where N is itself a variable, of which the value may be designated during the running of the program.

Figure 26 shows a simple routine to read in any number of numbers and to keep track of the order in which they are stored. A

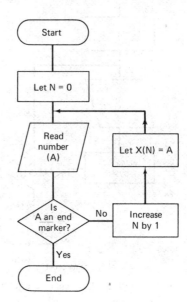

FIG. 26. Flow chart to read a list of numbers into store and count how many.

variable, N, is set initially at zero. The first number, referred to as A, is read and checked to see if it is an end marker; if not, N is increased by one, and the value of A is stored in position X(1). For the next positive value of A this is repeated, N becoming two, and the second number being stored in position X(2). This goes on until the negative number results in an exit from the read loop.

If it is desired to print out, say, the sixth number, then an instruction PRINT X(6) would be used. Similarly the sixth value of X can be called for calculation in the same way; we might have LET Z = Y *X(6); two or more subscripted values might be used, such as LET A(6) = B(1) * C(6) * D(10). The star is used throughout programming to avoid the confusion that would arise between X as a letter and as a multiplication sign.

The print out of a list of N numbers, where N is a known value, can be obtained as in the flow chart in Fig. 27(a). The counting variable used has been called M. This increases by one each time a value, X(M), is printed. When M exceeds N the print loop is abandoned by following the yes outlet from the decision involving IS M > N?

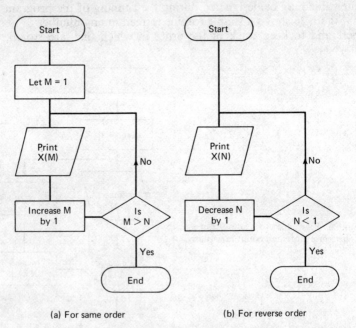

(a) For same order   (b) For reverse order

FIG. 27. Flow chart to print a list of N numbers held in store.

Part (b) of Fig. 27 shows the simple way in which the printing order can be reversed. The instruction PRINT X(N) results in the last stored value being printed. N is reduced by one after each number is printed, so that numbers stored in the (N−1), (N−2), (N−3) etc. positions are printed next. After the first stored value has been printed N is reduced to zero and the yes reply to the question IS N < 1? gives an exit from the print loop.

The BASIC versions of these simple routines are shown in Fig. 28. In the read routine the number most recently read is first called A so that it may be tested before being allotted its appropriate place as an X value.

```
10   REMARK READ ROUTINE
20   LET N=0
30   READ A
40   IF A<0 THEN 80
50   LET N=N+1
60   LET X(N)=A
70   GO TO 30
80   END


10   REMARK PRINT ROUTINE ORIGINAL ORDER
20   LET M=1
30   PRINT X(M)
40   LET M=M+1
50   IF M>N THEN 70
60   GO TO 30


10   REMARK PRINT ROUTINE REVERSE ORDER
20   PRINT X(N)
30   LET N=N-1
40   IF N<1 THEN 60
50   GO TO 20
```

FIG. 28. Programs for reading and printing an array of numbers.

Subscripted variables are often referred to as arrays. They may
also be regarded as lists of data. With BASIC the computer will
automatically find space for any list of items up to a limited
number, perhaps as low as ten, that are called for in the program.
It is also possible to state the number of items in the list anywhere
in the program by a dimension statement, such as DIM X(100),
Y(50) which would reserve space for 100 items of X and 50 of Y.
This is referred to as explicit declaration as compared to the implicit declaration when a dimension statement is not used. Other
programming languages generally require an explicit declaration
for all arrays, and often for all variables, before these can be used
in the program.

Tables, or matrices, involving more than one column, can be
handled by using a second subscript in the bracket. The first subscript refers to the number of the row and the second, separated by
a comma, to the number of the column. Thus X(7, 3) would imply
the seventh row and the third column. It will be remembered that
rows stretch from left to right while columns are vertical. To make
this clearer to the newcomer to these ideas suppose we have data as
follows:

6	12	1	9
8	4	10	2
7	6	1	4

There are three rows and four columns and the table dimensions could be declared as DIM X(3, 4). If X(2, 3) were specified in a calculation the number at the intersection of the second row and the third column, ten, would be selected. It must be clearly understood that (2, 3) refers to a position, rather like a map reference, and that in this location will be found an item of data.

"FOR" STATEMENTS

So important are subscribed items in programming that most languages include a special technique for processing loops, such as would be involved in reading in, for example, eight items. This can be done by statements such as:

```
FOR I = 1 TO 8
READ X(I)
NEXT I
```

which will cause I to vary from one to eight, in steps of one. A general form of read routine could be as follows:

```
FOR I = 1 to N
READ X(I)
NEXT I
```

which would require that the first data item read, by a preceding statement, READ N, would be the number of items, N (or eight in this case), after which would follow the eight numbers to form the list on a DATA line.

These FOR statements may be nested one inside the other. A simple case occurs when a table is being read, requiring the following statements:

```
FOR I = 1 TO 3
  FOR J = 1 TO 4
  READ X(I, J)
  NEXT J
NEXT I
```

which would read in the table used as an example above, if the data were presented as:

    DATA 6, 12, 1, 9, 8, 4, 10, 2, 7, 6, 1, 4

The effect is to allocate the first four numbers to positions (1, 1), (1, 2), (1, 3) and (1, 4) and the next four to (2, 1), (2, 2), (2, 3) and (2, 4), and so on. The second subscript varies within the first.

A general READ statement could take the form:

```
READ M, N
FOR I = 1 TO M
  FOR J = 1 TO N
  READ X(I, J)
  NEXT J
NEXT I
```

with data:

DATA 3, 4, 6, 12, 1, 9, 8, 4, 10, 2, 7, 6, 1, 4

in which the 3 and 4 at the start are the dimensions of the table. More than one line may occur between the FOR and NEXT statements (an example is given in Fig. 30).

Increases in steps other than one may be indicated by adding STEP, followed by the incremented number (which may be negative, calling for a decrease). Thus

FOR I = 1 TO 16 STEP 5

would increase I successively through 1, 6, 11 to 16 while

FOR I = 30 TO 10 STEP − 5

would decrease I successively through 30, 25, 20, 15 to 10.

An expression such as $2 * Y$, or $X + Y$, or N may be used for any or all of the initial and final values and size of step. For example:

FOR K = X TO Y + Z STEP 5 * A

will be valid, provided that the computer can evaluate the expressions used from data previously stored.

In connection with variables for use with BASIC programs it may be noted that the single letter variable, as so far used, whether subscripted or not, may be coupled with a single numeric digit, giving, as examples, A1, A2, X8, A1(1), A1(2). This enables the number of variables to be extended and also enables the same letter to indicate, say, different sets of data relating to the same subject by using a different number for each set. Subscripting is not affected and in the example just given, A1(1) would be the first item in an array of data collectively known as A1, while A1(2) would be the second item.

FUNCTIONS

Some mathematical functions occur so frequently in calculations that special provisions are made for them in most high level languages. Thus the programmer does not have to devise a means of calculating the square root of a number, all he need do is to put the number in brackets after the letters SQR. This can be extended to expressions of which the square root has to be found. Thus SQR (12), SQR(X), SQR(X + Y) would result in the square roots of 12, X and X + Y, respectively, being available. These would be included in statements such as:

LET Z = SQR(X + Y)

As well as the square root the following functions, among others, may be available in BASIC:

ABS(X)—the absolute value of X, disregarding any sign.
INT(X)—the whole number or integer part of X.
LOG(X)—the natural logarithm (to base e) of X.
LGT(X)—the logarithm of X to base 10.
EXP(X)—the value of e (the mathematical constant) to the Xth power.
SIN(X), COS(X), TAN(X)—trigonometrical functions of X in radians.
ATN(X)—the arctangent, in radians, of X.

In addition RND(X) calls up the next in a series of pseudo-random numbers. With some BASIC compilers it may be possible for the user to create his own functions within a program for use when required. The letters FN followed by a single letter, chosen by the user, can be defined as a function as follows:

DEF FNA(X) = X + X ↑ 2 + X ↑ 3

requiring its own numbered statement line. This would enable $X + X^2 + X^3$ to be calculated by a statement:

LET Y = FNA(X)

Since a computer is really only capable of simple mathematical operations, functions of any complexity have to be broken down to make them amenable to computer processing. This has become an important branch of mathematics referred to as numerical analysis.

SUBROUTINES

A subroutine is a set of statements forming a procedure that has been tested and is to be used one or more times in a program. In BASIC the subroutine is written as a series of numbered statements, ending with a RETURN statement. Thus:

```
100 READ M, N
110 FOR I = 1 TO M
```

```
120 FOR J = 1 TO N
130 READ X(I, J)
140 NEXT J
150 NEXT I
160 RETURN
```

converts the matrix read procedure, previously considered, into a subroutine. This could be called in the program by a statement:

    30 GOSUB 100

the result being that, on reading line thirty, the program will go to line 100, perform the subroutine, and then return to the line following line thirty. It might be easier to use the special MATRIX facilities next outlined for this purpose.

Subroutines can be very important in business programming for standard calculations, such as tax for payroll purposes. A library of subroutines may be on file. It may be possible to link with standard routines in a language other than that being used for the main program. Figure 32 gives an example of a BASIC program using subroutines.

MATRIX FACILITIES

BASIC contains powerful facilities for reading, operating on and printing matrices, which are really tables of rows and columns in which data is located.

The statement

    10 MAT READ A(3, 2)

suffices to enable a table to be read consisting of three rows and two columns, provided by a data line such as:

    20 DATA 1, 2, 3, 4, 5, 6

The sequence of this data is important. The data for the first row, going across the columns, must first be stated, followed by the second row, and so on.

A simple print statement

    30 MAT PRINT A

secures a print-out as follows:

```
1   2
3   4
5   6
```

Once the dimensions of the matrix have been established the whole matrix can be referred to by a single letter in a statement beginning with MAT. In the above example this letter is A.

If we wish to add together matrices A and B to give matrix C the statement would be:

60 MAT C = A + B

Subtraction is done by:

70 MAT D = A − B

The matrices would have to be conformable for these operations; that is one would have the same numbers of rows and columns as the other.

Multiplication (subject to there being as many columns in the first matrix as there are rows in the second) is achieved by a statement such as:

80 MAT E = A * B

Rows and columns of a matrix may be transposed by:

90 MAT F = TRN(A)

The involved process of matrix inversion, vital to some advanced business calculations, is achieved simply by:

100 MAT F = INV(A)

ALPHABETIC CHARACTERS AND STRINGS

We have seen that alpha characters may be included in a print-out by a statement such as:

PRINT "AVERAGE = ", A

where A is a numeric variable and AVERAGE = may be regarded as a constant sequence or string of alpha characters which is always printed when this program line occurs.

For many purposes in business it is useful to be able to treat words as variables which may be sorted, counted, etc.

Such alpha data is denoted in BASIC by a dollar sign following a letter, for example A$, B$, X$.

A statement

10 READ A$, B$

would cause words included in the appropriate sequence in data lines, e.g.

50 DATA JONES, BROWN

to be read in.

Lists of such items can be handled by first of all declaring the number of items by a DIMENSION statement:

10 DIM A$(20)

and then using, say, a FOR statement:

20 FOR I = 1 TO 20
30 READ A$(I)
40 NEXT I

The data line would, of course, require twenty names in this case.

Alpha characters are ranked in alphabetical order, so that, for example, C is "less than" F. This enables comparisons to be made, such as:

200 IF A$ < B$ THEN 250

If A$ were SMITH and B$ were THOMAS the effect of this line would be to transfer to line 250 of the program, since S is less than T. If the first letters of the names were the same then the second letters would decide, and so on. Thus, SMITH would be less than or come before SMYTHE. The numbers of letters in the name would not be significant, except if both names were the same apart from one or more extra letters at the end of one name.

Double subscript notation is not available for alpha data but the equivalent of a table with rows and columns can be created by using several alpha variables with single subscripts. Thus

DIM X$(15), Y$(15), Z$(15)

could be regarded as creating a table with three columns (X, Y and Z) and fifteen rows.

INTERACTIVE PROGRAMS

It is often useful in computing to "hold a conversation" with the computer. This really implies that at certain stages the computer indicates the need for extra information from the operator, who may guide it in the direction required, generally by typing information through the terminal or control keyboard. Examples of the practical use of this technique are given in Chapter 4.

Programs are written in such a way that, when certain stages are reached in the processing, a message is output through the terminal, requiring some response from the operator. This can be done with PRINT and READ statements. Some BASIC compilers have an INPUT statement which causes a question mark to be printed at the terminal, after which the operator types in the relevant data, in the order indicated by the program.

As an example, suppose that at one stage in the execution of a program, it is necessary for a date to be fed into the computer. This could be controlled by program statements such as

```
120 PRINT "TYPE, DAY, MONTH, YEAR"
130 INPUT, D, M, Y
```

resulting in output

```
TYPE DAY, MONTH, YEAR
?
```

to which the response might be

```
11, 12, 73
```

These would be interpreted as variables D, M and Y, respectively and would be handled as such by the program.

Without the INPUT facility, statement 130 would be replaced by a simple READ statement. A question mark could be printed by an extra statement PRINT "?" preceding this.

An important use of such techniques is in data- (or keyboard-) controlled programs where, for instance, a program may have various facilities, not all of which are required, and access to which is obtained by typing a pre-arranged number when called for by the print-out. A series of statements such as:

```
150 IF T = 1 THEN 200
160 IF T = 2 THEN 300
170 IF T = 3 THEN 400
```

would direct the computation to the appropriate part of the program.

More advanced interactive techniques can be used to program, say, business games. Here trainees make decisions that are fed into the computer, which is programmed quickly to assess the effect of these decisions and, possibly, to generate information on a basis not fully known to the players, as might occur in business.

Alpha input may be used, provided that this is indicated by alpha variables in the INPUT statement, e.g.

```
180 INPUT A$
```

One application is to control programs by typing YES or NO in response to questions, such as DO YOU WANT FURTHER INFORMATION? printed by the computer. The answers can be used in conjunction with IF statements to select the appropriate part of the program, as with the numerical responses above.

FORMAT

Automatic format

We have seen that BASIC has free format for input, implying that, provided the data is in the correct order according to the READ statements, it does not matter whether a number is an integer or real (with a decimal part) or how many letters are in alpha word. Individual items of data are separated by a comma, but if the data extends over several lines (each beginning with DATA) there must be no comma at the end of the lines.

Simple printing is achieved automatically in five positions across the page. These fixed tabulating positions, useful for lining up columns, can be destroyed by separating print items by semi-colons, when each item will take up just as much space as it needs.

Tabulating

A powerful means of controlling the printing position is to use the tabulating function (TAB). This indicated the position across the page (up to seventy-five characters) at which printing of specified items should start. Thus

50 PRINT X; TAB(10); A$; TAB(25); Y

would result in a variable X being printed starting at the extreme left, followed by alpha string A$ starting 10 characters from the left, followed by variable Y at 25 characters from the left. Notice the use of semi-colons.

This facility is very useful for precise control of format of tables and also for "drawing" graphs and bar charts, where a star or other character can be used on succeeding lines to denote, by its distance from the left hand edge of the paper, such things as frequency. This plotting shows independent variables (X values) vertically and dependent variables (Y values) horizontally. The tabulating position can be indicated dynamically by, say,

90 PRINT TAB(Y); "*"

which positions the star Y places to the right. Y can vary from line to line according to some formula. Thus, the following block of statements:

60 FOR X = 1 TO 10
70 LET Y = 20 + 4 * X

```
80 PRINT TAB(Y); "*"
90 NEXT X
```

will print the graph of $Y = 20 + 4X$ over the range of X values
from 1 to 10 in steps of 1.

"Print using" format

Ready control over format, up to a maximum line width of
seventy-two characters, is possible with a statement commencing
FORMAT, in which the precise use of each position in the line is
indicated. The FORMAT line is numbered in the normal way and
the program is directed to use this by a PRINT USING statement.
This indicates, first, the number of the format line (followed by a
colon), then any variables in the order in which they occur in the
format line. This approach is useful to combine text strings and
variables and to secure a desired format for numeric output, controlling the numbers of digits printed before and after the decimal
point, etc.

For example:

```
80 PRINT USING 90: X, Y, Y/Z
90 FORMAT "ANSWERS", # #, # #. #, #. # #
```

would result in the print of a line starting with the word AN-
SWERS. This would be followed by variable X printed as a two-
figure integer; by variable Y printed to one decimal place with two
figures before the point; and by the result of dividing Y by Z, printed to two decimal places with one digit before the point.

The hash mark (#) may also be used to control the length of
string arrays. A multiple may be indicated, e.g. 12# would reserve
space for a twelve character string.

Spaces may be indicated in the FORMAT either by blanks
within quotes or by stating a multiple of X, e.g. 6X would provide
for six blanks. This has nothing to do with the use of X as a variable.

Skipped lines can be obtained by the slash sign (/) preceded by
the number of lines involved, e.g. 6/.

The lines:

```
200 PRINT USING 210: X, Y
210 FORMAT "ANSWERS", 5X, #, 4/, 10X, # #. #
```

would result in a line starting with ANSWERS, followed by five
spaces and the single digit integer X. There would then be four
blank lines, followed by a line with variable Y having one digit
after the point and two before, inset ten spaces to the right.

FILES

Though much data in BASIC programs is obtained from DATA lines and INPUT statements it is possible to use "external" files created separately, if they are available to the terminal user.

The names of the files in the system are listed in the program in a FILES statement. Subsequent READ and WRITE statements show, first, the sequence number of the file in the FILE statement (preceded by a hash mark), followed by variables to be read from it or written to it, in order. Thus

```
10 FILES AFILE, BFILE
20 READ #1, X, Y, Z
```

would read variables X, Y and Z from the first file (AFILE).

After these variables have been used in the program, giving rise, say, to variables L, M and N, the instructions

```
100 SCRATCH #2
110 WRITE #2, L, M, N
```

will enable these values to be written to the second file, provided this does not already exist, in a form which can subsequently be used for BASIC input. The write file can be closed and made available for reading by the instruction

```
130 RESTORE #2
```

SORTING

Internal sorting

Arranging data in some predetermined order, or sorting, is one of the most important computer processes. Often in business data processing material that is to be used to update a master file has first to be sorted into the same order as the data in the master file.

The type of sorting used depends largely on the equipment available and the method of storing the data. We shall distinguish between data stored internally in the immediate access store and data stored externally on tape or on discs.

Internal sorting is a very efficient way of sorting. It implies that all the data can be drawn at one time into the immediate access store of the computer. Since such storage is limited by cost, much commercial data, which tends to be bulky, will have to be sorted by some other means, perhaps by punched card equipment, without using the computer, or by using computer peripherals controlled by a computer program. These methods are referred to in the Appendix. There are several approaches to the problem of internal sorting and two of these will be shown.

Figure 29 shows a flow chart for which the BASIC program is given in Fig. 30. A pre-determined number (N) of values is read and eventually printed-out in ascending order. Each number in turn, up to the (N − 1)th, or next to last, is compared with the following number in store. If it is not less than or equal to this then the fact is recorded by adding one to a counting variable, A, and the number is placed temporarily in location B, while the next number, which must be smaller, replaces it in its original location. The number in location B is then placed in the position of the

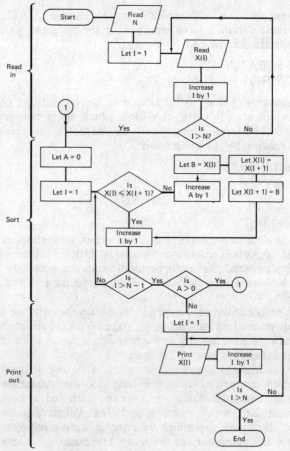

FIG. 29. Flow chart for internal sorting.

```
10   REMARK FIRST SORT PROGRAM
20   READ N
30   FOR I=1 TO N
40   READ X(I)
50   NEXT I
60   LET A=0
70   FOR I=1 TO N-1
80   IF X(I)<=X(I+1) THEN 130
90   LET A=A+1
100  LET B=X(I)
110  LET X(I)=X(I+1)
120  LET X(I+1)=B
130  NEXT I
140  IF A>0 THEN 60
150  FOR I=1 TO N
160  PRINT X(I)
170  NEXT I
```

FIG. 30. Program for internal sorting.

second of the two numbers. The effect is to reverse the order if the first of two numbers is not less than the second. This does not necessarily fully sort the numbers the first time; for example, an original series of numbers, 4, 1, 3, 2, 9, 8, 7, would become 1, 3, 2, 4, 8, 7, 9, after the first run through during which 4 changes with 1 and then with 3, and so on. A test is then made of whether any changes have been brought about during this sort. If so, shown by A exceeding zero, the process is repeated, giving in our simple example, 1, 2, 3, 4, 7, 8, 9, which can be seen to be in the correct order, but, since A will exceed 1, the computer will repeat the procedure, and finding A to be then zero, will print out the numbers as then stored.

An alternative form of sorting is shown in the flow chart of Fig. 31. Here an unspecified number of values are read in and counted (N). All the numbers are then searched to find the smallest, which is placed in the first position, while its own position is taken by the original first number. This is repeated, starting at the second, third, etc. numbers, until only one is left.

In the chart and program (Fig. 32) the nested FOR statements (lines 210 to 300) use I as the starting point of each search, becoming each time the minimum value of the items tested, while I signifies the item actually being compared. Notice that, for each search, J is initially made equal to I, so that the minimum values previously established are not disturbed. A variable, M, represents the minimum each time, and is set equal to the first value of the numbers to be tested (line 220). As the numbers are compared any less than or equal to the current value of M replaces M (line 250), while a note is kept of its position by making a variable K equal to J (line 260). When all the numbers have been compared (shown by J exceeding N, which is automatically handled by the FOR state-

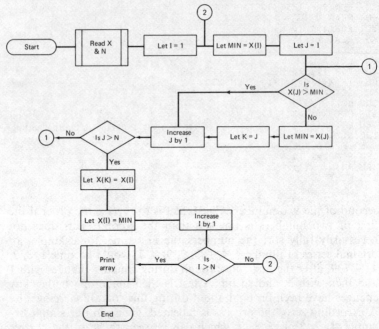

FIG. 31. Flow chart for internal sorting by alternative method.

ment), the program moves the number from the first position in that run into the Kth position (line 280) and then fills the first position with the M value (line 290). This procedure is then started at the next number by I becoming two, and so on. Finally the sorted items are printed.

With the numbers previously used, 4, 1, 3, 2, 9, 8, 7, the first run would start at 4 and set M equal to it. Comparison with the rest of the numbers would result in M becoming 1, which would be placed in first position, while 4 occupied the second. The six remaining numbers, starting at 4 would be surveyed and 2, located as the smallest, would be moved to the first place in this set, or the second place in the whole series, while 4 would replace it, giving 1, 2, 3, 4, 9, 8, 7. The next two passes would not upset this series since 3 and 4 are in correct order. The next pass would pull 7 into the fifth position and replace it by 9, so that the numbers would then be in order, but two more passes, starting at the sixth and seventh positions, would be performed.

It will be seen that the flow chart uses the symbol for a pre-defined process (*see* Fig. 42), for read and print-out, while the program, shown in Fig. 32, has been written as a set of subroutines.

```
10   REMARK ALTERNATIVE SORT PROGRAM
20   REMARK READ AND COUNT DATA
25   DIM X(50)
30   GOSUB 100
40   REMARK SORT
50   GOSUB 200
60   REMARK PRINT DATA
70   GOSUB 400
80   END
100  REMARK READ AND COUNT SUBROUTINE
110  LET N=0
120  READ A
130  IF A<0 THEN 170
140  LET N=N+1
150  LET X(N)=A
160  GO TO 120
170  RETURN
200  REMARK SORT SUBROUTINE
210  FOR I=1 TO N
220  LET M=X(I)
230  FOR J=I TO N
240  IF X(J)>M THEN 270
250  LET M=X(J)
260  LET K=J
270  NEXT J
280  LET X(K)=X(I)
290  LET X(I)=M
300  NEXT I
310  RETURN
400  REMARK PRINT SUBROUTINE
410  FOR I=1 TO N
420  PRINT X(I)
430  NEXT I
440  RETURN
```

FIG. 32. Alternative sort program as set of subroutines.

Sorting alpha data

The examples so far given have related to the sorting of numeric items. Alpha data may be similarly sorted by adjusting the programs. An example is shown in Figs. 33 and 34. The end-marker for the data has been fixed as ZZZ, being a combination of letters unlikely to feature in the data itself. The program has been designed to print out instructions of how the data is to be input. If the user knows the program he will have provided the data to be sorted, starting on line 400. He will answer "NO" to the query "DO YOU WANT INSTRUCTIONS?" and the program will cause the items to be printed in alphabetical order. In the case shown he has requested instructions and provided a new data line 400, subsequently running the program again to incorporate this.

The programs in this chapter illustrate the use of a sophisticated version of BASIC. On some microcomputers, for cheapness, such a

```
10    PRINT " SORT PROGRAM USING DATA LINES"
20    PRINT
30    PRINT
40    PRINT " DO YOU WANT INSTRUCTIONS?"
50    INPUT A$
60    IF A$=" NO" THEN 110
70    PRINT "PROVIDE DATA ON LINE 400 ETC AND RERUN"
80    PRINT " END WITH ZZZ"
90    GOTO 390
100   REM READ AND SORT ALPHA ITEMS FROM DATA LINES
110   LET C=0
120   DIM X$ (200)
130   PRINT
140   PRINT
150   PRINT
160   READ A$
170   IF A$=" ZZZ" THEN 210
180   LET C=C+1
190   LET X$(C)=A$
200   GOTO 160
210   FOR I=1 TO C
220   LET L$=X$ (I)
230   FOR J=I TO C
240   IF X$(J)>L$ THEN 270
250   LET L$=X$ (J)
260   LET K=J
270   NEXT J
280   LET X$(K)=X$ (I)
290   LEST X$ (I) =L$
300   NEXT I
310   PRINT
320   PRINT
330   FOR I=1 TO C
340   PRINT X$ (I)
350   NEXT I
360   PRINT
370   PRINT " NO, OF ITEMS =";C
380   PRINT
390   END
400   DATA TOM,DICK,HARRY,ZZZ
```

FIG. 33. Program for sorting alphabetic items.

compiler may not be available and an interpreter may offer a more limited version without such facilities as built-in matrix routines. Instead of automatic line-by-line interactive checking errors may be indicated at run time. With a V.D.U. the "print" will appear on the screen unless specially directed to an associated printer.

```
-RUN
SORT PROGRAM USING DATA LINES


DO YOU WANT INSTRUCTIONS?
-YES
PROVIDE DATA ON LINE 400 ETC AND RERUN
END WITH ZZZ
STOPPED AT LINE 390
-400 DATA JONES, BROWN, ROBINSON, EDGARS, WILLIAMS, THOMAS, ZZZ
-RUN
SORT PROGRAM USING DATA LINES


DO YOU WANT INSTRUCTIONS?
-NO


BROWN
EDGARS
JONES
ROBINSON
THOMAS
WILLIAMS

NO. OF ITEMS = 6

STOPPED AT LINE 390
```

FIG. 34. Run of the program shown in Fig. 33.

Specimen Examination Questions

1. "BASIC is an approach to the ideal form of programming in which the programmer will use his normal language." Discuss.

2. Explain what is meant by an interactive programming language and show how such a language can considerably assist in the "debugging" of programs.

3. "Commercial tabulations are really matrices but it is only when they are processed by computers that it is worth considering them as such." Critically discuss.

4. Explain how subroutines may facilitate the writing of programs and avoid programming errors.

5. Explain the purpose of loops in computer programs and show how FOR statement may simplify the procedures.

6. "Format is one of the chief problems of writing business computer programs." Discuss this statement making explanatory references to methods of handling format in any programming language with which you are acquainted.

N.B. This question could equally apply to Chapter 7.

Chapter 4

TERMINALS AND TIME SHARING

BASIC CONCEPTS

A terminal is an input/output device at the end of a communication line linked to a computer. We have already seen that a normal means of controlling a computer is through a console with a keyboard, which may also be used for the input or output of low-volume data. If we imagine several such keyboards linked to the computer and operating at different locations, possibly many kilometres apart, we have the basic concept of terminal operation as it strikes the user.

Such terminals generally have the characteristic that the user seems, almost immediately, to have the full use of the computer, despite the fact that many other users may be operating simultaneously. This is achieved, generally, by having a master program which rotates the computer facility round the terminals which happen to be live at any time. Each terminal has a time slice during which it has access to the central processing unit and during which the whole or part of its own particular program will be dealt with. Because of the slowness of peripherals this can give the effect of the computer being continuously available, though, at peak usage times, with many terminals operating, there may be an appreciable delay. Priorities can be allocated to terminals in a way similar to that used in multiprogramming.

Such systems may be run on an in-house or on a bureau basis. In the former case the terminals will be linked to the user's own computer, either in the same building or at a distance. Post Office lines may be used, and brief details of these facilities are given later. With a bureau, a contract is made with a selected time-sharing company to which the terminals will be linked over Post Office lines.

To bring about the interface, or link, between several remote terminals and the central processor a small computer called a multi-channel communications controller or processor is used.

Many technical problems arise in connection with data transmission. There are three transmission modes which are:

1. *simplex*, implying that data can be transmitted in one direction only without possibility of reversal;

80

2. *half duplex*, in which data can pass in only one direction at a time, but this can be reversed. This allows linked devices either to transmit or receive;

3. *duplex*, where data can travel in both directions at the same time, using two channels for transmission.

The basic terminal looks like a rather large typewriter and, when connected, it is on-line to the computer system. Telephone networks, which are designed to handle speech, require that the connection be made through a modem (modulator/demodulator), rented from the Post Office, which is used to convert the pulses, representing the digital form of computer data, into up and down movements (modulations) of a carrier wave.

Such a typewriter or teleprinter, in addition to its use for transmitting data, will be able to print out information received from the computer comparatively slowly, one character at a time, as with an automatic typewriter.

As well as using such terminals to communicate with a computer they may be used back-to-back, in which case messages are passed to and fro between terminals. This, similar to telex, gives rapid communication with hard copy (printed matter).

Terminals with paper tape punches are very useful. The punch may be disconnected when communicating through the keyboard. If left on it will give a paper tape copy of messages sent and received. This can be useful for remote job entry. Programs or data are received in a punched form over the line and the tape can be processed as convenient. When disconnected from the network (in "local" mode) the terminal can be used as a paper tape punch for off-line data preparation. The program or data tape can be checked beforehand so that, when transmitted through the terminal, valuable time is not wasted in correcting errors.

Terminals having visual display units, like small television screens mounted behind and above the keyboard, have made a big impact. The information transmitted and received appears as lines of characters on the screen, instead of being printed in the conventional way. Hard copy can be provided as well by linking in a suitable print unit.

TIME-SHARING BUREAUX

The provision by time-sharing bureaux of computer facilities which could be accessed over telephone lines gained popularity towards the end of the 1960s. Among the merits of such systems may be listed the following.

1. The speed with which a terminal can be installed (and removed). The existing telephone may be used to provide the link and the only extra equipment is a Post Office modem and the terminal itself, which may generally be carried or wheeled about.

2. The fact that, apart from certain fixed charges, the costs depend on the time during which the facilities are used, and it is often possible to allocate these to specific departments or staff members.

3. Firms without computers can gain some experience in using them without a heavy capital commitment, while those already having their own in-house computer (i.e. located on their own premises) can channel jobs such as special calculations and program development externally.

4. The possibility of trying out languages for which compilers are not available on the user's system or of handling powerful computers when the in-house installation is small or out-of-date.

The Post Office provides an essential link in such systems. The services provided go under the name of Datel and are outlined later in this chapter.

Circuits and systems

Figure 35 shows a simplified version of a typical time-sharing terminal system. At the user end there may be only one terminal which can be linked via a modem with the nearest telephone. The multiplexor enables several terminals to be operated by the same user. At the computer end there is usually a powerful computer controlled by a smaller computer called a communications controller or processor. Considerable backing storage is provided on discs or drums from which compilers and stored programs can be drawn into the main computer's store, as required by the users. Facilities for linking magnetic tape units and paper tape and punched card readers, all of which require manual intervention, may also be provided. A terminal service can combine batch processing of clients' data with the time-sharing services which are the main concern of this chapter.

TERMINAL OPERATION

A simple terminal will have a teleprinter with a normal keyboard for alphabetic and numeric characters and some special control keys. It may have a visual display unit. After making contact with the bureau whose facilities are being used, by dialling the telephone number, the terminal is switched, through the modem, into the

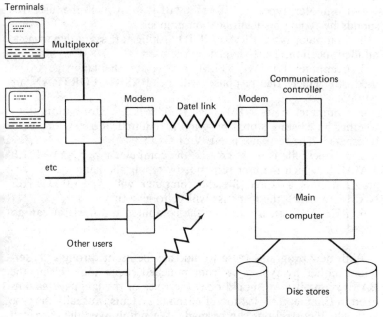

Terminals
Multiplexor
Modem
Datel link
Modem
Communications controller
etc
Other users
Main computer
Disc stores

FIG. 35. Schematic layout of time-sharing system.

telephone circuit, and the user will have to type his contract number. On some systems a security test is brought in at this stage by the system automatically checking if that number should originate from that particular terminal. At the bureau end the usage will start to be logged to provide a basis for billing. The user then types, as appropriate:

1. command instructions, in a command language whose details he will be given by the bureau. This gives control over what is happening, such as the input of programs, the display of stored programs at the terminal, the execution and amendment of programs, their saving for future use or purging from the system, the incorporation of such compilers as are available, etc.;

2. programs, in a high-level language appropriate to the system being used. He may also call up stored library programs;

3. data, either numeric or alphabetic.

The GEIS system (later Honeywell Information Systems, Ltd.) was a pioneer in the use of terminals and of BASIC and evolved a very simple command language which we shall use as an example. The standard sequence (which can be abbreviated) is as follows.

1. Computer types USER NUMBER to which the user responds by typing his identification number.

2. Computer types PROJECT ID, asking for, say a departmental identification. This is typed by the user.

3. Computer types SYSTEM, asking for the language to be used, to which the response will be BASIC, FORTRAN or ALGOL.

4. Computer types NEW OR OLD, seeking information as to whether an existing stored program is required or a new one is to be created. The response is NEW or OLD.

5. If a new file is to be created the computer types NEW FILE NAME to which the user responds by typing the name of his program. If it is a stored file the computer will type OLD FILE NAME to which the response will be to give this.

6. READY is then typed by the computer and the user can go ahead.

With new programs these would then be input through the terminal, either by typing or from punched paper tape. Using the BASIC compiler we should obey the rules of the language as outlined in Chapter 3. A feature of terminal systems is usually the ease with which corrections can be made. We simply type the corrected version of a line, with its line number, at some stage after the line containing the error, whereupon the new line is substituted for the old. Lines may be inserted by using line numbers providing the appropriate locations in the program. This is the reason for numbering originally in tens, to allow up to nine "spaces" for such insertion between each pair of lines.

Mistakes recognised during typing may be corrected by pressing appropriate keys which back-space and delete characters as required. A fair copy of the program, eliminating such deletions and other changes and bringing the lines into numerical order may be obtained by typing the instruction LIST.

When the program has been input the message RUN is typed, when it will begin to operate unless it has syntactic errors. These will be indicated by error messages and corrections will have to be typed (*see* Fig. 24). This "debug" facility is very useful for program development and also for training programmers, though thinking out corrections over the teleprinter can run up the charges.

Programs may be saved on the time-sharing bureau's storage by typing SAVE; old programs may be destroyed by typing UNSAVE. A coding system protects files from being altered or destroyed by unauthorised users. To sign off the user types BYE and presses the RETURN key.

Each system, whether operating as an in-house facility or using an outside bureau, has its own peculiarities, which usually can be easily mastered. For example, on one system the program name is created at the same time as the save instruction by typing SAVE AS followed by the required name. Some systems have useful facilities for reassembling and merging programs. An instruction such as RESEQUENCE 100(10) may be available to renumber the first line of the program as 100 and space all the subsequent lines at multiples of 10 from it. The use of facilities such as DELETE 120–180 to delete a sequence of lines, and MERGE WITH *aaaa* AS *bbbb*, where *aaaa* is the name of another program available on the system and *bbbb* indicates the starting point of the numbering of the transferred material therein, should be explored.

The operation just described is an example of conversational mode or interactive mode, where action by the user creates a response from the computer which in turn indicates what should be done next by the user. It is not necessarily unique to time-sharing systems, as a computer may be programmed to give this mode of operation through its control console, but this is probably wasteful of C.P.U. time. This is a particularly important consideration where large mainframe computers are involved. However, with the introduction of cheaper minis and especially with microcomputers it is becoming increasingly possible to offer small local systems, working independently of any mainframe computer, having powerful programming and data facilities. Such systems may themselves have a small number of local terminals. Many business systems really amount to using special suites of programs to control posting and manipulation of data and text.

TIME-SHARING LIBRARY PROGRAMS

Library programs and packages are available to the user to save him the trouble of writing his own programs. If a suitable program is in the library it may be cheaper to use it than to input a special program, though the latter might be more streamlined from the point of view of terminal print-out.

A specimen from the GEIS library is shown in Fig. 36. We must first select the version of the program required by typing the appropriate number, as indicated. Notice that mistakes in format are signalled automatically and have to be corrected by the user. A full tabular print-out showing the month-by-month position has been called for by the user, but only that relating to the first year has been shown in this example.

Programs related to management decision-making of quite a sophisticated kind may be available, such as critical path analysis and linear programming.

Figure 37 shows the operation of a network planning program

```
MORTGE          12 10        GEIS A 16/04/79

TO FIND:          TYPE:
     RATE            1
     LIFE            2
     AMT. BORROWED   3
     MONTHLY PYMT.   4

WHICH DO YOU WANT ? 4,

WHAT IS THE NOMINAL ANNUAL RATE [DECIMAL]? 0.0875,

WHAT IS THE LIFE OF THE MORTGAGE  YEARS, MONTHS? 20.0,

INPUT DATA NOT IN CORRECT FORMAT, RETYPE IT,

? 20,0,

WHAT IS THE AMOUNT TO BE BORROWED? 4000,

WHAT IS THE MONTH (JAN=1,ETC.) AND YEAR OF THE LOAN? 1,79,

HOW MANY CALENDAR YEARS DO YOU WANT THE MORTGAGE TABLE PRINTED? 2,

TYPE '1' FOR AN ANNUAL MORTGAGE TABLE; TYPE '0' FOR
A MONTHLY TABLE.? 0,

                   ***MORTGAGE TERMS***

NOMINAL ANNUAL RATE= .0875

LIFE OF MORTGAGE= 20 YEARS 0 MONTHS

AMOUNT BORROWED= 4000

MONTHLY PAYMENT= 35.3484

                   ***MORTGAGE TABLE***
                   BEGINNING
                   PRINCIPAL                     PRINCIPAL
MONTH              OUTSTANDING    INTEREST       REPAYMENT


                        CALENDAR YEAR 79
    2              4000           29.1667        6.18177
    3              3993.82        29.1216        6.22684
    4              3987.59        29.0762        6.27224
    5              3981.32        29.0305        6.31798
    6              3975.         28.9844        6.36405
    7              3968.64        28.938         6.41045
    8              3962.23        28.8912        6.4572
    9              3955.77        28.8442        6.50428
   10              3949.27        28.7967        6.55171
   11              3942.71        28.749         6.59948
   12              3936.11        28.7008        6.6476

INTEREST PAID DURING YEAR= 318.299
PRINCIPAL REPAID DURING YEAR= 70.5336
PRINCIPAL OUTSTANDING AT YEAR END= 3929.47
```

FIG. 36. Library program print-out for mortgage repayment (showing table for only one year).

```
-OLD NETP
OK
-1 DATA 1,2,4,   2,3,2,   2,4,2,   2,5,1,   2,7,2,   3,6,4
2 DATA 3,8,36,   4,9,24,   5,8,10,   6,8,0,   7,11,10, 8,10,3
3 DATA 9,11,2,   10,11,3,  11,12,0,  9999
-RUN
NETWORK PLANNING  CPA   PERT   NETP
TYPE "YES" IF PERT IS NEEDED, ELSE TYPE "NO"
-NO
PROJECT TIME = 48
DO YOU WANT TO AMEND ANY ACTIVITY TIMES?
-NO
DO YOU NEED FURTHER INFORMATION?
-YES
DO YOU WANT SPECIAL SORT?
-NO
TYPE - ALL - FOR FULL PRINT OUT
     - ACT - FOR EARLY, LATE, FLOAT, AND CP
     - CP - FOR C.P. ACTS
     - EV  - FOR EVENTS
     - DATA -FOR ACTIVITY LISTING
-ACT
```

ACTIVITIES, START AND FINISH TIMES, FLOAT, AND C.P.

ACTIVITY		TIME	START		END		FLOAT			C.P.
			EARLY	LATE	EARLY	LATE	TOTAL	FREE	IND.	
1	2	4	0	0	4	4	0	0	0	*
2	3	2	4	4	6	6	0	0	0	*
2	4	2	4	20	6	22	16	0	0	
2	5	1	4	31	5	32	27	0	0	
2	7	2	4	36	6	38	32	0	0	
3	6	4	6	38	10	42	32	0	0	
3	8	36	6	6	42	42	0	0	0	*
4	9	24	6	22	30	46	16	0	0	
5	8	10	5	32	15	42	27	27	0	
6	8	0	10	42	10	42	32	32	0	
7	11	10	6	38	16	48	32	32	0	
8	10	3	42	42	45	45	0	0	0	*
9	11	2	30	46	32	48	16	16	0	
10	11	3	45	45	48	48	0	0	0	*
11	12	0	48	48	48	48	0	0	0	*

```
IS FURTHER INFORMATION NEEDED?
-YES
DO YOU WANT SPECIAL SORT?
-NO
TYPE NEW INSTRUCTIONS
-CP
```

ACTIVITIES ON CRITICAL PATH

ACTIVITY		TIME	START	END
1	2	4	0	4
2	3	2	4	6
3	8	36	6	42
8	10	3	42	45
10	11	3	45	48
11	12	0	48	48

```
IS FURTHER INFORMATION NEEDED?
-NO
STOPPED AT LINE 400
-BYE
OK
15,53,42-LOGOUT

CONNECTED FOR      25 MINS
MILL TIME USED     12 SECS
```

FIG. 37. Network planning program run on an in-house system.

available on an in-house system. The user has previously signed on and called up the BASIC compiler. The program on this system is retrieved by typing OLD followed by the program name NETP. The user knows, from operating instructions, that data must be shown on lines from 1 onwards and must consist of the tail and head numbers for each activity, followed by the relevant time. The

```
WOULD YOU LIKE TO SEE A GRAPH OF THE FIVE-YEAR
FORECAST WITH LINEAR AND PARABOLIC GROWTH RATES?
REPLY = YES

PLOT KEY:
      ACTUAL SALES FIGURES      - (')
      LINEAR SALES FORECAST     - (.)
      PARABOLIC SALES FORECAST - (*)


                MONTHLY SALES FORECAST

------------------------------------------------------------
MONTH    0                    35000                    70000
------------------------------------------------------------

    2     '                                              (
    4     )'                                             (
    6     )'                                             (
    8     )'                                             (
   10     ) '                                            (
   12     )   '                                          (
   14     )   *                                          (
   16     )  .*                                          (
   18     )   .*                                         (
   20     )   . *                                        (
   22     )   .  *                                       (
   24     )    .  *                                      (
   26     )    .  *                                      (
   28     )    .    *                                    (
   30     )    .    *                                    (
   32     )    .      *                                  (
   34     )     .      *                                 (
   36     )     .       *                                (
   38     )     .        *                               (
   40     )     .         *                              (
   42     )      .         *                             (
   44     )      .          *                            (
   46     )       .          *                           (
   48     )       .           *                          (
   50     )       .            *                         (
   52     )        .             *                       (
   54     )        .              *                      (
   56     )         .              *                     (
   58     )         .               *                    (
   60     )          .                *                  (

------------------------------------------------------------

PROGRAM ENDED
```

Fig. 38. Graphical output from a teleprinter terminal using Time Sharing Ltd. "TELFIT" curve-fitting program.

end of the data is signalled by 9999. He has a choice of print-out, and can also amend activity times and arrange for the data to be sorted on selected columns. This is the data used in connection with the computer installation in Chapter 8, Fig. 63. The print-out shows times in weeks from the starting date. Programs are available to convert these figures into dates, taking into account the length of working week, holidays etc. It is interesting to note that the time-sharing system was reacting slowly, due to overloading, when this program was run. The computer was working for 12 secs (mill time) but 25 minutes were needed at the terminal (connect time).

Some programs will convert data into graphical or bar chart form and the graphs of equations can also be traced. There are two main methods of doing this through a terminal. One is to print the shape in the form of dots or characters through the teleprinter (*see* example in Fig. 38, which is from the end of a sales forecasting program by Time Sharing, Ltd.). The other is to display the graph on a visual display screen from which it may be photographically captured for permanent retention (*see* Fig. 39 again by permission of Time Sharing, Ltd.).

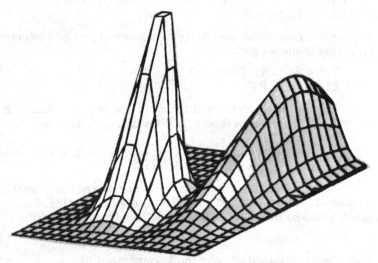

Fig. 39. Print of "solid" graph from display terminal of Time Sharing, Ltd.

REPORT PROGRAMS

The use of time-sharing terminals in management information systems is greatly enhanced if data can be readily arranged in rows and columns (appropriately titled) as would occur in accounting and financial reports and also reports concerned with other branches of management, such as machine loading, manpower scheduling and materials requirements analyses.

We have seen that BASIC automatically lines up print output into five columns. Report programs, such as the Leasco Response REPORT, which is used as the basis of what follows, were developed to enable users with no programming experience to define layout in terms of rows, columns and tables and to specify accumulations and summations of row and column elements. The steps in specification are as follows.

1. Provide control information of the number of lines per page, date and type of teletype.

2. Define title lines by responses such as:

T1? XYZ LTD
T2? PROFIT FORECAST

3. Define row and column headings by responses such as:

C1? JANUARY
R1? DIRECT COSTS
R2? OVERHEADS

4. Define rules which govern the calculation of row and column entries by responses such as:

?R10 = SUMR1 THRU R9
?R5 = ACC R10

(The question mark precedes the code in the case of calculating rules and data entry, but follows it in the case of definitions).

5. Enter data.

6. Possibly change structure and use editing characters to control spacing and number of decimal places.

File storage space for new reports must be reserved based on the number of "records" or "sectors". This is done by an OPEN command, followed by the file name and the number of sectors (n):

OPEN—name, n

Such files are disposed of, when no longer needed by:

KILL—name.

Three files are needed as follows.

1. Report file, containing the specifications.
2. Data file, containing the data.
3. Work file, handling the calculations involved.

Developments along these lines may help to bridge the gulf between accountants, managers and other business users of computers and specialist programmers. They represent further progress along the road to controlling computers using terminology in ordinary use.

TERMINALS FOR COMMERCIAL DATA PROCESSING

The rapid access facilities (chiefly discs), essential to the applications of time-sharing terminals so far discussed, tend to be expensive when large volume data has to be handled and stored. The use of terminals for data banks is bound up with the cheapening of such storage media and the development of mammoth storage facilities.

Though it may not pay a firm to do its bulk processing through a time-sharing network it can, nevertheless, make use of terminal facilities to ease the load connected with such processing. Some systems offer compilers for commercial languages, such as COBOL and PL1, and with these will go facilities for checking new programs or making amendments to old ones.

Any syntactic errors detected during attempted compilation will result in an error print-out at the terminal, indicating the line where the error occurs, the code number of the error, and a short statement describing the error, such as, using COBOL on the I.T.T. system:

> 13 IEQ 10551-E VALID FILE-NAME NOT PRESENT, DESCRIPTION IGNORED.
> 24 IEQ40021-E CLOSE STATEMENT INCOMPLETE, STATEMENT DISCARDED.

Sometimes small errors can generate a stream of error messages. As an example, with COBOL, if a period is placed immediately after FD in the FILE SECTION, the effect is that the description is eliminated, so that, whenever the file is mentioned in the program, an error message indicating that it has not been defined will appear.

As has previously been explained in Chapter 3 the fact that a program has passed a syntactic check is not a proof that it will run satisfactorily to give the required results.

Such further testing may be done through the terminals if the system has facilities for using magnetic tape units and discs so that we may simulate the user's own configuration.

The I.T.T. system, in which all commands are preceded by /,

allows up to four discs to be used, files being created by a command instruction through the terminal such as

/FILE DISC = 1, DSNAME = STCKFL, RES, DISP = NEW, SPACE = (1,2314), UPDATE

which has the effect of assigning to disc number one a restricted file called STCKFL (which can be used in a COBOL program) being a new file, with one track reserved on an I.B.M. 2314 disc and being capable of being updated or altered. Such a file will be reserved until purged by an instruction such as

/FILE DISC = 1, DISP = PURGE

Temporary work files, which are automatically purged, can be created by an instruction such as

/FILE DISC = 2

which would assign a file to disc number two.

Such instructions are input through the terminal before the program which is to use them is input, though the compilation of such a program can, of course, be performed without the files on which it is to operate. An attempt to run such a program without its files will result in a message:

I/O REQUEST ON UNIT 001, FILE NOT DEFINED.

The use of magnetic tape files requires that tape unit be available after which the designated tape or a new one will be loaded manually for processing at the computer end of the terminal service. Availability is checked by a /INQUIRY command which will result in a reply such as

01 7-TRACK TAPES AND 04 9-TRACK TAPES AVAILABLE FOR ASSIGNMENT

being received at the terminal. The user wishing to avail himself of a new tape may then type

/ATTACH TAPE 9 = 1

to which the reply will be

YOU NOW HAVE 0 7-TRK and 1 9-TRK TAPES ASSIGNED.

This will take perhaps two or three minutes, since the loading is manual. A /FILE command such as

/FILE TAPE = 1, MOUNT = RTS064, TRK = 9

will then follow, to assign this work file in a manner similar to that for assigning a disc file.

COBOL programs will generally call for one or more master files which are to be updated. Such files will have to be created previously for test purposes, using trial data. This can be done by a suitable program run through the terminal.

TIME-SHARING CHARGES

Though details vary as between different bureaux the basic elements of cost of a time-sharing service are bureau charges, Post Office charges and terminal equipment charges.

1. *Bureau charges*, which break down into charges for the following.

   (*a*) Central processing time (C.P.U. time) to cover the time the computer itself is used. At an hourly rate these charges seem high but they apply only to the short periods, perhaps of a few seconds, when the central processing unit is employed on the user's programs. It is because multiple usage enables the c.p.u. to be employed more fully that individual firms may gain, compared with having their own computer.

   (*b*) Connection time, during which the user is linked to the bureau facilities, from "signing on" to "signing off". These charges can be minimised by reducing delays in transmission by having work planned and programs and data prepunched on tape, if this is possible. Some bureaux calculate all their charges apart from storage on this basis of connection time.

   (*c*) Storage of programs and data on the discs or tapes of the time-sharing bureau. These charges can mount up, especially if programs or data files are left in storage when this is not really justified. On some systems old stored items may be erased automatically after a stated period, unless they have been specifically designated to be kept. The alternative to such bureau storage is for the user to feed in the programs and data through the terminal each time they are required. This is much slower than accessing them through the system. Since it also involves connection charges the economics of the situation are to use the terminal to feed in programs unless the connection charges make this more expensive than bureau storage.

2. *Post Office charges*, involving:

   (*a*) rental of modem;
   (*b*) standard telephone charges;

(*c*) special charges for private speech circuits (if used) on a distance basis.

3. *Terminal equipment* costs. Such equipment may be rented or purchased, in which latter case provision will have to be made for routine maintenance and overhaul.

It is difficult to assess the use that will be made of terminals and their total weekly costs before they are in operation, so that installation for a trial period may be desirable. Links may be established with several time-sharing bureaux to compare the facilities, though it takes some time to become familiar with any one system and to operate it effectively and cheaply. Factors to be considered in selecting a time-sharing bureau are:

1. costs, including special facilities such as cheap off-peak rates;
2. power of the computer and the size of its store;
3. availability of compiler languages;
4. facilities for training in operation and for answering the queries that will inevitably arise. A good bureau will have knowledgeable and helpful staff who can be telephoned to help to solve the user's problems, often within minutes;
5. availability of packages for standard calculations and operations, which can be called into use through the keyboard by means of an appropriate code;
6. simplicity of command language, which will be a factor in the acceptability of the system to staff who are not computer specialists;
7. terms of the contract regarding minimum charges (if any) and notice required to discontinue;
8. clarity of billing so that the user can see where the charges have arisen;
9. facilities for putting a stop on usage after so many hours so that bills will not exceed budget.

POST OFFICE DATEL SERVICES

The Post Office provides the essential links for time-sharing bureaux and for the operation of an organisation's own multi-access facilities over a distance.

The Datel services are numbered according to the maximum speed in bits per second (bit/s) at which information can be transmitted. For the higher speed ranges (2,400 bit/s and over) the operating mode is synchronous, that is the transmission rate is automatically controlled.

The following services are provided.

1. Datel 100. This can be used over the telex system (a switched public teleprinter system on which calls are dialled) or over telegraph private circuits provided on a point-to-point basis for customers' exclusive use. The operating speed is fifty bit/s. A five-bit alphabet is used and the terminal may have a teleprinter with a tape punching attachment, a tape perforator for receiving data and an automatic transmitter which reads paper tape. No modem is needed.

2. Datel 200. This uses the public telephone network and will probably be the system by which a user is introduced to terminal working. The bureau is dialled in the ordinary way and, on establishing contact, the user switches over to the modem and terminal equipment. The modem converts the signals generated by the terminal equipment into transmissible form. Normal S.T.D. telephone charges apply.

It is also possible to hire private speech circuits for customers' exclusive use, though these may be more applicable to a centralised processing system operated by the user rather than to a bureau system.

3. Datel 600. This operates over the public telephone networks or private speech circuits, with a speed range of 600 to 1,200 bit/s. It is suited to data collection applications and can provide telemetry facilities for the collection of information from a number of remote points, such as storage tanks or reservoirs where the level of contents is measured. An optional backward or auxiliary channel (at 75 bit/s) can be used for control or for input from a V.D.U. keyboard.

4. Datel 2400. This uses four-wire private telephone circuits to achieve 2,400 bit/s working, but the public telephone system may be used for standby at the rate of 600 to 1,200 bit/s.

5. Datel 2412 uses either private circuits or public networks to transmit at 2,400 bit/s and has an optional 150 bit/s backward channel supervisor. It is not compatible with Datel 2400.

6. Datel 48K. This wideband service has a capacity of 48,000 bit/s and may be provided with a special channel for co-ordination and control. Wideband circuits have a capacity many times that of ordinary speech circuits and are intended for high speed data transmission or for bulk communication facilities. For example, transfers may be made from disc to disc, or files may be dumped. A wideband circuit may be split into different channels, by means

of approved channelling equipment. Whole page facsimile transmission equipment may also be used. The cost is less than the combined cost of the equivalent number of separate speech circuits.

Dataplex services provide for concentration on to one telephone line of a number of terminals from a distant area, providing for the economical extension of a computer service catchment area. Dataplex 3 was announced towards the end of 1978 as an enhancement of Dataplex 1 and 2.

Multipoint circuits may be rented from the Post Office. They enable up to twelve outstation terminals to be connected to a central site. On this system terminals cannot communicate directly between themselves. International services are available over public telephone and telex systems, while circuits may also be leased for customers' exclusive use.

NETWORKS AND PACKET SWITCHING

Networks of linked computers have been established, often operating across national boundaries. The Society for Worldwide Telecommunications (SWIFT) was set up by over 200 banks. EURONET serves the European Community, providing scientific, technical and socio-economic information through access points available to users of terminals in its member countries.

Computer control of telephone exchanges is displacing the electro-mechanical systems. Stored program control (S.P.C.) of exchanges has been claimed to facilitate modular design of exchange equipment, which can be adapted to specific needs. In Britain the Post Office expects System X to make an impact in the early 1980s, while P.D.X. (Private Digital Exchange) can offer a computer-controlled fully digital system.

Packet switching routes information between the modes of a network until the correct destination is reached. An approach to this is to fit messages into packets of fixed length, the latter being calculated to give optimum response for a particular set of uses. Each packet contains details to route its information to its destination and a system for eliminating transmission errors. The Post Office operated an Experimental Packet Switching Service (E.P.S.S.) during 1978, to be replaced by Packet Switched Service (P.S.S.) late in 1979. An aim of such systems is to go beyond DATEL and eliminate the problems arising from differences in computers and terminals when they are linked into a system. Manufacturers of computers and peripherals can help by standardisation, such as is provided by Systems Network Architecture (S.N.A.) of I.B.M.

PRESTEL SERVICES

The Post Office PRESTEL service was originally publicised under the name of Viewdata. It is designed to provide (from 1979 for general use) computer banks of information on a variety of topics to be accessed using the telephone together with either a modified television receiver (with a pushbutton control unit or keypad, which may be held in the hand, to control selection and display of material) or a standard visual display unit. A combined telephone and small screen display may also become available. The interactive information retrieval facilities are available both to business and domestic users. National and local database structures are envisaged. Interconnected computers will have databases comprising not only data of national interest which is replicated throughout the network but also information of local interest, not stored elsewhere. Independent agencies are to supply the information to be displayed and the Association of Viewdata Information Providers (AVIP) was therefore formed. The information providers pay a yearly tariff and they may recoup from the viewers. Advertisements may be provided free to users but other information can incur a charge, this being displayed at the end of each call, for which the user also pays the normal telephone call charges to the Post Office.

Information is selected by the viewer, guided by instructions on the screen. From a numbered list of topics one is chosen, which itself can be broken down, and so on, using the "tree" structure of the data base, until the appropriate page is found. This can be accessed directly if its number is known. The interactive features of the system seem to offer interesting possibilities, not only for the retrieval of information, but also for problem-solving (where the user is guided through a routine requiring responses at each stage until an answer to the problem is obtained), for calculations and for programmed learning. The public system can be combined with an in-house system, controlled privately by a business firm which uses terminals in connection with its own database.

Information services, known as TELETEXT are provided by the broadcasting organisations. The B.B.C. has CEEFAX and the I.B.A. has ORACLE. These do not, however, provide interactive services. They are also limited to about 120 pages, each of up to 150 words, whereas the Post Office system claims an initial capability of 60,000 pages which can be expanded almost indefinitely.

SPECIMEN EXAMINATION QUESTIONS

1. Explain, in outline, how a time-sharing bureau operates and discuss the advantages of using such facilities compared with an in-house system.

2. Write notes explaining the use of modems, multiplexors and video units in connection with time-sharing systems.

3. Outline the routine you might expect to have to follow in running a program available on an external time-sharing system.

4. How may management best take advantage of the opportunities available for data transmission at a distance?

5. Briefly explain what is meant by Post Office Datel Services and show how they are essential to a variety of computer applications.

6. Compare the organisational implications of using (*a*) an in-house terminal system and (*b*) distributed processing based on small computers.

7. Assume you are head of management services in a medium sized organisation which has computer facilities exclusively devoted to commercial applications. Write a report to the managing director advocating what you consider to be an appropriate policy regarding a computerised approach to some of your problems.

8. In connection with time-sharing systems distinguish between: (*a*) command language and programming language, (*b*) simplex and duplex operation, (*c*) library programs and special (user) programs.

9. Discuss the possible role of Post Office Prestel services in widening the appreciation and use of computerised information systems and compare these with information services based on broadcasting.

Chapter 5

MANAGEMENT INFORMATION SYSTEMS AND SYSTEMS ANALYSIS

SYSTEMS CONCEPTS

This book is primarily concerned with data processing for business purposes. It must always be borne in mind that such processing is not an end in itself, but is used by management to assist in achieving its objectives of providing goods and services, making profit, dealing fairly with employees, customers and suppliers and satisfying legal requirements regarding the keeping of records.

The satisfactory operation and control of business systems rests to a great extent on information or data, using this term in the widest sense. Very simple examples occur when invoices are prepared and when records are kept of how much customers owe the business and of how much should be paid in wages to each employee and how much tax should be deducted. More complex uses occur when the various aspects of business are brought together in the form of final accounts and balance sheets, showing the profit resulting from the business operations and the over-all position relating to capital, assets and liabilities. Still further examples are concerned with business statistics where attempts are made to study aspects of business operations and to come to logical conclusions about them, including studies of external conditions that may affect such things as sales and marketing policy.

The term "system" implies some arrangement, with regularity and order, and the word "systematic", with its connotation of regular method, provides a good indication of the approach relevant in the case of data processing. More precisely a system may be considered as a set of things chosen by an observer to form the subject of his study and related in such a manner as to form a whole when considered from the appropriate point of view.

We may have a purely mechanical system (such as the keys and levers of a typewriter); a man/machine system (such as formed by an operator using a teleprinter); a social system, where individuals are related within an organisation by the roles they fulfil. A business organisation (*see* Fig. 40) is a system, consisting of a number of subsystems (such as the various departments into which it is

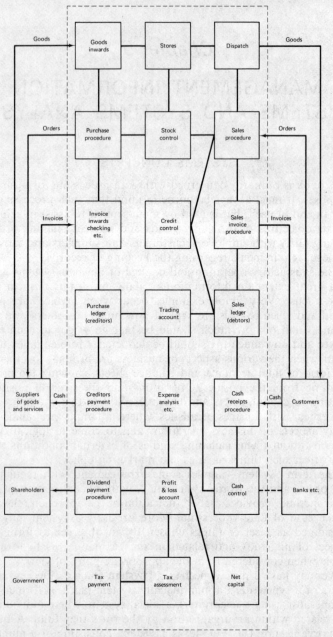

FIG. 40. Some of the systems and procedures involved in a commercial business, showing internal relationships and links with the environment.

divided) and itself forming part of larger systems (such as the industry, the national economy and the world economy).

From the point of view of the present book, the study of the data requirements of business units and of the departments within these units is of particular interest. Systems analysis, in its business sense, is concerned with these problems, especially when a computer is to be involved in the data processing. A general theory of systems has been developed and it attempts to find similarities in varying situations so that the same basic approach can be used with modifications suited to particular circumstances. All systems have the characteristic of parts which are related to each other, being interdependent to an extent, and interacting to give a total effect, which is the outcome of the system. The whole is more than the sum of its parts considered in isolation. Systems must generally be considered in relationship to other systems which form an environment, from which the system being studied draws "inputs" and to which it passes "outputs". This is exactly in line with the terminology of computing. A computer system processes information, for which the information must be input to the computer and, when processing is complete, the results are meaningful only when output to the management environment.

An important aspect of systems is their control. This implies that events are assessed as they occur and their effect on the planned progress of the system towards its objective is evaluated, so that any appropriate action may be taken, if possible, to bring the system back on to course. Computers, by their speed of processing data, should have a significant contribution to make in this respect. "Real-time computing" is the name given to computer processing where data is adjusted for any changes sufficiently quickly for management to be able to exercise this control effectively. Control is usually considered as depending on communication, which, in this context, can be considered as the passing of information from one part of a system to another. With electronic processing of data, in an appropriately designed system, communication may be practically instantaneous. An often-quoted example is the case of aircraft seat reservations by real-time computing.

The information on which control is based is often termed "feedback", which implies that, whatever the system being controlled, information about it is used for monitoring to check whether deviations significant enough to threaten the required outcome of the system are arising. If this is the case remedial action must be taken or the plan must be revised if increased information, which influences subsequent planning, shows it to be unrealistic. This self-adjusting approach is called "negative feedback" implying that a bad tendency generates forces which will counteract it. When control depends on the output of the system (as with a thermostat in a greenhouse) it is referred to as "closed-loop" control. The term "open-loop" control is applied when the output is not monitored but some independent criterion is used for control (as when a heating system is switched on at a specified date).

INFORMATION LEVELS AND FLOW

From the data-processing point of view business organisation consists of a number of information systems linked together. These systems should be related to organisation in the more conventional sense of a network of persons, each fulfilling a particular role, such as sales manager, accounts clerk and production engineer. This relationship involves a recognition of what are often termed different levels of information. The chief categories relate to the following.

1. *Degree of sophistication* of the data, ranging over:

(*a*) routine processing;
(*b*) the control of business activities by comparison of results with plans; and
(*c*) the use of mathematical models to assist in planning.

2. *Reporting level* or the level in the management hierarchy at which the information is made available, ranging from the chairman and board of directors to departmental and section heads and rank-and-file workers. The importance of decisions, judged by the risks to the business of their being wrong and by the length of time over which the decisions operate, tends to depend on the level of management. At higher levels a wider view has to be taken, and many more different items of information may have to be related than at lower and more specialised levels. At the top, questions of policy affecting the total business organisation must be settled; at the bottom the problem areas are more specific.

Computer systems can be particularly good at producing the information appropriate to each level. An example is the use of by-product encoding where information from a routine process is retained, often punched on paper tape, to be used later in processing by a computer. Again, in the routine processing of magnetic tape files, totals may be accumulated and analyses made.

At lower levels decisions are said to be programmable; that is, all possible eventualities are provided for and the action to be taken is predetermined. At higher levels the manager may be faced with unprogrammable, many-sided problems, calling for considerable judgment. More sophisticated data processing techniques can remove some decisions from the unprogrammable into the programmable region.

3. *Functions within the business unit*, such as marketing, finance, production, etc., and also external functions related to the industry and market area. In each of these spheres peculiar problems arise and traditional methods of recording and processing data may have become established. In computing, such a division exists between scientific computing and commercial computing, even to the extent of using different languages in which to write computer programs. Computer systems tend to evolve at the functional level, probably because such functions have traditionally been regarded as independent and each can define its objectives.

4. *Accessibility of information.* This varies from information in the archives, where delay in finding what is needed may be considerable, to information available on a departmental basis and, in some cases, that immediately accessible to individual workers. The use of computers may help to break down such barriers, especially when real-time systems are used.

5. *Frequency of use.* This is related to accessibility, since frequently used data should be on hand to avoid waste of time. The two do not always go together, however, since certain vital information (such as indicating that a chemical process is reaching a dangerous state) may occur rarely, if ever, but it has to be conveyed quickly to the management when it does.

An important decision regarding information concerns how frequently it is produced and to what extent management should be involved with it. For control purposes data that confirms the satisfactory working of a plan is of no use to management other than as a source of comfort. When something occurs that deviates so far from the plan as to require management action then the management should know of this. Concern with exceptions can conserve managers' time. The exception principle is also used in connection with the reporting level, already considered. A manager will require to be kept informed of variations occurring in systems for which his subordinates have responsibility when these deviations are so great as to threaten the larger system of which they are part.

6. *Technical nature of the information process.* Data has to be collected, transmitted, stored and made available as output, while it may also be processed to rearrange it (as in sorting), to combine items (as when a file is updated) and for analysis and interpretation (as when statistical methods are used).

In the field of information storage and retrieval computerised systems compete with up-to-date filing (vertical, lateral, sliding, circular and mobile units), card indexes (which may be rotary and power-assisted) and strip indexes and also needle-sorted notched or punched card systems, in which parts of the card are removed according to an information code, so that a needle pushed through specific holes in a set of cards will allow those so punched to drop, thus selecting cards with specific information. Automatic filing units are available where the touch of a button conveys the required file into position. The use of microfilm saves space and makes for quick retrieval; its use in conjunction with computers is dealt with in Chapter 2.

Information may be used by managers for the related topics of forecasting, planning and control. Much attention has been devoted to developing control systems but the forecasting and planning aspects of management also seem to offer major opportunities in connection with improved management decision making. Business operates in changing, dynamic conditions characterised by uncertainty as to the future. Forecasting can never be guaranteed as completely accurate but fuller information and its adequate and speedy processing by computer should leave management less prone to surprise. This in turn should improve management planning (decision as to what is to be done) which itself can benefit enormously from rapid processing of complex data. As for control (comparing what is happening with the plan and taking appropriate action), speed is essential, since too great a lag between a variation from the plan and its discovery may render the remedy ineffective.

Decisions, analysis and planning

The analysis of problems facing managers depends, to a large extent, on the information available and its treatment. Modern data processing can help to improve decisions by enabling more information to be processed in more sophisticated ways and with much less delay than was possible in the past. The following stages may be distinguished in decision-making.

1. Decide the objectives. What is to be achieved? Some problems may be exploratory in nature, the objective being to obtain information and to study its implications. Decision problems, on the other hand, are those involving a choice between two or more possible lines of action.

2. Consider the information available or obtainable, perhaps involving a special investigation. Examine the scope of the problem in relation to this information and decide the minimum information that is needed to provide an adequate study.

3. Determine the type of investigation and the techniques to be used.

4. Conduct the investigation.

5. Compare possible solutions and decide between them.

6. Implement the decision.

7. Follow up the decision to see how it works out in practice.

Decision-making may occur at three levels.

1. *Strategic.* High level decisions concerned with the business in its environment and covering long time spans. Problems tend to be novel and involve uncertainty and risk.

2. *Tactical.* Managerial decisions to achieve objectives within the strategy, involving choice between alternatives and medium time span. Problems tend to recur and information to be more under the control of the organisation.

3. *Programmable.* Related to operations planned within the tactics, with little choice and short time span. Problems tend to be eliminated by standardisation and predetermined decisions cover anticipated variations.

Computers can assist at each of these levels. Strategy may be improved by sophisticated studies of the firm in relation to its markets and sources of supply; tactics may employ techniques to determine, say, the best "marketing mix" of goods for the business to produce and sell; programmable decisions may be available at the shop floor or design office through a computer terminal.

Problems of the efficient organisation of work in factory and office occur so frequently that special techniques have become established to deal with them. The rest of this chapter is largely concerned with such techniques applied to data processing, in which context they are often termed "systems analysis". Since they must be related to other office and clerical processes the following chapter deals with the essentials of the subject of Organisation and Methods (O. & M.) which was developed for the study of work in offices long before computers were invented, but which still has an important role to play.

SYSTEMS ANALYSIS

Systems analysis is concerned with converting the objectives of management, as far as information and data are concerned, into methods that are amenable to processing by a computer (or other data processing equipment).

Figure 41 shows the position of systems analysis as a link be-

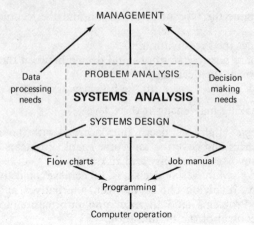

Fig. 41. The place of systems analysis.

tween management and the software and hardware of computing. It is sometimes itself divided into three different levels.

1. *Problem analysis*, which is more oriented towards management problems, and which tries to define the problem and outline a solution.

2. *Systems analysis proper*, which converts this solution into a practical system, capable of being run on the available equipment.

3. *Systems design*, which is concerned with the detailed procedures implicit in the system.

It should be noted that this terminology is not universal. Sometimes the term systems designer is used to denote the person responsible for what is above called problem analysis, while the computer analyst deals with the detailed conversion into computer processes.

Systems analysis, which will be here regarded as embracing all three of the above stages, is often considered as a branch of the organisation and methods aspects of work study, though, since the advent of computers, it is generally used to imply the design of computerised systems. Systems analysts require both a knowledge of business and its procedures and also of computers and how to use them in a business environment.

The systems analyst is concerned with the following.

1. *Finding the objectives* of activities, which will involve discussions with management and the interviewing of key members of staff. The precise needs of management should be clarified. The scope of the computer application must be defined; it may vary

from a limited, fairly isolated data processing function, through schemes that may require considerable integration, up to total systems concepts, where the whole data processing of the business is to be built into a single system. Considerable ability in human relations will be called for, as well as a good appreciation of business organisation and of the problems faced in different departments and the responsibilities of their managers.

Often the systems analyst will have to devise his systems for a known computer configuration, but a very important exception occurs when management is considering either replacing a non-computerised system by a computer or improving its existing computer facilities. This special problem is dealt with later under feasibility studies.

2. *Establishing facts* about the organisation, policy, methods and problems of the user departments. The flow of information and the procedures used are studied, together with the documents involved and the volumes and frequencies of data. Any legal and auditing requirements will be noted as will controls that are used. Exception conditions must be defined and the methods used to cope with them should be fully understood. The success of business computing depends largely on standardisation. It is often not appreciated how much a clerk, making almost automatic decisions, may contribute to the smooth working of a non-computerised system. The computer system must take account of all eventualities. Basically this recording and analysis is on the lines of normal organisation and methods work (*see* Chapter 6).

3. *Designing systems* and selecting the best. This involves the design of input and output layouts and, similarly, of records to be stored, as well as the planning of the flow of information and the procedures and runs required for its processing. Some of the main results of systems design are the charts, perhaps broken down in increasing detail from block diagrams of complete systems, to flow charts to be used by the programmers.

A comprehensive account of the system, sometimes called a systems definition, provides, for users, operators and programmers, all the information they may require. It must not be forgotten that computer operating staff and other clerical workers will be involved. This document will be the basis of management's decision to approve the system or not. The writing of program specifications, in which the aims, methods and controls, together with timings for each program are given, and the compilation of a job manual may be considered at this stage. There will be considerable liaison with the programmers and test data will be provided to validate the programs.

4. *Developing, implementing, operating and maintaining the system.* It is difficult to divide this stage precisely from that just considered, which is sometimes restricted to design of outline systems and the preparation of block diagrams, together with timing and estimation of resources needed. If this definition is adopted the preparation of program specifications and more detailed flow charting will be included under the present head. Discussion with the user department may result in modification of the original proposals.

Eventually a detailed plan for implementation will be needed and job procedures for the user department and for the data preparation and computer operating departments will have to be written. Programs and systems will have to be tested and, probably, modified, while the timing estimates will be checked by dummy runs. The systems analyst will be involved in all this and will have a general interest in maintaining and monitoring the application of the systems he has devised. He will also advise on the training of staff in user departments and will often find he has to explain his system to staff who may be affected.

In connection with consultancy the term "turnkey" operation is used to denote a system whereby the user is completely relieved of all systems analysis and programming problems, the consultancy firm engaging to lay on a system to produce the required results. This may even go as far as providing operating staff for the computer installation and seeing to its running.

DATA PROCESSING FLOW CHARTS

The most obvious products of systems analysis are the flow charts which indicate, with varying degrees of detail, how a system is supposed to work. It is difficult to define precise boundaries between the different levels of such charts but the following is a guide:

1. *Total systems* charts, which show the inter-relationships of the various sub-systems entering into the over-all data processing (*see* Fig. 40). Each of these can be represented by a block, linked by arrowed lines to other blocks, to show the information flow in the over-all system. Each block will represent a routine of work that forms the subject of more detailed flow charts.

2. *Block diagrams* of each of the routines entering into the total system will show information flow, its sources and destinations, and a broad outline of the processing sequence. These charts may involve only a broad statement of the processing and are built up of rectangles, though the term "block" is often used to describe diagrams using flow-chart symbols.

3. *Systems flow charts*, giving more detail of the procedures and using standard flow chart symbols. Input, output and storage devices may be shown, as well as decisions and main processes. (*See* Fig. 42 and the flow chart in Fig. 43.)

4. *Detailed flow charts*, giving sufficient detail to enable programs to be written, are the final stage.

So far, in this book, the flow chart examples have been of the detailed type, and the appropriate BASIC programs have been shown. The situation has been simplified since input and output through a keyboard terminal has been assumed. In the present chapter the practical problems of using the peripheral devices outlined in Chapter 2 must be faced.

Payroll example

A payroll calculation may be taken as a simplified illustration of data processing. Suppose a magnetic tape file contains the standard pay information for each man on the payroll, showing his payroll number, the standard hours and the standard rate of pay. These details are recorded in ascending order of payroll number. Each week a magnetic tape is prepared showing the payroll number and actual hours worked for each man, again assembled in payroll number sequence. The object is to output a third tape showing details of standard and overtime hours worked for each man, together with his standard, overtime and total pay. In this simple case deductions for tax and other purposes will be ignored. The flow chart can be extended to cover these, including a special routine to calculate the P.A.Y.E. liability of each worker.

The broad outline of the operation is shown in the systems flow chart (Fig. 43), which indicates the data conversion from punched cards to magnetic tape, the sorting of this tape and, finally, the main computer run, of which fuller details are provided in the flow chart in Fig. 44. This flow chart is chiefly taken up with the problems of linking the standard data file with the weekly tape of hours worked. The calculations are shown in one block and are detailed in Chapter 7, Fig. 54, in the PAYCALC paragraph.

The layout of input and output files are indicated in Fig. 45. The records on the master file (HRRTFL) each show payroll number (M), standard hours (STHR) and rate of pay (RATE), while those on the weekly work-record file (HRWKFL) show payroll number (NM) and hours worked (HRS). The output file (PAYFL) will have records showing payroll number (ROLL), standard, overtime and total hours (STD, OT, TOT) and standard, overtime and total pay (ST-PAY, OT-PAY, TOT-PAY). The letters represent the

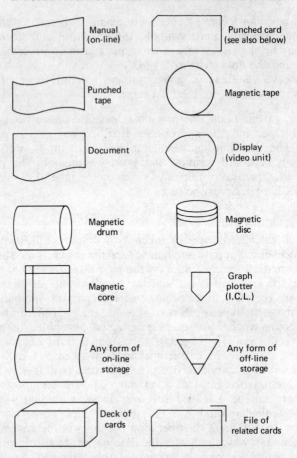

FIG. 42. Flow chart symbols (2). Basic symbols are shown in Fig. 3.
(a) Relating to type of input and output. (b) Relating chiefly to process.

names given to these items in the COBOL program shown in Chapter 7.

Suppose, to check the program, that the master file has payroll numbers from one upwards, while the weekly file happens to have workers numbered, say, 2, 3, 5, 6 etc. Each tape has an end marker which is recognised by the computer.

The program commences by making the value of M in store equal to zero. Next the first record of the weekly file (NM) is read and checked for being the end of the tape. It is compared with M

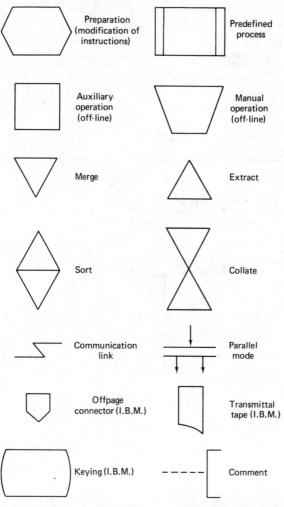

Preparation (modification of instructions)

Predefined process

Auxiliary operation (off-line)

Manual operation (off-line)

Merge

Extract

Sort

Collate

Communication link

Parallel mode

Offpage connector (I.B.M.)

Transmittal tape (I.B.M.)

Keying (I.B.M.)

Comment

and, since this is zero to start with, the program branches to the right to read the first number (M) on the master file, which will replace zero in storage (if it is not the end of the tape). The situation with the specimen numbers is that M = 1 and NM = 2. The comparison is again made; M is still less than NM, so the next record of the master file (where M = 2) is read. Now both M and NM are equal to 2 and the question Is M < NM? receives the answer No. The next question, Is M = NM?, receives the answer Yes, so the calculation is performed and details printed on to the

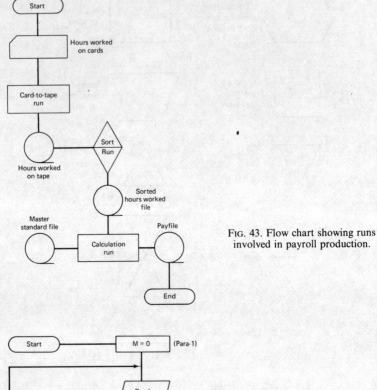

FIG. 43. Flow chart showing runs involved in payroll production.

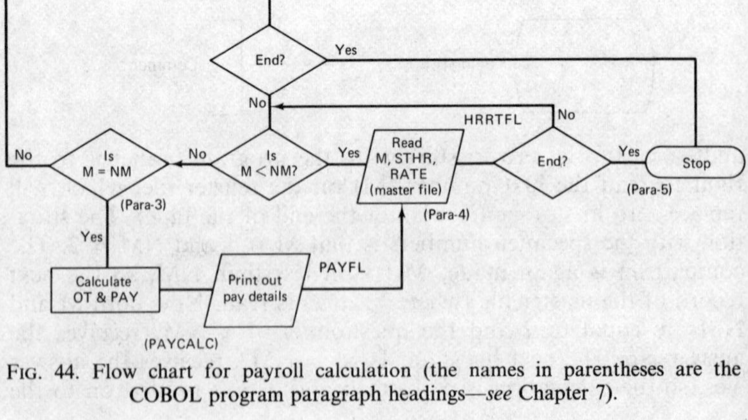

FIG. 44. Flow chart for payroll calculation (the names in parentheses are the COBOL program paragraph headings—*see* Chapter 7).

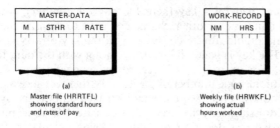

(a)
Master file (HRRTFL)
showing standard hours
and rates of pay

(b)
Weekly file (HRWKFL)
showing actual
hours worked

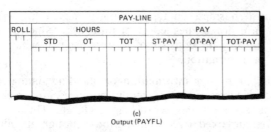

(c)
Output (PAYFL)

FIG. 45. Tabular equivalent of layout for payroll files.

output tape. The next record on the master file, where M = 3, is read and the consequences of this are that the line going up to loop into the instruction to read NM on the weekly file is followed.

The reader should test for the effects of items out of order in the weekly file and also of items in that file that have payroll numbers beyond these recorded in the standard file. He should amend the chart to ensure that it keeps track of such cases and to provide a print-out at the computer console when they occur. No provision is made explicitly in this flow chart to cover the situation when less than the standard number of hours are worked. This could be included in the calculation or the condition might be tested at an appropriate stage in the program, which could be directed into alternative calculations. The simple COBOL program in Chapter 7 does not provide for this and readers interested in COBOL programming may like to amend this program to cover their proposed solution, after reading that chapter.

FILE HANDLING

The simple payroll case just considered illustrates the use of a master file of standing data, in conjunction with transactions data (in this case the number of hours worked), to produce required output data at weekly intervals. The link between the two sets of data is provided by a key (here the payroll number), which is a group of numbers, or other characters, used to identify and locate items. This should not be confused with the key of a typewriter or console. The key is generally recorded along with the data to which it relates. For example, each record on magnetic tape will commence with the code number of the item. With direct access disc files, if records are in strict sequence and of fixed length, the system of direct addressing may be used. In this case the code number is not recorded, the location or address being calculated from the key.

In practical business data processing a master file will be the equivalent of a firm's sales ledger or purchases ledger or stock records, etc. Such a file consists of records each of which contains two kinds of information:

1. Static or master information or standing data (there is a wide choice of terms), such as account numbers, customers' names and addresses, stock codes, reordering levels, etc. This information tends to remain fixed over long periods, though it will require keeping up to date. Such updating can be done by a variations run, under the control of a special program, during which mistakes in the master data can be corrected and other modifications, additions and deletions may be made.

2. Transactions data, that is information to be updated, such as customers' balances or the amounts and values of stock items.

Master files, such as described, may be stored on one of many forms of storage media, such as punched cards, magnetic tapes or discs. Magnetic tape files are probably the most popular, combining cheapness with speed of reading. When discs are used for processing the data is often dumped on to magnetic tape for cheap storage and for security.

A typical processing run would involve mounting the old master tape on a magnetic tape deck, reading the records into the computer memory one at a time, or more probably in blocks of records, matching these with the updating information, and, finally, outputting a new master file on another tape deck. This new master file would be a copy of the old file as far as the static data is concerned. This is the basis of the "father and son" security precaution. If anything goes wrong during the computing run the old file is available and there is not a disastrous loss of data. In systems where the old records are overwritten by the new, as is often the case with disc systems, special attention must be paid to this problem (*see* Chapter 9).

The updating material, or movement data, gives details such as sales, purchases, stock receipts and withdrawals, etc., depending on the particular processing run. This data will be assembled in appropriate order as, say, a deck of punched cards or as records on magnetic tape. Usually the movement data must be marshalled in the same order as the master file data to which it relates. This may be done mechanically by sorting, in the case of punched cards, but it is perhaps preferable to sort by a special computer run, using magnetic tape. This sorted tape is used as updating input for the main computer run.

Updating of master files often involves several updating records for any given master file record. For example, each stock item may have been subject to several withdrawals since the last updating run. In such cases the total effect of all the transactions will be evaluated in the computer and only the final result will be output, this being triggered off when a movement record with a higher key (or an end marker if it is the last record) is read.

Straightforward updating of master records may be supplemented by the generation of other information at negligible cost in extra time, if appropriate peripherals are available. For example, when updating a stock file it would be possible to output files, or direct print-out, covering:

1. items requiring re-order, because the predetermined ordering level has been reached;
2. costs of items withdrawn from stock for works orders. A material costs print-out on the basis of work order numbers would be useful to the cost accountant. Since the data would be in stock code order it could be profitably sorted on the basis of works order numbers by a separate computer run;
3. analysis of stock usage;
4. stock items with very low activity.

In this connection it should be appreciated that totals may be easily accumulated in the computer memory by suitable programming, to be printed out as required. The calculation of ratios and percentages, often of use for management control purposes, may similarly be easily performed. The need for such information should be recognised in the early stages of systems analysis.

The processing just described is generally organised on a batch basis. Updating material is accumulated until there is sufficient to make a computer run economic. Runs for updating different files are scheduled for different times of the week or month, as described in Chapter 8, a main consideration being the avoidance of bottlenecks in the processing. This batch system has the obvious drawback that records are only up to date at the time of the updating run. The deficiencies of the batch method have caused real-time systems, considered in the next section, to be developed.

REAL-TIME v. BATCH PROCESSING

The traditional approach to processing business data by computer was to batch the work, as described in the previous section. This follows the practice adopted earlier when ledger-posting and punched card equipment began to be used. Such batching may be the obvious solution, especially when data requires conversion, such as card punching, before it is acceptable as computer input. It does not, however, make full use of the potential of computers and treats them just as advanced calculating machines.

Real-time computing attempts to keep the data system as up to date as management feels to be necessary and provides for accessing of relevant information in the system as and when required by those who have authority to do so.

The quality of instantaneous updating of records when new movement data occurs may not always be worth while. It is a matter of the significance of any time lags. An early example of the application of real-time computing was in connection with aircraft seat reservations. In such a case instantaneous updating is clearly an essential. The same might apply if a computer were used to control a factory process. In many cases, however, the use of a computer overnight to process, for example, stock data, so that the position is correct each morning, might be satisfactory.

Real-time computing poses many problems for the systems analyst. Fundamentally it is a matter of strategically based terminals for input and output, coupled with rapid access facilities to the files to be used, generally implying the use of disc backing stores. If a computer can be "dedicated" to a particular job, that is, used solely for that purpose, the problem is greatly simplified. Otherwise systems of varying complexity may be devised using methods such as:

1. multiprogramming, with direct access to the computer, (achieved by hardware or by a resident software system);

2. multiplexors, really small computers, acting as buffers between terminals and the computer, and also between files and the computer;

3. communications processors, which are computers concerned with scheduling and housekeeping for the main computer, which is responsible for the major computational work;

4. dual systems, where a standby computer can be utilised in the event of break-down of the main system;

5. mixed systems, operating partly on real-time and partly for batch processing. The standby computer of (4) may be used on batch work in the normal course of events. Processing of magnetic tape files may be an extra facility of a time-sharing system.

Among special factors to be considered in real-time feasibility studies and systems design are the following.

1. redundancy of equipment. The cost of protection against system failure by standby equipment may be high;
2. provision must be made for re-establishing the system in the event of partial or total failure.
3. low utilisation of terminal hardware. Real-time implies that there are many terminals located with reference to the requirements of the user departments. Utilisation may be high in cases such as a seat booking system but low in the case of an executive's desk terminal.
4. Speed of response to terminal enquiries and input. A study of the queue situation may be required. Work was done on this, long before the invention of computers, in connection with the loading of telephone exchanges. This is an operational research technique. The simplest situations can be handled by formulae. Suppose, during interval of time, there are a arrivals (that is requests through the terminals) and the average number of such items that can be processed, or serviced, during a similar time interval is s.

The ratio, $\frac{a}{s} = i$, is called the intensity of traffic, and must be less than one for the formulae to apply. The implication of this is that the system can deal with all the requests, in the long run, but, since these arise in a random way, a queue may develop. A number of formulae are available, among which may be noted:

(a) average waiting time $= \dfrac{a}{s(s - a)}$

(b) probability of having to wait $= i$

(c) average number of items in the queue $= \dfrac{i^2}{(1 - i)}$

More involved situations arise in practice. If formulae are not available they may be studied by the operational research technique of simulation (see Chapter 10). Complicated data networks may have to be dealt with.

5. Failsoft techniques are required to cope with data faults, where suspension of the process is not enough and the processing on hand requires concluding in an orderly way.

6. The structure of the data available to the system must be carefully considered. Real-time may call for a set of data common to various types of processing, instead of the departmentalised data common to batch processing. This may yield opportunities for savings in data storage by centralisation. Directly accessible data necessary for a system is sometimes referred to as a data bank. The term data base is used in a similar context, with emphasis on the organisation of the data so that it may be used for one or more applications programs.

7. Access to the data base involves consideration of its purpose (is it just for reading or for updating?) and security. It is clearly important that only authorised persons should have access, and essential that changes in the data base should be brought about only in an approved way. The use of identification codes and badge readers may assist security. Data may be partitioned so that different programs have access to different parts. Decisions must be made as to what content of different records is available on line; this may vary as between departments and grades of staff. The design of the output format is important, varying, possibly, from a simple digital display, through teleprinter print-outs and their video unit equivalents, to sophisticated reproductions of records and graphical displays.

DECISION TABLES

In the design of systems it frequently arises that predetermined sequences of conditions require specified actions to be taken. It is important that the outcomes of all possible combinations of conditions should be taken into account and decision tables show all these together with the required actions.

Such tables take many forms. The basic approach is to specify the conditions in such a way that "yes" (Y) or "no" (N) can fully express the situation for each. With only one condition there are two possibilities (Y or N); with two conditions there are four possible outcomes, since with both Y and N for the first condition there may be a Y or N for the second, and so on. It will be seen that the number of different sequences is 2n, where n is the number of possible conditions.

As an example, suppose that a firm has introduced a credit control system for its customers, but all customers have not yet been vetted. The details of the control system are not significant to this illustration; what is significant is that four conditions will be tested each time an order is placed.

1. Is a credit rating available? If not this is assessed and the customer's order is then checked in the routine way against this rating.

2. Will the outstanding credit, including the new order, exceed the credit limit?

3. Has there been any adverse indication in the past six months?

4. Has there been any activity in the account in the past six months?

The aim of this system is either to clear orders or to list information on such orders as may require rejection or special action. The second condition clearly results in such a listing, while the third and fourth conditions are intended to ensure that credit ratings are alive to the up-to-date position. The system has been devised for purposes of illustration of decision tables and would not necessarily be satisfactory in all circumstances. Various versions of decision tables to cover this situation are shown in Fig. 46.

The full version is like a football pool permutation. There are sixteen columns, since these are required to cover four different actions ($2^4 = 16$). Each row of the "condition" section has eight Y and eight N, arranged to cover all possible sequences. The action consequent on each sequence is shown by placing a cross in the appropriate position in each column of the "action" section of the table.

In several cases certain conditions are irrelevant in view of the state of other conditions in the table. This situation may be shown by placing a dash against the conditions that need not be checked. Thus, if a rating is not available, the action required is to obtain such an assessment, and the second condition cannot be determined until this is done, when the order will be resubmitted, and the answer to the first condition will then be yes. Again, if the rating is exceeded, the order will not be approved, regardless of the state of the account and its activity. The full table can be reduced to five columns. A numerical check can be applied at this stage. If there are m dashes in a column then the number of columns eliminated from the full table is $2m - 1$. The number of columns in the condensed table, together with these calculated values, where dashes occur, should total 2n. In this example this is the sum of

$$5 + (2^2 - 1) + (2 - 1) + (2^3 - 1) = 5 + 3 + 1 + 7 = 16$$

which agrees with the number of columns in the full table. When such tables are used as a guide to action they may sometimes be rearranged as shown in Fig. 46(c).

CONDITION

1. Rating available?	Y	Y	Y	Y	Y	Y	Y	Y	N	N	N	N	N	N	N	N
2. Rating exceeded?	Y	Y	Y	Y	N	N	N	N	Y	Y	Y	Y	N	N	N	N
3. Adverse indication?	Y	Y	N	N	Y	Y	N	N	Y	Y	N	N	Y	Y	N	N
4. Activity in last 6 mths?	Y	N	Y	N	Y	N	Y	N	Y	N	Y	N	Y	N	Y	N

ACTION

a. Assess and reprocess									+	+	+	+	+	+	+	+
b. Approve order						+										
c. Print out details	+	+	+	+	+	+		+								

(a) Full version

CONDITION

1. Rating available?	Y	Y	Y	Y	N
2. Rating exceeded?	Y	N	N	N	–
3. Adverse indication?	–	Y	N	N	–
4. Activity in 6 mths?	–	–	Y	N	–

ACTION

a. Assess & reprocess					+
b. Approve order			+		
c. Print out details	+	+		+	

(b) Condensed version

Rating available?			Y		N
Rating exceeded?	Y		N		
Adverse indication?		Y		N	
Activity in 6 mths?			N	Y	
ACTION	PRINT		OK	AS	

(c) Re-arranged table

Fig. 46. Decision tables.

Decision tables may be classified as:

1. limited entry, where each possible condition and the required actions occupy a separate row (see parts (a) and (b) of Fig. 46);

2. extended entry, where the row statements are incomplete and columns provide for a variety of conditions or of actions. In the example part (c) is in extended entry form as far as the action is concerned. A form of extended entry condition would be:

Is the order valued at more than £50, £100, £500, £1,000, so that a particular column would be chosen depending on which of these values applied?

PROCEDURE MANUALS AND STANDARDS

Data processing, at all its stages, should be subject to standards. These standards may be incorporated in a set of manuals, useful for reference and for training, and aimed at achieving efficient working and the prevention of error and fraud, while enabling performance standards to be set and responsibilities to be allocated.

Standards may relate to apparently trivial matters which, in practice, may be very significant. As an example, in writing programs, it is important to distinguish between characters such as the letter O and 0 (zero), and the letter I and the number 1. Standards vary as between users; for example in the first case either the letter or the numeral may have a line drawn across the normal character. The use of a programming language is an example of standardisation, as is the use of standard flow chart symbols. Beyond this the individual data processing department may produce standards covering, for example, the layout of programs, the indentation of lines, etc.

Obviously any full illustration of procedure manuals would involve far more pages than the present book contains. Of great significance is the need for clarity in writing the manual, which implies that the knowledge and abilities of the users have been carefully considered, whether the standards cover forms design, input preparation, systems analysis, programming, operating or performance. This subject is developed further in Chapters 6 and 9.

MODULAR AND STRUCTURED PROGRAMMING

It is not surprising that attempts have been made to standardise approaches to programming and to lay down rules aimed at simplifying and speeding-up the process, reducing the risk of program failure and making modification easier. This is especially important when large programming projects have to be co-ordinated from the work of many programmers or teams of programmers. The modular technique builds up larger programs from modules or smaller programs, which are known to produce stated results and are linked together with a minimum of statements. Some programming languages encourage this approach, examples being ALGOL and PL1. In ALGOL subprograms can be created between the words BEGIN and END, and sets of programs can be nested.

A feature of structured programming is that jumping about between parts of the program, using GO TO statements, is avoided. Basic constructions are used having a single entry and a single exit, rather like plugging electronic components together. Programming is seen as a rational, rather than inspirational process, using component types such as sequence of parts, iteration or repetition of parts and selection of parts, which are used to build an hierarchical structure. Flow charts, as part of the standard system, recognise this and are drawn to solve the programming problems and with a view to subsequent testing of the programs. It should be emphasised that the process is a "top-down" one, where we start with the input and output requirements of the system and progressively break this into simpler functions. This is analytical and the opposite of the "bottom-up" approach, which synthesises the final result.

DATA BASES AND STRUCTURES

Data bases ideally contain all the information needed for a set of applications, or for the fully integrated control of a large business (or other) unit. Duplication is avoided. Data are assembled independently of particular uses, and applications programmers do not need to know the data base structure, being linked with it through a system called a data base handler. One approach is to have separate languages, one concerned with the format and structure of the data base and the other with manipulating it.

Early thinking on data bases was much influenced by centralised information concepts related to mainframe computers. Such ideas are still significant but distributed processing techniques have altered the picture, so that we may think more in terms of integrating, when necessary, the contributions of many localised data bases. To do this effectively probably implies that such distributed systems should be planned to be compatible both technically and from an information point of view. Autonomous subsystems may be linked and controlled so that the one most appropriate processes a request from a user of the data base.

Any set of data requires some structure to enable information to be retrieved. Sequential and random structures of information have been considered in Chapter 2. Problems of classifying information and indexing it for easy retrieval, especially in real-time systems and data bases, have given rise to many special techniques.

At the simplest level classification resembles the systems already well-developed, in connection for example, with stores part numbers and employees. A sequential code may be built up where different numbers (or characters) in a given sequence represent different aspects of information relating to the item. The first two digits may represent, say, the particular factory at which the worker is employed, the next three may record the particular department, and so on.

Data may be regarded as forming a matrix in which the row names give the record sequence in the master file while the column names relate to the aspects or terms or fields of the files.

Progress from record to record in a "list", can be achieved by including the address of the next record as part of the listed information, so that, once the correct trail has been reached by finding the address of the first record the rest follow automatically. For example links may enable all workers in a particular department, or with particular skills, to be traced. This may be called simple list structure.

Alternatively a record or index may be kept for each field, listing all the records in which it occurs. This is called an inverted file. A tree structure can be used to show the relationships between items of information, in a manner similar to that in which a "family tree" enables the relationships between generations to be traced. In the "binary" form each branch splits successively into two.

A management information system may well be restricted to standard information of value to management and retrievable in a clearly predetermined way. For example standard reports may be available through terminals on typing the appropriate code name. Retrieval of more general information, such as references to books and articles dealing with many aspects of assorted topics may cause more problems, since the titles may not be fully indicative of the contents. One approach is to prepare a system of standard words, sometimes called a thesaurus. Such words are used for indexing and the person seeking information selects the word or words nearest to the subject matter that concerns him.

From a programming point of view, when information is "moved" within a store, conventionally the source remains undisturbed and the information is written over whatever existed at the destination, destroying this. Thus an instruction such as LET Y = X results in the value of X being left at X while Y also takes on this value. Another approach is to have long registers where information already stored remains and new information is added to it, either before or after (left or right of) the existing information. When information is extracted from such a register it is actually erased from the source. At the destination it is added to what is already stored, not overwriting this. If information can only be added or removed at one end the arrangement is called a stack or pushdown store. With this arrangement "movement" of data is in line with the everyday use of the term. It is similar to a physical store where "last in first out" has to operate. The computer simulates this by using consecutive registers having a fixed lower position and a variable upper position.

Developments such as content addressable memory (CAM) (*see* Chapter 2) are increasing the sophistication of data bases. New approaches in data base structures reduce or even eliminate the need for sorting. Relational data bases seem likely to become significant and have the feature that criteria for sequence and selection can be designated when the logical file is created. An aim is to facilitate the interaction between managers, clerks etc. and the data base with the mimimum of specialist programming intervention. Common factors, attributes and links can be built into the data. Theory tends to be well in advance of general usage.

SPECIMEN EXAMINATION QUESTIONS

1. Explain what is meant by saying that a business organisation is a system operating in an environment and itself consisting of subsystems. Briefly comment on the significance of this to the development of practical business computer systems.

2. Discuss the relevance to management of there being different levels of information and comment on how the flow of such information may be planned.

3. Outline the role of systems analysis and give some details of the stages involved in practical analysis.

4. Files and their updating may be regarded as the basis of all commercial data processing. Explain this statement, giving examples based on four distinct types of business record.

5. (*a*) Distinguish between standing (or master) data and transaction data. (*b*) Briefly indicate the difference involved in updating master files held on magnetic discs compared with those held on magnetic tape.

6. Explain what is meant by a decision table and discuss the circumstances in which it may be used in connection with computing. Distinguish between limited and extended entry versions.

7. Discuss the need for standards in connection with systems and programming work.

8. Compare batch processing with real-time processing, explaining how these approaches depend on the equipment available and how they should be related to the particular application involved. Give practical examples.

9. "Real-time computing is beneficial to management but poses special problems for the systems analyst." Comment.

10. Describe the features of hardware and software that may be involved with real-time applications.

11. Explain how the data base approach to information differs from the traditional methods of building up a computer system and assess its possible advantages and disadvantages.

12. "The systems approach to business is closely related to the development of equipment for processing management information and making it quickly available." Discuss.

Chapter 6

ORGANISATION AND METHODS

WORK STUDY AND O. AND M.

Work study is concerned with improving the efficiency and economy of work by systematic investigation. Its chief techniques are method study and work measurement.

1. *Method study* is concerned with the manner in which work is done. Existing ways of doing work are systematically recorded and critically examined, as are possible alternatives, with a view to using more effective methods at lower costs. At one time a distinction was made between "method study", concerned more with the flow of work through factory or office, from process to process, and "motion study", concerned with individual workers and processes within this flow.

2. *Work measurement* is concerned with the time work should take, assuming the worker is qualified and does a specified job at a rate achievable without over-exertion over the working day. The standard time can be used as a basis for costing, for planning and job scheduling and for calculation of piece rates, if applicable.

Systematic study of work is usually considered to have originated at the end of the nineteenth century in the work of the pioneers of "scientific management", F. W. Taylor and F. B. Gilbreth. Very slow progress was made in Britain until the 1930s. "Time and motion study", which was a term often used, was regarded very suspiciously, particularly by the workers. Nowadays work study is accepted as a service to management. It is also recognised that office work is amenable to improvement, as is work in the factory. The term O. & M. (Organisation and Methods) is generally used in this case. In some ways office work presents difficulties, especially in the measurement of output and productivity. Scrap in a factory tends to reveal itself whereas, in the office, its equivalent in the form of unnecessary communications, irrelevant statistics, wordy letters and the like, may be linked with an appearance of hard work and conscientiousness.

The relevance to computing is obvious, since a computer can generate massive quantities of records and documents, perhaps far

126

beyond the capacity of management either to assimilate them or to use the information effectively. The term "systems analysis" was associated with O. & M. to imply the study and design of business systems, including the staff and office equipment involved, before the advent of computers. In the 1960s its use became associated with computerised business systems, though many O. & M. specialists do not agree with this limited definition.

Method study

This is concerned with improvement of methods and involves the following stages.

1. *Selection of the work to be studied* and definition of the scope of the study. Jobs where the greatest economies seem likely will reasonably have the highest priority, unless bottlenecks are more urgent.

2. *Recording information about the work*. This may be the most time-consuming part of the study. Paying particular attention to O. & M. in the examples it is possible to note the difference between the primary "note-book" data produced by the investigator and the systematic version of this generally referred to as a process chart or flow process chart. Examples of such charts are shown in Figs. 47–50 in this chapter.

Photography may be used. Time-lapse photography (memo-motion study) records what is happening on cine film exposed at a much lower number of frames per time interval than is normal. This gives a speeded-up version of, say, office activity when projected at the normal speed. Frame-by-frame inspection of cine film may be used. Alternatively, using chronocyclegraphs, a single exposure may cover, say, hand movements involved in a job, these appearing as a trace on the photograph as small electric light bulbs are attached to the fingers.

3. *Critical examination of the facts*, challenging what is done and seeking alternatives. This generally involves some version of the so-called "questioning technique". Primary questions look into the facts and the reasons behind them; secondary questions examine the alternatives. In turn are challenged the purpose (what is done?), the place (where is it done?), the sequence (when is it done?), the person (who does it?) and the means (how is it done?). Each of these questions involves the further questions of "why?" and "what else could be done?", with a final decision on "what should be done?" In considering a data processing system, challenging the "purpose" might reveal that the data was not really needed so the system might be eliminated in part or completely. The "place"

might refer to data processed in a number of separate offices or under the control of separate departments; the alternative might be central processing. The "sequence" might involve an existing system of saving data until there is enough to be processed economically and the alternative might be to use a real-time computer system, processing each item as soon as the updating requirements of the system indicate the need for this. The "person" might be a skilled accountant doing a difficult calculation manually or a clerk using a computer to obtain the same result. The "means" might vary from hand-written book-keeping to the use of ledger machines, punched cards and computers.

4. *Development of improved methods*, including standards relating to the procedures, the equipment, the staff and their training requirements, the stationery, the quality of work, the instructions and the working conditions.

5. *Installation of improved methods*, involving planning and implementation.

6. *Maintenance of improved methods*, involving regular checks that the standards are being adhered to.

Human aspects

An important consideration in all change is the human factor and efforts must be made to secure acceptance and support of the change. This involves effective communications, involvement of the workers concerned in deciding on the changes, adequate training for and explanation of the new systems and, above all, assurances of the security of the workers' position, based on good faith. An expanding industry, such as computing in its early days, can offer opportunities for men and women versed in the new skills, who may be in short supply for several years. The early stages of introducing computers in industry were not associated with large reductions in staff, rather the reverse. As computer installations grow in sophistication there may well be radical changes in the office labour situation amounting to a data processing or communications "revolution" (*see* Chapter 11).

Attention must be paid to the personal factor throughout any investigations. This will include obtaining the approval of managers and of trade unions (or other forms of worker representation) to the investigation. The persons conducting the survey should be properly introduced to managers concerned and, through them, to their staff.

Work measurement

Work measurement is concerned with establishing time standards. The three different approaches, which may be used in combination, are as follows.

1. *Time study*, traditionally associated with the use of stop watches. The job is broken down into cycles of work, including all the elements necessary from start to finish of a complete job. The elements are timed over a number of cycles. Usually a performance rating is noted as this is done, being the time study man's assessment of the rate of working and subsequently used to adjust the observed time to basic time. The time for similar elements is totalled and averaged. Allowances are added for relaxation (for recovering from fatigue and attention to personal needs) and for contingencies (delays, unoccupied time, etc.) to give a standard time. This may be further stretched by the addition of a policy allowance to give the allowed time, used for payment purposes so that a worker can obtain agreed bonus earnings.

2. *Synthesis*, using the experience obtained from other jobs to provide data for element times.

3. *Predetermined standards*. Various schemes are used. M.T.M. (methods–time measurement) considers the nature of each motion and the conditions under which it is made and assigns a predetermined time to it. The "Work-Factor System" provides tables for estimating times to perform movements and mental processes. Such predetermined motion time systems (P.M.T.S.) require training in their use and are identified with the consultants who originated them.

The timing of data processing runs is outlined later. As mechanical and electronic equipment is involved in most stages attention tends to concentrate on the speed of operation of, say, a card reader or a printing device. The operator time needed to collate documents and to set up machines is, however, a major factor in the efficient operation of a data processing department.

CHARTING PROCEDURES AND ROUTINES

Systems may be described in a number of ways. Some form of procedure record is generally used for business systems giving, in sufficient detail, all the operations involved in the procedure, laid out in sequence and indicating the links with other systems or other parts of the same system.

Suppose there is a simple ordering procedure for a company selling to a number of retailers. The orders come through the company's travellers who visit each shop once a week. They carry supplies of order forms (made up in sets with three carbon copies) on which the order is entered in consultation with the customer. The traveller retains one copy (number four) and leaves the top three copies with a sales control clerk at pre-arranged times. After credit vetting one of these forms (number three) is used as a packing guide for the warehouse while copies one and two are priced, extended (price multiplied by quantity) and totalled, appropriate checks being applied. Copy three, the packing guide is marked to indicate any shortages or alterations and returned to the invoice section so that such changes can be incorporated in copies one and two before they are finally released. The top copy acts as an invoice while the second is passed to the accounts department for book-keeping, a control total being first established to act as a check on the subsequent posting operations.

A simple way of conveying part of this information is illustrated in Fig. 47, showing the routing of documents. Columns are used for each separate section and the routing of the forms (shown as rectangles, each copy being numbered) is indicated by arrows. Retention is shown when no arrow leaves a numbered rectangle. Such a chart itself is insufficient to convey what is happening at the different stages. An extension of this principle uses actual forms, with real or dummy transactions which are pinned on a large

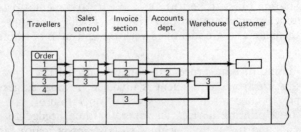

Fig. 47. Form routing chart for ordering and invoicing.

board and the connections indicated by tape or lines drawn by chalk or felt-tip pen. This can be photographed for a permanent record. It is sometimes called a form routing or routine chart.

Figure 48 shows a flow chart, while Figs. 49 and 50 provide written descriptions or narratives. A full set of process chart symbols is shown in Fig. 51. The chart shown at Fig. 49 is more suited to detailed analysis of the kind used in method study. Each operation is described on a separate line and is classified under one or more of the five main process chart symbols by placing a tick. On

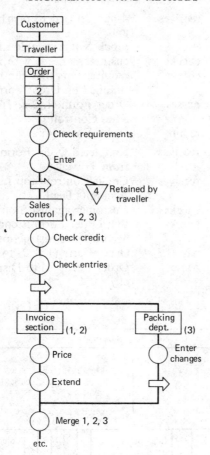

FIG. 48. Flow chart for ordering and invoicing. (Checking might be shown by the symbol for inspection☐.)

the right is provision for systematically questioning every stage, recording that this has been done by placing a tick in each space.

The use of diagrams and symbols clarifies the flow of work and assists any analysis that may be needed to improve efficiency. There is still much to be said for a clear, written statement of the procedure (a procedure narrative), giving information about the purpose and principles of the routine together with the persons and forms, indicating precisely how each is involved.

Order and Invoice Procedure

Traveller	receives	4-part set Order Form blanks and
		Stock Not Available List
	checks	customer's needs with List
	enters	requirements that can be supplied on Order Form
	passes	Order Form (1, 2 & 3) to Sales Control
	retains	Order Form (4)
Sales Control	receives	completed Order Form (1, 2 & 3) from Traveller
	receives	Credit Control Stop List from Accounts Dept
	checks	Customer against Stop List
	checks	that Order Form is completed according to instructions
	passes	Order Form (1 & 2) to Invoice Dept
	passes	Order Form (3) to Dispatch Dept etc.

FIG. 49. A procedure narrative.

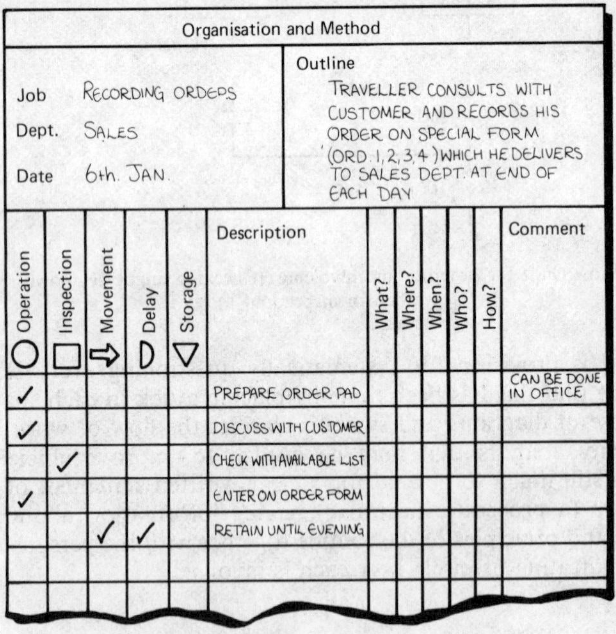

FIG. 50. A process chart.

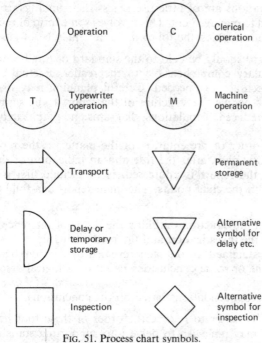

FIG. 51. Process chart symbols.

INVESTIGATIONS AND REPORTS

The stages involved in method study have already been outlined.
As far as investigation into methods generally is concerned these
stages may be considered as fitting into a sequence.

1. Establishing the objectives of the study. These may be to raise
efficiency and reduce costs of an existing system, to enable a
system to cope with more or less work, to set up a system to provide a new service, or to study the possible impact of new techniques.

2. Preliminary survey to assess the scope of the proposed investigation and the methods to be used, taking into account the
likely costs and the possible savings. In business, investigations
must be economically justifiable, not merely exercises in technical
expertise.

3. Method study, as previously outlined, resulting in a report to
the management which will guide them in making a decision, and
in the installation and maintenance of the new system, if this is
favoured.

Investigations are of little use unless their findings can be communicated to management. This involves some form of report, in the preparation of which the following points may be of guidance.

1. Regard should be paid to the standard of English and the use of vocabulary comprehensible to the reader. Factual and grammatical accuracy are needed. Careful planning may improve the clarity and enable the structure of the report to be simplified and its length reduced. Tabulations, diagrams and graphs may be desirable.

2. The order of presentation of the matter in the report is important. One plan, after the title and an indication of the persons to whom the report is addressed, is to include first a summary dealing with the chief points. The main report can follow, consisting of:

(*a*) an introduction outlining the terms of reference, the reasons for the investigation and the methods used;

(*b*) a statement of the facts revealed by the investigation;

(*c*) one or more conclusions based on a logical assessment of the facts;

(*d*) recommendations based on the conclusions.

It may be better to reverse the order of these four items, since managers may not wish to delve into supporting statistics, unless their appetite is whetted by interesting recommendations.

3. The persons to whom the report is addressed, together with restrictions on its circulation if it is confidential, should be clearly indicated, as should the persons responsible for the report, the period of time covered and the date of issue.

4. Any expressions of opinion should be clearly stated as such so that they are not confused with facts. Some communications may set out to change the opinions of the reader and to induce action on his part.

5. Lengthy reports tend to be shunned by busy managers who are generally keen to see clear answers to their problems.

Often management decisions will depend on balancing a number of factors. Though managers should be able to rely on the facts and advice of, say, O. & M. specialists, decisions on developing new systems and replacing old ones are ultimately their responsibility.

FEASIBILITY STUDIES

Every proposed computer application should be subject to a preliminary study to see if it is feasible before management approval is given and more detailed planning set in motion. However, the term feasibility study is often restricted to the special case where a decision has to be made on whether or not to go over to computerised methods, with the implications that a major policy decision on capital equipment and processing methods will be involved. Such a study will also occur when the question of replacing an existing computer system arises.

Much more computer experience is now available than in the early days of computers, and systems consultants may be engaged, or computer specialists may be available among the proposed user's staff. The method originally favoured of setting up a study team from the user's own staff is still often followed. Such staff may find their work is increasingly involved with computing, if the feasibility study appears favourable, and they may form the nucleus of a data processing department. A danger of this is that it may give the team a vested interest in producing a favourable report. Such a team requires some members with a specialised knowledge of computers together with representatives of the chief activities of the organisation. Since high level staff cannot normally be spared for this time-consuming work the team must be sure of top management interest and support. A steering committee of directors and senior staff may set objectives for the study team, perhaps in terms of investigating the feasibility of systems to achieve stated results with a given cost ceiling. The study team will produce interim reports to be considered by the steering committee. A preliminary survey may be conducted, followed by more detailed surveys if this seems worth while. If a consultant or specialist is entrusted with this work he will probably similarly produce interim and final feasibility reports. An interim report will generally cover topics such as:

1. introduction, outlining the reason for conducting the study and the terms of reference;

2. basic assumptions made, such as those related to the expansion expected in the organisation by the time the computer becomes available;

3. broad description of the equipment likely to be required, mentioning any essential characteristics;

4. outline of the systems to be installed and their procedures, with an indication of the expected work levels and schedules;

5. time-table for installation of equipment and implementation of systems;

6. likely costs of equipment and systems, with a comparison with costs of continuing present methods;

7. the effect on organisation and staff, and on methods, including improvements or deteriorations in availability of information (for example some batch processing systems may make access to accounts difficult in the period between processing). The impact on accommodation must also be considered.

The final report may contain more precise and detailed information on these topics. The study team will have contacted computer manufacturers giving them details of requirements and job specifications and asking for proposals to meet these. The systems requirements will be given in terms of procedure requirements, file lengths and contents, method and frequency of updating, and controls and security requirements. The workload may be outlined over a suitable period, say of four weeks.

An attempt will be made to obtain precise information from equipment suppliers regarding the type of equipment advocated, with full specifications of this and any ancillary equipment, together with programming facilities available (or promised), delivery expectations, acceptance testing, maintenance provisions (with costs) and a clear indication of the extent to which the configuration is out of action when individual units go down, with details of standby facilities, and also the facilities afforded for training staff and providing advice. The costs of equipment, programs and services must be indicated. Some manufacturers develop pricing based on a complete deal, including for example, the software in the computer costs. The use of separate quotations for the different components of cost, called unbundling, has tended to replace this.

COSTS AND FINANCE OF COMPUTER SYSTEMS

Feasibility studies are very much concerned with the costs of providing the recommended facilities and their comparison with the the costs of existing or alternative systems. The purchase of a computer and its associated equipment will involve a significant investment decision on the part of the user. Major points to be considered are:

1. initial outlay;
2. life of the equipment. With computers a maximum practical life of seven years might be normal. The policy of the manufacturer with regard to maintenance and the provision of new software and of interfaces to enable new hardware to be connected is very important;
3. residual value, if any, of the equipment when the user wishes to replace it. This will be very low towards the end of the expected

life span. The general popularity of the make and type of computer will be a factor. There may be special trade-in values when the equipment is exchanged for new equipment;

4. remaining life and resale value of the existing equipment to be replaced by the computer;

5. tax considerations, depending on the current fiscal policy of the government;

6. building costs involved in housing the computer;

7. delivery, installation and testing costs;

8. training costs.

Considerable immediate savings may be made by purchasing second-hand equipment but the software and maintenance position must be carefully considered.

The investment decision may best be made on a discounted cash flow basis (*see* page 139). Alternatives to outright purchase may be considered. These are renting from the computer manufacturer or leasing from a finance company. In the former case the rent will generally be a monthly charge (including maintenance), estimated to recover the capital and maintenance costs for the manufacturer in about four years. In the case of leasing the calculation is similar to that for hire purchase, interest being added to the purchase price and the total being spread over the months of the lease, with a much reduced charge if the user keeps the equipment beyond the agreed term. Payment may be quarterly, in advance. So-called risk or operating leases are for a fixed term, during which the user will pay at a monthly rate sufficient to repay the leasing company over an appropriate number of years. They tend to be restricted to the most popular equipment, to ensure that the leasing company will have few problems of re-leasing.

The running costs of a computer system may be broken down in the conventional way between fixed, variable and semi-variable costs.

1. Fixed costs, which do not vary with the volume of work done by the system. Costs associated with the capital equipment, such as lease or rental payments or depreciation will fall under this head, though rentals may increase for extra shift working. Charges for floor area occupied by the computer and tape libraries and punch rooms will also be fixed, as will the salaries of key members of the staff.

2. Variable costs, which tend to depend directly on the volume of work. Punched cards, paper tape, stationery and power fall into this category, as do payments to staff for overtime working.

3. Semi-variable costs, falling between (1) and (2) and having

the characteristic of tending to be fixed in the short run but variable over a longer period. For example, staff salaries will tend to be constant but the number of staff will, ultimately, vary according to the volume of work. Magnetic tapes may be re-used but will eventually require replacement.

The degree of utilisation of the computer system will affect the apparent cost of the work it does. New computers require a considerable period of time to operate at anything like their full load potential. It will be of interest to do the equivalent of a break-even analysis to find how much work the computer must handle to justify its installation. After this point there is a clear gain to the user from loading it with other jobs. This is, obviously, a major consideration with firms offering computer processing services, either for batches of work or on a time-sharing system. The possibilities of using bureau services for some or all of a firm's data processing activities should be considered. It may also be feasible to link with other users, either by hiring time on another user's computer, or by combining to purchase one. The power of mainframe computer systems tends to increase at a rate greater than the increase in costs needed to achieve this increase, so that a large system, effectively shared, might be a better proposition than several small systems. Against this may be set possible scheduling difficulties and problems arising from break-down; some equipment will be downgraded by component break-down, still remaining operational but at reduced speed, while other systems may be put completely out of action. With chip technology costs of equipment tend to be proportional to memory size for machines of similar design. It can be cost effective to link several minis or microcomputers.

CHOICE BETWEEN ALTERNATIVES

Management, having studied such reports as considered necessary, is faced with making a decision, which really amounts to a choice between alternatives.

1. An existing system may be replaced by a new one, involving expenditure on equipment and running costs, which must be compared with the costs involved in continuing the old system.

2. An entirely new system may be created, providing services not previously available.

3. Often an existing system may be replaced by a new one providing different facilities, so that it is impossible to make a straight cost comparison.

In all comparisons attention must be paid to the volume of work and how this is spread. Expensive equipment may be only justified by a large volume of work, so that different companies may find themselves served best by different systems and equipment. Work that is evenly spread and all of one kind may be dealt with more easily and cheaply than work tending to create peak loads and requiring frequent resetting of machines. The reliability of rival systems should be taken into account as should also the costs of checking results and making any necessary corrections. Involved systems, such as may apply with sophisticated data processing by a computer, will require long periods of preparation and testing, a factor that is often under-estimated, which may account for many unsatisfactory installations.

Success of systems often depends on some key factor, such as the availability of specialised staff, and the implications of such factors should be fully considered.

When equipment is being bought and systems devised that will produce a saleable service or commodity, then the yearly benefits arising may be estimated and compared with the cost of installing the system. For each year the difference between the income from the new system and the direct costs of using it may be calculated. The difference is termed the "cash flow" or "net annual gain". The total cash flow over the life of the equipment should exceed the initial investment involved for the latter to be worth while, on the simplest basis of calculation. A more sophisticated approach ("discounted cash flow" or D.C.F.) is to discount (or reduce) each year's net gain by a factor that allows for a rate of interest. Instead of using the actual value for the year the present sum of money needed to be invested at compound interest to amount to that value is taken. This is beneficial in estimating, since future circumstances, which may be difficult to forecast, count proportionally less than more immediate events which are more precisely known.

Alternative approaches, somewhat out of favour, are to calculate the pay-back period (the number of years over which the gains will balance the equipment costs), or the average rate of return as a percentage of the new equipment costs.

In the case of data processing this simple "saleable commodity" approach may apply to a business contemplating selling computer services, for example as a computer bureau. For the majority of computer users data processing represents a cost to be minimised, taking into account the basic needs for records and the effect on general operating efficiency of information services beyond these. Such things are difficult to assess.

If identical results to those produced by the existing system are expected then a straight cost comparison may be made, preferably on a discounted basis. Such a comparison would take account of the costs of operating the existing system and equipment over future years and of any money arising from the sale of equipment.

A factor in most decisions based on cost is what this would be if provided on a bought-out basis by a bureau. Here gain with data processing, factors that cannot be measured, such as desire for secrecy and for control over a company's own data processing and for prestige, will probably enter into the decision. Another such factor is the experience gained in running systems, which may eventually be essential to the company's progress and the cost of which the management may be prepared to write off. It is useful to list the factors to be taken into account (such as financial, technical, personnel, etc.) and show against each the favourable and unfavourable aspects.

Investigations rarely leave the existing system unchanged. The comparison may best be between a suggested new approach and the existing approach on an improved basis.

Before making decisions it is as well if all feasible alternatives are explored. A salesman for a particular type of equipment can hardly be expected to draw the attention of possible customers to the products of competitors. In studying the desirability of introducing computers it may well be found that a hybrid solution, using a computer together with other forms of equipment and manual methods, is best.

The full costs of running existing and proposed systems must be taken into account for comparisons to be valid. With computers, attention tends to concentrate on the outlay involved for equipment ("hardware"). The cost of providing systems ("software") to run on the computers can be substantial, as can the running costs, including staff to operate the computer and to prepare data for it. Maintenance and costs involved when the computer is out of action must also be taken into account.

Data processing services may be charged to the departments involved, if such internal accounting is favoured, and this may provide a basis for comparison. It is also useful to study what has to be foregone in the form of other expenditure of value to the firm if a particular project is favoured.

FORMS DESIGN

Business systems have, inevitably, required the use and control of forms for recording data and one of the chief factors to be considered when a computer is introduced will be the redesign of the forms employed. Aspects of form design to be considered are listed below.

1. How does the form fit into the system? Information may be entered at different stages and copies of forms may go to a variety of destinations. Colour coding to distinguish the various uses and the build up of sets of forms, with interleaved carbon paper or other method of obtaining duplicates, will be considered at the design stage.

2. What information is to be recorded and is this best done on one form or several?

3. What should be the layout and order in which the information appears? This will be related to factors such as the manner of making entries (handwritten, typed, computer print-out, etc.) and who reads the form. If the form is to be optically scanned as a form of computer input the exact positioning of marks made on it may be vital. The order should generally allow a left to right sequence of entry and reading moving from top to bottom of the page. The special requirements of any equipment should be considered, an obvious example being the space required for each character with any mechanical printing device.

4. The appearance of a form is an important factor in its acceptability. Both outside and within the business unit the company image may be related to this. Much can be done by attention to the format in which computer output is printed, for example the alignment of data. Titles may be preprinted on stationery or may be printed under the control of a computer program.

5. Paper quality may be important. An absorbent surface is not suited to entries in ink while too glossy a surface may make pencil entries difficult. For optical reading devices (see Chapter 2), thickness, opacity and surface texture may be critical, as may also the printing ink used.

6. Training in the use of forms should be given and instruction manuals may be prepared. Errors can frequently arise when data is entered or extracted because of lack of instruction, the insufficient provision of space and because data is not segregated sufficiently within the form. Before the layout is approved it should be tested under working conditions or as close to these as may be possible. Clear horizontal and vertical positioning in columns and rows, with perhaps a blank row after every tenth line of a print-out or a thickening of every fifth line of a form to be completed is desirable.

7. Costs will generally be a major factor. These will depend on

the quality of paper and printing (including the preparation of special blocks if used) and on the size and quantity of forms used. The special costs of setting a form up for printing will be spread over the number of forms printed. Modern methods of office reproduction tend to make businesses less dependent on specialist printers than they used to be. Word processing (*see* Chapter 10) is a significant development. The use of combined forms may reduce the variety of forms to be stored and controlled, with a saving in costs. A frequently neglected aspect is the clerical and other costs arising from the use of badly designed and inadequate forms.

8. Forms should bear a title briefly indicating their function and the department involved. They may also have a code to simplify reference in procedure manuals and for reordering.

A form designed for clerical use, from which computer input will be prepared in the form of punched cards on which the position of the information is rigidly predetermined, is shown in Fig. 52, with instructions for completion as shown in Fig. 53.

STANDARDS

Standards, in data processing as in any other field, attempt to state what is desirable in the light of experience and of current techniques, and to provide uniformity where variety is pointless or is too costly compared with the benefits it brings. The following aspects of standardisation are especially important.

1. Design standards of equipment, especially when achieving compatibility and interchangeability. Computer manufacturers have gone a long way in this direction. The modular approach to design, where items of equipment can be linked together to form operating units of varying sizes, and the use of common interfaces, so that equipment can be electrically linked without difficulty, are examples.

2. Standard terms, symbols and definitions. Progress has been made, examples being the standard flow-chart symbols used in this book which follow the B.S.I. (British Standards Institution) recommendations, except where indicated. Standard terminology is really essential if misunderstanding is to be avoided. The use of standard programming languages may be considered under this head.

3. Standard codes of practice. These may cover, for example, the operation of a computer system to ensure that it is correct and that security is maintained and fraud detected (see Chapter 9). Such codes will also apply to the testing of computer installations and the location and correction of faults.

orth East London Polytechnic
rolment/Registration Card   To be completed for all courses other than special

| gistration Number | 2   1042 | FACULTY
BUSINESS | DEPARTMENT | Office use only
MODE OF ATTEN.
LOCN. OF STUDY |

CTION A—to be completed by student—see overleaf

name

manent Address   Tel. No.

m-Time Address   Tel. No.

Forenames

Mr
Mrs
Miss

Date of birth (figures only)

al Education Authority (L.E.A.) _____ Country of Origin/Birth _____ Country of Domicile _____

ionality _____ Date of first entry to U.K. _____ Are you an L.E.A. Award holder   Office use only

ental Occupation (This information is required for a research programme and once processed will not be linked with individuals) _____ YES/NO

ne, address, telephone no. of employer _____ Nature of Employer's business _____
ase give Postal Code, if known) _____ Your occupation/title of post _____
_____ Name of training officer _____
_____ Address (if different from
you sponsored (i.e. released and/or have fees paid) YES/NO   Tel. No. _____ employer address) _____ Tel. No. _____
Section A is continued overleaf

CTION B—to be completed by member of staff accepting enrolment

Enrolment accepted by
Signature _____
rse _____ Course Code   Repeat in block capitals

CTION C—to be completed by administrative staff

mployer/Sponsor   Nature of Business   L.E.A.   Country   C   O/S   Pooling Status   Date of Enrolment

Courtesy the Director, North East London Polytechnic

FIG. 52. Part of a student enrolment card designed to assist card punching and subsequent computer processing.

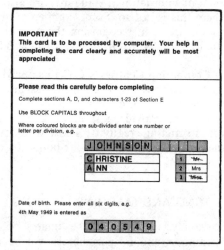

IMPORTANT
This card is to be processed by computer. Your help in completing the card clearly and accurately will be most appreciated

Please read this carefully before completing

Complete sections A, D, and characters 1-23 of Section E

Use BLOCK CAPITALS throughout

Where coloured blocks are sub-divided enter one number or letter per division, e.g.

J O H N S O N

C HRISTINE
A NN

1 ~~Mr~~
2 Mrs
3 ~~Miss~~

Date of birth. Please enter all six digits, e.g.
4th May 1949 is entered as

0 4 0 5 4 9

FIG. 53. Instructions for completing the enrolment card.

4. Standards of fitness for purpose. Examples are the quality and thickness of punched cards so that they will run satisfactorily through card reading and sorting equipment.

5. Performance standards, relating to work done in a factory or office, where local conditions may be important, can be fixed, often using standard techniques. These standards of volume and performance may relate to topics such as the time to be taken for setting up, testing and running jobs, the costs of materials and maximum percentages of faulty work, as well as equipment performance, down-time and maintenance (which may be the subject of specifications by the equipment manufacturer). Management control depends on well-established techniques, such as budgetary control and standard costing. The tendency is to bring performance standards into line between different organisations as information becomes available on what is happening throughout industry. The use of ratios and percentages (based on, say, estimated : actual, as a measure of efficiency) may be helpful.

Standards may arise at various levels. Internationally there is the International Organisation for Standardisation (I.S.O.), while the B.S.I. is well-known in Britain. The American National Standards Institute (ANSI) is influential. Standards also become established within individual business units and between equipment manufacturers or users. An example is the European Computer Manufacturers Association (ECMA). Local standards may relate to topics for which national or international standards are also available or to situations where this is not so. Some companies may be in advance of their competitors in recognising the need for standards. This may eventually give rise to proposals for new B.S.I. or other standards.

The National Computing Centre (N.C.C.) has produced a manual of standards "for all those involved in the design, development, testing, implementation, use and maintenance of computer-based systems". An aim is to provide a framework of documentation standards without restricting creativity. Those who devise software are noted for their general reluctance to be bound by charting and programming standards.

TIMING AND MACHINE LOADING

Effective systems analysis requires that estimates be made of the time that the computer and its peripherals will be occupied by work that is planned.

In estimating the hardware requirements in feasibility studies it is essential that the capacity of the equipment should be able to cope with the planned work load, with appropriate allowances for contingencies. In the case of adapting a system to a given configuration the work will have to be scheduled to fit in with existing demands on the computer, which may themselves require modification.

Problems arise in run timing for computers similar to those with factory machinery. The position is complicated by the fact that different activities may be overlapped, for example reading and printing may proceed simultaneously by normal buffering or by multi-programming. In this case it is the longest of concurrent times that is significant. Off-line activities, such as the punching of data on cards, can be scheduled separately from actual computer runs, but the encoded material must be available when the appropriate computer run is scheduled, while off-line print facilities must be scheduled to handle computer output according to any dead-lines. The components of total runtime will be as follows.

1. *Set-up time*, covering activities such as loading the peripherals, reading programs into computer store, switch setting, typing console messages to initiate the run and, possibly, the running of test packs.

2. *Peripheral time*, covering on-line activities such as the reading of cards and tape and the generating of output on card punches and line printers. The speed of the peripherals, which may be overlapped, is often the determining factor in total timing with business data processing, where the calculations tend to be simple, so that central processing unit time is short; in the case of some scientific and operational research calculations this may not be so. Sorting, a very important feature of business data processing, may be very time-consuming if it is done using four tape decks as described in the Appendix. Equipment manufacturers quote speeds at which their equipment will operate but much depends on the way in which data is organised. If a whole tape, or just a block of several records, is read into the computer at once this will provide for quicker operation than when records are read one at a time. Rewind time for tape must be taken into account, though its effect can be reduced by using two tape units alternately.

Under this head may be included time for drawing information from direct-access backing stores (such as discs) into the immediate-access store, and vice versa. When programs are stored in this way their loading time, previously included under set-up time, may be considerably reduced. A feature of time-sharing systems is the use of quick-access store so that the user of a terminal can rapidly set up the facilities he requires.

3. *Central processing unit time*, can be estimated, theoretically, from consideration of information of the times required for standard operations on data, included in the computer manufacturer's technical specification, but this is by no means a simple matter. The programming language and the effectiveness with which it is used will be a consideration. Since the computing time is usually over-shadowed by the peripheral time it may not call for accurate estimation, just a check that it need not be included in the allowed time.

4. *Contingency time*, arising from errors, mis-reads, etc. A percentage based on experience may be added to the estimated time, but the aim should be to reduce the need for this by effective "house-keeping", implying that data is rigidly controlled. These controls, ranging from data validation to control over such activities as tape library operation, are considered in Chapters 8 and 9.

The performances of different computers can be compared by the use of benchmark tests, which consist of sets of test problems, typical of the runs that will be involved, and of which the actual timing may be found by actual computer runs, with the co-operation of the computer manufacturers.

It is possible to program a more powerful computer to simulate the performance of a less powerful one. This may be used to provide timing estimates, though it is chiefly applied where programs, already available on one computer, are to be used on a different machine. When the same effect is attained by control of hardware, rather than by programming, it is referred to as emulation.

SPECIMEN EXAMINATION QUESTIONS

1. Explain the need for work study in connection with the improvement of office methods.

2. You have been asked to look into a particular clerical procedure with a view to its ultimately being incorporated in an evolving electronic data processing system. Briefly outline possible alternative ways of describing the procedure and state, with reasons, which you would select.

3. Discuss the uses of work measurement in relation to clerical work and comment on the ways in which its impact may be affected by the growth of computer systems.

4. Outline the difference between flow charts used in connection with general O. and M. and those evolved for computers. Try to account for the need for two types of chart.

5. List, with brief comments, the essentials of a good report and consider the possible uses of reports in connection with the installation or development of computer systems.

6. Why are feasibility studies usually so important in connection with computer systems? In the course of your answer explain clearly what such studies contain and by whom they may be prepared.

7. Explain the significance of the main costs involved when an organisation decides to run a computer system of its own.

8. "Deciding on a computer system is just a matter of logical choice between alternatives." Do you agree? Give reasons.

9. "Good forms design is necessary in any clerical procedures. It becomes even more relevant with computer systems." Discuss, with examples.

10. Write notes on: (a) overlapping, (b) off-line working, (c) central processing unit time, explaining their significance in connection with the timing and planning of computer runs.

11. "Planning for computer output is very similar to that involved in factory scheduling and machine loading." Comment, with examples.

12. Explain what has to be taken into account when preparing time standards for scheduling of computer work.

Chapter 7

BUSINESS PROGRAMMING WITH COBOL

BACKGROUND

COBOL (**CO**mmon **B**usiness **O**riented **L**anguage) was introduced in 1960 as a result of CODASYL (Conference on Data Systems Languages) set up in the U.S.A. the previous year. The original version has now been considerably improved.

It is a language that aims at readability, perhaps at the cost of length and verbosity compared with more compact languages such as BASIC. A consideration seems to have been the assumption that the average commercial programmer will be unhappy with statements in mathematical form. Sometimes both mathematical and verbal forms are available to achieve the same effect. For example, on some systems, the statements

1. COMPUTE TOT = L + M and
2. ADD L, M GIVING TOT

are alternative ways of achieving the same result.

This implies a duplication of approaches which tends to make the language complex. On the credit side full COBOL seems capable of coping with all likely business data processing problems, no matter what configuration is being used. This richness of COBOL tends to make COBOL compilers lengthy and complicates the problem of training programmers.

WRITING COBOL PROGRAMS

Originally COBOL was conceived in terms of standard eighty-column punched cards. Each card represents a separate line of a program sheet, of which a typical example is shown in Fig. 54 with a specimen card in Fig. 55.

The first six columns are used to indicate the sequence numbers of the lines, the numbers being in ascending order. These numbers may be inserted by the programmer or, more generally automatically by the computer in the course of compilation. The first three columns may indicate page number and the next three the line number of the page.

COBOL PROGRAM SHEET

TITLE PAYROLL TRIAL
SYSTEM 360
PROGRAMMER N.E. BODY

SHEET NO. 3
OF 3 SHEETS
IDENTIFICATION

```
       PROCEDURE DIVISION.
       PARA-1.
           OPEN INPUT HRWKFL, HRRTFL, OUTPUT PAYFL. MOVE ZERO TO M.
       PARA-2.
           READ HRWKFL AT END GO TO PARA-5.
       PARA-3.
           IF M LESS THAN NM GO TO PARA-4. IF M IS EQUAL TO NM PERFORM
           PAYCALC. IF M GREATER THAN NM GO TO PARA-2.
       PARA-4.
           READ HRRTFL AT END GO TO PARA-5. GO TO PARA-3.
       PAYCALC.
           SUBTRACT STHR FROM HRS GIVING OT.
           MULTIPLY STHR BY RATE GIVING ST-PAY.
           COMPUTE OT-PAY = OT * RATE * 1.5.
           ADD ST-PAY, OT-PAY GIVING TOT-PAY.
           MOVE NM TO ROLL. MOVE HRS TO TOT. MOVE STHR TO STD.
           WRITE PAY-LINE.
       PARA-5.
           CLOSE HRWKFL, HRRTFL, PAYFL.
           STOP RUN.
```

FIG. 54. Program sheet with procedure division for payroll calculation based on flow chart in Chapter 5.

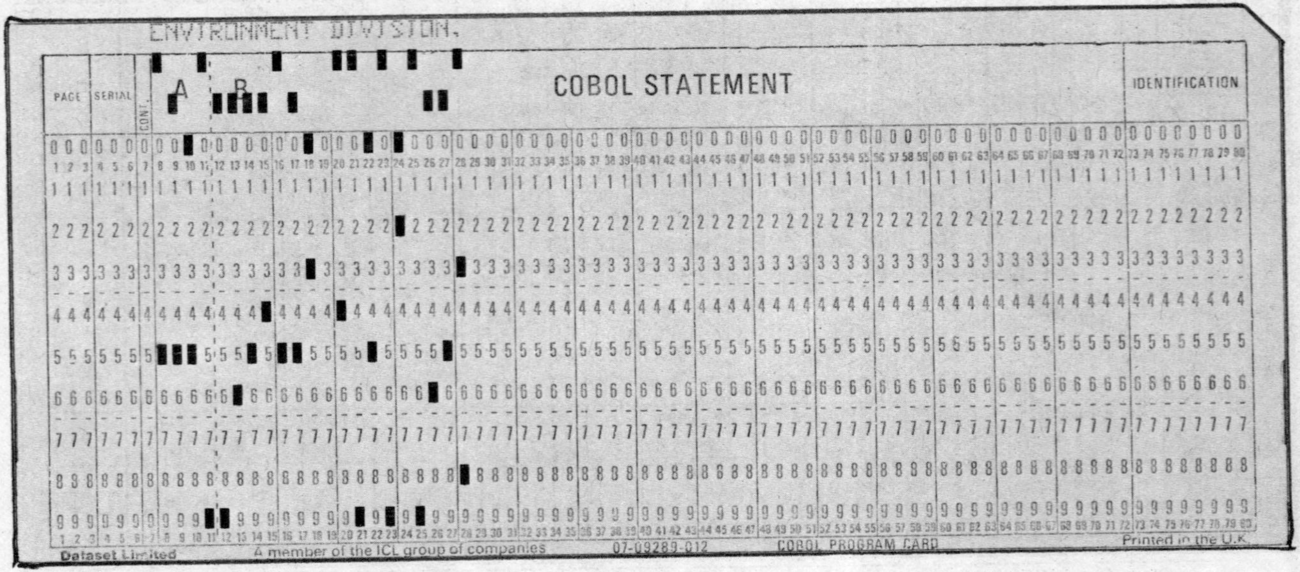

Fig. 55. A card out of a deck forming a COBOL program. This represents one line of the program.

Column seven is used when a word has to be split at the end of the previous line. A hyphen is placed in this column on the continuation line.

The text of the program is written in columns eight to seventy-two. This will occupy the bulk of our attention. Column eight is referred to as margin A, and the names of divisions, sections and paragraphs commence here. Inset a further four columns (column twelve) is margin B, which is used as the starting point for most other lines. Any further indentation is in multiples of four columns.

The last eight columns (seventy-three to eighty) can be used for program identification purposes. Since this remains the same throughout the program coding sheets often include these spaces only once in the heading. Thus, for programming, the sixty-five columns from eight to seventy-two inclusive are effectively available. For data cards, of course, the full eighty column width may be used.

The text of a COBOL program will consist of letters, numbers and symbols. Certain key words have a special meaning to the compiler and must not be used unless this meaning is intended. Optional words are available which may be incorporated to make the text more readable. As an example PICTURE IS and PICTURE have the same effect, PICTURE being a key word and IS being optional. Some words may be key or optional depending on the context. These words together constitute the reserved words. A specimen list is shown in Fig. 56.

In addition to these words the programmer can invent his own names for data, conditions, procedures, etc. These data names, condition names and constants are dealt with later in this chapter under data division. Procedure names are required in the procedure division (see below) to name the sections and paragraphs. This leaves what are called literals, a name implying that the words are taken literally and do not have to be separately defined by the programmer. If "STOCK", enclosed in quotes occurs, it is a nonnumeric literal which could be used to print-out this word in part of the program. Up to 120 characters can be included between the quotation marks. In contrast the data name STOCK, without quotes, would be defined (as explained later) to indicate a location in the computer system which would take on different numerical values from data input or from calculations performed by the computer. Numeric literals consist of numbers, with possibly a sign and decimal point. When used for computation the maximum length is eighteen digits; no quotes are needed and the value is the actual number. Special literals, known as figurative constants, are available to the program by name, examples being ZERO, SPACE and

ABOUT	COPY	IDENTIFICATION	ORGANIZATION	SEQUENCED
ACCEPT	CORRESPONDING	IF	OTHERWISE	SEQUENTIAL
ACCESS	CYCLES	IN	OUTPUT	SIGN
ACTUAL	DATA	INCLUDE	OVERFLOW	SIGNED
ADD	DATE-COMPILED	INDEXED	PAGE	SIZE
ADVANCING	DATE-WRITTEN	INDICATE	PAPER-PUNCH	SOURCE-COMPUTER
AFTER	DELETE	INITIATE	PAPER-READER	SPACE
ALL	DEPENDING	INPUT	PERFORM	SPACES
ALPHABETIC	DESCENDING	INPUT-OUTPUT	PIC	SPECIAL-NAMES
ALPHANUMERIC	DIGITS	INSTALLATION	PICTURE	STANDARD
ALTER	DIRECT	INTO	PLUS	STOP
ALTERNATIVE	DIRECT-ACCESS	INVALID	POINT	SUBTRACT
AND	DISPLAY	I-O	POSITIVE	SUM
APPLY	DISPLAY-number	I-O-CONTROL	PROCEDURE	SUPPRESS
ARE	DIVIDE	IS	PROCEED	SYMBOLIC
AREA	DIVISION	JUSTIFIED	PROCESS	SYNC
AREAS	EDS	KEY	PROCESSING	SYNCHRONIZED
ASCENDING	ELSE	KEYS	PROGRAM-ID	TALLY
ASSIGN	END	LABEL	PROTECTION	TALLYING
AT	ENTER	LABELS	QUOTE	TAPES
AUTHOR	ENTRY	LEADING	QUOTES	TAPE-number
BEFORE	ENVIRONMENT	LEAVING	RANDOM	THAN
BEGINNING	EQUAL	LEFT	RANGE	THEN
BIT-number	EQUALS	LESS	READ	THROUGH
BITS	ERROR	LINE	READY	THRU
BLANK	EVERY	LINE-COUNTER	RECORD	TIMES
BLOCK	EXAMINE	LINES	RECORDING	TO

BY	EXCEEDS	LINKAGE	RECORDS	TRACE
CALL	EXHIBIT	LOCK	REDEFINES	TRACK-AREA
CARD-PUNCH	EDIT	LOW-VALUE	REEL	TRACKS
CARD-READER	FD	LOW-VALUES	REMARKS	TYPEWRITER
CASSETTES	FDS	LOWER-BOUND	RENAMES	UNEQUAL
CHANGED	FILE	LOWER-BOUNDS	REPLACING	UNIT
CHARACTERS	FILES	MEMORY	REPORT	UNIT-RECORD
CHANNEL-number	FILE-CONTROL	MODE	REPORTING	UNTIL
CHECK	FILE-LIMIT	MOVE	REPORTS	UPON
CHECKING	FILLER	MULTIPLY	RERUN	UPPER-BOUND
CLASS	FINAL	NAMED	RESERVE	UPPER-BOUNDS
CLOSE	FIRST	NEGATIVE	RESET	USAGE
COBOL	FLOAT	NEXT	RESTRICTED	USING
CODE	FORM-OVERFLOW	NO	RETURN	UTILITY
COLUMN	FROM	NOT	REVERSED	VALUE
COMP	GENERATE	NOTE	REWIND	VALUES
COMPUTATIONAL	GENERATION-NO	NUMERIC	REWRITE	VARYING
COMP-1 or 2 or 3	GIVING	OBJECT-COMPUTER	RIGHT	WHEN
COMPUTATIONAL-1	GO	OBJECT-PROGRAM	ROUNDED	WITH
COMPUTE	GREATER	OCCURS	RUN	WORDS
CONFIGURATION	GROUP	OF	SAME	WORKING-STORAGE
CONSOLE	HEADING	OFF	SECTION	WRITE
CONSTANT	HIGH-VALUE	OMITTED	SEEK	ZERO
CONTAINS	HIGH-VALUES	ON	SEGMENT-LIMIT	ZEROES
CONTROL	HOLD	OPEN	SELECT	ZEROS
CONTROLS	ID	OR	SENTENCE	

FIG. 56. Specimen list of COBOL reserved words (not all available on any one system).

QUOTE representing respectively the value zero, a space and a quotation mark.

Punctuation marks and some special characters are also available. Generally a space will follow a punctuation mark. The full stop ends a heading or sentence and its presence or absence is vital to the sense of the program. Commas and semi-colons are ignored by the compiler. Parentheses, (and), have special uses in controlling the order of mathematical operations. The hyphen can be used to link two or more words into a single data name, for example STOCK-ON-HAND.

PROGRAM STRUCTURE

COBOL programs are divided into four divisions in the order given.

1. IDENTIFICATION DIVISION
2. ENVIRONMENT DIVISION
3. DATA DIVISION
4. PROCEDURE DIVISION

The headings of these divisions are written on the program sheet, starting in column eight.

Identification division

This contains the program name, of which the length and composition are subject to restrictions. For example, with one series of computers, it must be six characters in length, of which the first must be alphabetic. The first four characters identify the program at run time; the last two, which must be numeric, give the priority code for multiprogramming computers. The name is written in the

(a) Full outline
IDENTIFICATION DIVISION.
PROGRAM-ID. name.
AUTHOR. name of programmer.
INSTALLATION. name of company.
DATE-WRITTEN. month, day, year.
DATE-COMPILED. month, day, year.
SECURITY. description.
REMARKS. descriptive comments.

(b) Basic Requirements
IDENTIFICATION DIVISION.
PROGRAM-ID. name.

FIG. 57. Identification division format.

A position on the line below the division heading, following the paragraph heading **PROGRAM-ID**.

For some systems this is all that is required, though extra information identifying the author, installation (e.g. user company name), the dates written and compiled, security arrangements and other remarks may be included. A specimen is shown in Fig. 57. Such of this information as is standard for a particular installation may be pre-punched.

Environment division

An aim of COBOL is to provide a language that is independent of the particular computer and configuration being used to run it. The ENVIRONMENT DIVISION provides the link between the rest of the program and the specific installation being used. This division consists of two sections.

1. CONFIGURATION SECTION
2. INPUT–OUTPUT SECTION.

In the former are shown the names of the computers used for compilation and for running (often the same equipment) and also, optionally, any special names that will be used in the program to refer to specific items of equipment. If the SPECIAL-NAMES option is used then COPY followed by the library name (if the program library has a list of special names) or followed by IS and the name given by the programmer for each device is needed.

The second section is concerned with the allocation of various specified peripherals to named files. This is done by SELECT . . . ASSIGN TO . . . or by COPY . . . if a full description is in the library. It will be appreciated that in business data processing there will probably be several files, generally on tapes or discs, which are brought into operation at appropriate points in the program. The computer must be told to which particular peripherals it is to look to for these files. The manufacturer's manual should be consulted, since this division is dominated by the hardware involved.

An optional I–O–CONTROL statement can allow the re-use of an area of a closed file, cope with page overflow on a line-printer, specify the dumping of information on to a peripheral and enable files to use the same storage area for processing.

Figure 58 shows a skeleton of this division.

With the introduction of disc drives various ways of file organisation have emerged, for example sequential (which must be accessed in order), direct (accessed randomly) and indexed sequential (which may be accessed in either way). This is handled by ACCESS and ORGANISATION clauses. KEY clauses provide a reference pattern of digits to enable an item to be located.

ENVIRONMENT DIVISION.

CONFIGURATION SECTION.
SOURCE COMPUTER. name of computer.
OBJECT COMPUTER. name of computer.
SPECIAL NAMES. COPY library name.
   or name of device IS name given by programmer.
    (repeat for each device)

INPUT–OUTPUT SECTION.
FILE-CONTROL. COPY library name
or
FILE-CONTROL.
SELECT file name ASSIGN TO device number
ACCESS IS SEQUENTIAL (*or* RANDOM) ⎫ for   ⎫ repeat
ORGANISATION IS INDEXED (*or* DIRECT)⎬ direct ⎪ for
ACTUAL KEY IS name   ⎧ access ⎬ each
SYMBOLIC KEY IS name.   ⎭ devices ⎪ file
                                            ⎭

I–O–CONTROL. (optional)
SAME AREA FOR file name
APPLY input/output technique.

Fig. 58. Environment division format.

Data division

Some high level languages such as BASIC allow new data names
to be introduced as and when required in the program, while
others demand that a declaration be made of all data names early
in the program before they can be used. COBOL is of the latter
type and the DATA DIVISION is used to give a detailed description of each file, record and item of data. This division may well
exceed in length the procedure division, which gives effect to the
flow chart. COBOL insists on this detailed description largely because the business data with which it is concerned generally occupies specific positions on documents, often in the form of headed
columns. Similar results can be achieved by other programming
languages but the COBOL DATA DIVISION provides a clear, if
somewhat lengthy description, suited to the thinking of programmers with a commercial rather than a mathematical background.
The DATA DIVISION may consist of four sections.

    1. FILE SECTION
    2. WORKING-STORAGE SECTION
    3. CONSTANT SECTION
    4. LINKAGE SECTION

File section. A file is a set of data, usually in order, which is in a form that can be input to (or output from) the computer. An example would be a STOCK-MASTER-FILE containing, on magnetic tape, or on a disc or in the form of punched cards arranged in order, details of the stock items, quantities and values, etc.

Each file has a name which is written on the program sheet after the letters FD in the FILE SECTION. This file name must agree with the appropriate SELECT statement file name in the environment division.

The file will be broken down into a series of "records" or complete units of information, each representing, say, the individual sales ledger accounts or persons on a payroll.

Each record will consist of data, or elements of information, which may be in the form of numbers, letters or symbols, up to thirty characters in length. A stock file would have individual stock records for each stock item, each record consisting of data items such as code number, balance quantity, balance value, re-order level, etc.

The relationships between these items are controlled by the use of data "levels", indicated by two-digit numbers, after the heading FD (file description) which is used in conjunction with each file. Each record is associated with the level 01, which is indented four columns. Different "areas" within the record (that is groupings of the data that are considered convenient) are indicated by a higher number, such as 02, indented a further four columns. Within these groupings further sub-groups may exist shown by higher level numbers, inset a further four columns. Finally individual data items will each have the same level number.

The important point to grasp is that the same level number must apply to data which occupies the same topic/sub-topic relationship or "level". The level numbers do not refer to any sequence off the data. The only satisfactory way of coming to grips with this is through practical examples; one is given in Fig. 59.

Data names must not be COBOL reserved words. They may consist of up to thirty characters of which at least one must be alphabetic. Spaces must not occur within a name, hyphens being used if a name is split to aid recognition e.g. STOCK-BALANCE, but the hyphen cannot be used at the beginning or end of a word.

When the same data occurs in two or more records the same name may be used provided it is qualified. Thus, if a material stock code, named SCODE, occurs in a STOCK-RECORD and in an ISSUES-RECORD we can distinguish between these by referring to SCODE OF STOCK-RECORD and SCODE OF ISSUES-RECORD, linking the name of a higher member of the hierarchy.

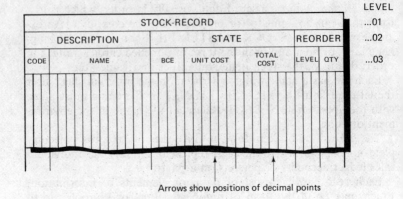

(a) Proposed Format of One Record

```
01   STOCK-RECORD
     02 DESCRIPTION.
          03 CODE              PICTURE 999.
          03 NAME              PICTURE X(12).
     02 STATE.
          03 BCE               PICTURE 9(4).
          03 UNIT-COST         PICTURE 9(3) V99.
          03 TOTAL-COST        PICTURE 9(4)V99.
     02 REORDER.
          03 LEVEL             PICTURE 9(3).
          03 QTY               PICTURE 9(3).
```

N.B. 999 has the same effect as 9(3).

(b) Record description of above in File Section of Data Division

Fig. 59. Data levels and record description.

It is often preferable to ensure that each data-name is unique. One method is to use a six-letter code, the first two letters being unique to the particular file for all its record and field names, while the other four letters are unique for the record or field. We might have STFILE for the stock file and STCODE for a material code number of an item in that file, while the issues file could be ISFILE and the same code occurring in that file would be ISCODE.

Condition-names show the values of data-names, generally to save space. Four different products sold through a chain of shops may be named but referred to by number, say one to four or by letter, say A to D. The level eighty-eight is assigned to condition names, as in this example.

02 PRODUCTS PICTURE 9.
    88 SWEETS VALUE IS 1.
    88 CIGARETTES VALUE IS 2.
    88 TOBACCO VALUE IS 3.
    88 SUNDRIES VALUE IS 4.

The name may be followed by REDEFINES and another data-name. The effect is to reallocate the storage previously used by this data-name, which must be of the same level.

Information which may be found under the FD includes the following.

1. RECORDING MODE, which refers to the method of recording information on external media, such as cards, paper or magnetic tape, discs, etc. Generally a standard mode, as prescribed by the computer manufacturer, will be used and this clause may be omitted. With one system letters F, V or U are used indicating, respectively, fixed length, variable length or undefined records.

2. BLOCK CONTAINS, which describes how many records have been blocked or grouped together to be handled at one time by the computer with the object of conserving space on magnetic tape by reducing the number of inter-record gaps, of which one is needed each time the computer starts to read a new set of data. If the records to be blocked are of variable length then the number of characters in the block must·be specified. In the more usual case of fixed-length records the number of these records which will constitute a block is indicated. With unblocked records or where standard block sizes are available this clause may be omitted.

3. RECORD CONTAINS, which can be used to indicate the number, or minimum and maximum number, of characters in a record, but may be omitted, since the record description (*see* below) gives a detailed account of this.

4. LABEL RECORDS, which apply to magnetic tape and direct access files. These may be header labels (at the start of a file) giving information such as file name, number of reel and date of updating the file or trailer labels (at the end of a file) relating to the number of records on the reel, identification of continuation files etc. Computer manufacturers now tend to use standard formats and discourage user-defined labels. The appropriate entry indicates the label is STANDARD or STANDARD WITH GENERATION NUMBER (*see* note 5).

Label records do not apply to files held on character peripheral devices in which case the clause may be omitted or shown as LABEL RECORDS ARE OMITTED.

5. VALUE OF clause, which enables the programmer to specify

what is to be included in the file labels. These will include the file name (or identification), the retention period (or active time) and the generation number. For input the system will search until a file with the specified identification is reached; there may be several files on one tape, though systems will often not permit this. For output it will write the identification on the output file. The retention period is specified for output files and prevents the file being over-written during the time specified. The generation number (specified in the LABEL clause) is used to distinguish between input files and output files, which are updated versions of these with the same identification. If used, it is specified when the program is being run.

6. DATA RECORDS ARE, which is used to list the names of the records in the file and is followed by data description entries which indicate the level of the data and its format. Each entry begins with the level number followed by the data name (or FILLER for a space to which no name is being assigned). These levels have been dealt with above.

7. SIZE (on some systems) and PICTURE clauses enable the length of an item to be specified. Figure 59 shows typical entries. The PICTURE clause (which makes a SIZE clause unnecessary) can be used to describe the appearance of each item in detail. Some of the chief symbols used are.

(a) A for alphabetic characters or blanks;
(b) X for alphanumeric characters (alphabetic or numeric);
(c) 9 for numeric characters;
(d) V for assumed decimal point;
(e) S for a signed (+ or −) value.

One or more of these symbols will appear after PICTURE IS or PICTURE for each item to indicate the type of character in each position. Where several similar adjacent characters are involved the number of these may be placed in brackets after the appropriate symbol. Thus, five alpha characters followed by six numeric characters may be shown as:

(a) AAAAA999999 or
(b) A(5) 9 (6).

An alternative may be to use a CLASS IS clause followed by ALPHABETIC, NUMERIC or ALPHANUMERIC, as the case may be.

Editing facilities exist to make data more meaningful and easier to grasp by inserting additional signs, suppressing leading zeros, etc. For example a four figure number 0065 would print as 65 if the picture were ZZ99, since Z indicates suppression of the zero.

8. USAGE IS clause can be very important to the way data is handled. It may be used at any level to indicate the manner of recording information in a field as far as the computer is concerned. COMPUTATIONAL or COMP is applied to numeric fields on which arithmetic operations will be performed. DISPLAY denotes alphabetic or alphanumeric fields where each character or decimal digit is represented by six bits.

9. OCCURS . . . . . TIMES, which may be used when repeated data, such as in a table, is required. If the table has 200 rows and a column is headed SCODE the record description would show OCCURS 200 TIMES and we could refer in the program to any particular row by subscript notation. Thus SCODE (50) would refer to the fiftieth row of the column headed SCODE.

10. VALUE IS or VALUE clause, in the file section, which is followed by the condition-name (*see* above) giving the value of the data name.

11. JUSTIFIED RIGHT, which aligns data from the right and is used only if this is required rather than the normal left-justified data, which starts at the left of the "space" it is to occupy. With some machines right justification may considerably speed up certain operations.

The other three sections of the data division can now be briefly considered.

Working storage section. This section is used to define storage areas which are not part of any file but which are used for intermediate processing of data. Thus we might wish to accumulate a total of amounts posted during a run in an area called ASUM. We should define this with a data description entry in the working storage section. For single items which are independent of other items in this section the data level seventy-seven is used, for example:

```
77   ASUM    PICTURE 9 (8)
COMPUTATIONAL VALUE ZERO
```

It is important that an initial value, generally zero, be given to all summation items in this section, otherwise whatever happens to be stored in that location from a previous run will be added in. After such independent (level seventy-seven) items come any grouped items in this section for which a file is not required each record name (at 01 level) being unique.

Low volume data items for which a file is not required and

which may be input or output through a keyboard are described in this section. They will be handled by ACCEPT and DISPLAY statements respectively.

Constant section. Similar rules apply as in the working storage section (77 and 01 levels). A constant remains of the same value, numeric or non-numeric, throughout the program.

Linkage section. Here links are provided with separately compiled programs stating the names and descriptions to be found in them. All sub-routines, that is programs that are called in to supplement a main program, generally providing standard calculations, must have a linkage section immediately before the procedure division.

A skeleton data division is given in Fig. 60.

(*a*) General Layout

DATA DIVISION

FILE SECTION.
FD file-name (*or* file-name COPY library-name.)⎫ repeat for
followed by descriptions of records in file ⎬ each file

WORKING-STORAGE SECTION.
followed by details

CONSTANT SECTION.
followed by details

LINKAGE SECTION.
followed by details

(*b*) Specimen File Section For Records In Fig. 59

FILE SECTION.

FD STOCK-MASTER (this is the file name)
BLOCK CONTAINS 10 RECORDS
LABEL RECORDS ARE STANDARD
DATA RECORDS ARE STOCK-RECORD
01 STOCK-RECORD
followed by the rest of Fig. 59(*b*).

FIG. 60. Data division format.

Procedure division

This division is concerned with handling the data in such a way that the required results are achieved. It puts the logic of the flow chart into program form. The logic is built from statements (each beginning with a COBOL verb), which are combined into sentences (followed by a full stop and a space). These in turn are combined into paragraphs (each of which must be named). Finally, the paragraphs may be combined into sections (which must again be named).

Imperative sentences are executed completely, being followed by the next statement, unless a GO TO statement transfers to another paragraph or section, from which the continuity will similarly be maintained. In the case of a PERFORM statement the paragraph referred to will be taken out-of-sequence, and, when it is completed, control passes back to the statement following the perform statement.

A specimen PROCEDURE DIVISION is shown in Fig. 54. Section names (if any) followed by paragraph names, are written in the A position. Sentences commence in the B position. Statements may be used for a number of purposes, of which the chief are now listed.

1. *Input.* COBOL has built-in I.O.C.S. (Input/Output Control System). For file processing an OPEN INPUT statement is used incorporating the precise file name used in the data division. This name will be searched for in the header label of magnetic tapes and direct access (disc) files. With punched cards or paper tape a typed message will instruct the operator to load the file on the correct peripheral.

Following this will be a READ instruction which pulls in the next record from a tape file or a specific record from a direct access file. Thus for sequential files, READ STOCK-MASTER RECORD AT END GO TO END-RUN will read the next sequential record and continue to do this as required by the program, until all records are exhausted, when it will go to the instructions in the paragraph labelled END-RUN (a name devised by the programmer) while, for random files, READ STOCK-MASTER RECORD INVALID KEY GO TO END-RUN performs a similar function, ending when a record cannot be found. After RECORD we may inset INTO followed by a data-name, which has the effect of moving the record read into the area required.

For low-volume data, such as from a console typewriter an ACCEPT instruction is used to read one logical record into a data area. Thus ACCEPT PRICE FROM CONSOLE. This can be used for punched card and paper tape readers.

In the case of disc files organised and assessed on a random basis an appropriate statement (such as SEEK) must precede every READ statement. The effect is to read the index tables.

Input processing is ended by a CLOSE statement incorporating the file name. This releases the peripheral from the program, after rewinding in the case of a tape deck. Specific options may be included, such as LOCK, where operator intervention is needed before the tape deck becomes available.

2. *Output.* This is dealt with in a manner similar to input, with OPEN and CLOSE statements. WRITE is used to copy on to an external medium the information in the record area. A hard-copy record may be output on to a line printer, or the output may be on to cards, tape or direct access files.

For low volume data DISPLAY followed by the item results in output on the console typewriter. If the statement is followed by UPON and the name of another peripheral, as in the SPECIAL NAMES section of the ENVIRONMENT DIVISION, this will receive it. When the USAGE (data division) is DISPLAY the print-out will correspond to the characters in the computer store; when COMPUTATIONAL usage has been specified this may appear as if moved into a field with DISPLAY usage.

3. *Mathematical operations.* These may be performed by ADD, SUBTRACT, MULTIPLY and DIVIDE statements or, alternatively, by COMPUTE statements (if available) using symbols ($+$, $-$, $*$ and $/$ and also $**$ for exponentiation or raising to a power).

Examples are:

ADD A, B, C GIVING D.

equivalent to COMPUTE $D = A + B + C$.

ADD A TO B.

equivalent to COMPUTE $B = A + B$. (i.e. B becomes $A + B$)

It should be noted that both TO and GIVING should not appear in the same statement.

SUBTRACT A FROM B GIVING C.

equivalent to COMPUTE $C = B - A$.

SUBTRACT A FROM B.

equivalent to COMPUTE $B = B - A$. (i.e. B becomes $B - A$).

SUBTRACT A, B FROM C GIVING D.

equivalent to COMPUTE $D = C - (A + B)$.

MULTIPLY A BY B GIVING C.

equivalent to COMPUTE $C = A * B$.

MULTIPLY A BY B.

equivalent to COMPUTE $B = A * B$.

DIVIDE A INTO B GIVING C.

equivalent to COMPUTE C = B / A.

DIVIDE A INTO B.

equivalent to COMPUTE B = B / A.

It should be noted that options ROUNDED and ON SIZE ERROR may be added to the above statements. If the number of decimal places in a result is greater than the space provided in the data name the excess will be dropped unless ROUNDED is used, in which case the last available digit will be increased by one if the next digit is five or more. The ON SIZE ERROR, followed by a statement such as GO TO ERROR-ROUTINE copes with the problem of numbers to the left of a decimal point being too many for the data-name. These would be dropped with an unpredictable result unless a suitable routine were adopted.

An example of the use of these options might be:

MULTIPLY A BY B GIVING C ROUNDED ON SIZE ERROR GO TO ERROR-ROUTINE.

For a COMPUTE statement we have COMPUTE C ROUNDED = A * B ON SIZE ERROR GO TO ERROR-ROUTINE.

When the COMPUTE statement is used brackets are an aid to securing the correct result. Thus COMPUTE A = ((B + C) ** 3) / (D + E) results in $\frac{(B + C)^3}{(D + E)}$ being calculated and placed in field A; while A = (B + C ** 3) / D + E would give A = $\frac{B + C^3}{D}$ + E.

4. *Data management.* MOVE is used to transfer data from one area to a new area, and care must be taken if the areas are not the same size. For non-numeric data the digits are moved from left to right, while, for numeric data, they are aligned on the decimal point. A statement such as MOVE COST TO PRICE will shift whatever is in the area called COST into the area called PRICE, without destroying the information in the original COST area.

EXAMINE is used with data defined as DISPLAY to tally the number of times a character is encountered and record this in a tally register. An example is EXAMINE CODE TALLYING ALL A., if applied to area CODE containing 35A467B9A would result in a tally of two. EXAMINE may also be used with a REPLAC-ING option. Thus EXAMINE CODE REPLACING ALL A BY D would transform the code into 35D467B9D.

After a READ statement REWRITE can be used on a direct access device to replace the last record read by one specified, thus REWRITE .... FROM .... On some systems DELETE can be used to delete a record from a direct access file.

5. *Sequential control.* The program will be performed in the sequence in which it is written. If a statement starting GO TO followed by a procedure name appears the program branches as instructed. An IF statement is often used in conjunction with this (*see* below). A very powerful form of this branching is to use GO TO ... DEPENDING ON followed by an identifier. The result is to cause the program to branch to procedure-name-1 if the identifier is 1, to procedure-name-2 if the identifier is 2, etc. For example:

> GO TO CALC-1, CALC-2, CALC-3, DEPENDING ON COUNT

would channel the program to the paragraph called CALC-3 if COUNT were read as 3.

PERFORM followed by a procedure name directs the program to this procedure (or sub-routine), returning to the original statement when the sub-routine has been completed. With a GO TO direction on the other hand, the program will run on from the particular paragraph to which it has been directed. With no qualification the sub-routine is performed once. If we specify a number of TIMES this will be obeyed, as will an instruction to perform UNTIL some condition is satisfied.

Thus we can have PERFORM ROUTINE-A 30 TIMES, and

> PERFORM ROUTINE-A UNTIL COUNT EQUAL TO 40.

We can thus achieve looping in programs. A further development is as follows:

> PERFORM ROUTINE-A VARYING X FROM 20 BY 5 UNTIL 300.

Which performs the routine specified with values of X starting at twenty and increasing in steps of five until it has the value of 300. If several routines are to be followed we can write PERFORM ROUTINE-A, THRU ROUTINE-D followed by TIMES, UNTIL, etc. We specify the first and last routines in the desired sequence.

STOP RUN brings the execution of a program to an end. STOP followed by a literal temporarily halts the program (until restarted by the operator) and causes the literal to be displayed on the console.

The one word paragraph EXIT, to which a name must be given, is used to end a PERFORM procedure containing one or more conditional exits before the last sentence.

As an example:

Somewhere in the program may be found

    PERFORM TEST-1.

and later in the program a paragraph

    TEST-1.
        IF A LESS THAN B GO TO FINAL.
        IF A EQUAL TO B COMPUTE C = X + Y GO TO
        FINAL.
        PERFORM CALC-A.
    FINAL. EXIT.

The effect of this will be:

(*a*) if A is less than B the rest of TEST-1 is ignored;

(*b*) if A = B the calculation C = X + Y is done and the PERFORM CALC-A is ignored;

(*c*) if A is greater than B then CALC-A (another procedure) will be performed, after which the program will return to the next paragraph, which exits from the procedure TEST-1.

In each case the program will return to the next line following PERFORM TEST-1.

An ON statement may be available, such as:

    ON 20 AND EVERY 5 UNTIL 300 PERFORM ROUTINE-A ELSE PERFORM ROUTINE-B.

6. *Conditional statements.* The IF statement tests one or more conditions and channels the program in one of two directions depending on the result. It copes with the decision part of a flow diagram. The conditions are GREATER THAN, LESS THAN, EQUAL TO (or =), EQUALS, POSITIVE, ZERO, NEGATIVE, NUMERIC, ALPHABETIC and the statement links these with IF by IS, IS NOT, AND, OR NOT, ending with THEN (optional) or ELSE (synonymous with OTHERWISE) and an imperative statement or NEXT SENTENCE.

Examples of these conditional statements are:

(*a*) IF BALANCE GREATER THAN REORDER GO TO
      READ-ITEM.
(*b*) IF A LESS THAN B, OR A LESS THAN C NEXT
      SENTENCE ELSE PARA-2.

Notice that, after LESS THAN C, we cannot have GO TO and NEXT SENTENCE together since GO TO being a key-word must be followed by a paragraph name; it is omitted.

7. *Compiler directing instructions.* These do not affect the object program itself. CALL, followed by a subroutine name, with USING, followed by one or more identifiers corresponding to the names of records, transfers control to a COBOL subroutine.

ENTER enables a COBOL program to incorporate subroutines written in another language. It is followed by the subroutine name. NOTE can be followed by a paragraph of comment which will not affect the object program but is used to help human understanding of the program.

PROGRAM SEGMENTATION

Segmentation of a COBOL source program is used to reduce the size of memory required by the program in the immediate access (internal) store. The program is divided into permanent and over-lay segments. With the former the object code resides permanently in store at run-time; in the case of overlay segments these are held on a backing store and are called into the internal store, as required, being overwritten when another such segment is needed.

For segmentation the procedure division is written as a series of sections under which all paragraphs will be contained. Priority numbers (0 to 99) are assigned to each section, those with the same number belonging to the same segment. These numbers follow the section name which has been given by the programmer, thus:

section name SECTION 21.

Division into permanent and overlay segments is typically achieved by a SEGMENT-LIMIT clause in the environment division. Any section with a number less than that stated in this clause will be permanent. A limit of fifty applies automatically if it is not stated.

MICROCOBOL AND COBOL SUBSETS

Because of the large internal storage requirements of a full COBOL compiler compact versions or subsets, containing a condensed version of the language, are often used. The range of the programming will be restricted to what is included in the particular compiler available and the manufacturer's programming manuals must be consulted.

The popularity of small business computers, coupled with the widespread knowledge of COBOL among business programmers, has led to the development, for example, of MICROCOBOL with its operating system BOS and its file management and reporting facility AUTOCLERK.

An ingenious simplification of the writing of COBOL programs, called RAPIDWRITE, was produced by I.C.L. for its computers. Preprinted forms and dual purpose cards are used to enter the program information, which is punched into cards to form the source program. This can then be automatically compiled in COBOL and the program in COBOL form may be listed by the computer.

OTHER COMMERCIAL LANGUAGES

Programming Language 1 or PL1 has been produced by I.B.M. as a general purpose language of use to both commercial and scientific programmers. A chief feature is its modularity, implying that simple programs can be written without a full knowledge of the language, as long as the programmer knows enough for his particular requirements. Programs consist of blocks, which may be contained within other blocks. Each block which is not so contained is compiled separately and may be used as a procedure in several different programs. PL1 shares several of the features of COBOL along with those of FORTRAN and ALGOL and it is claimed that the costs of programming and of program maintenance are reduced, as well as the cost of training programmers.

Report Program Generator (R.P.G.) is a language suitable for use on smaller computers and claimed to be easy to use and learn. Its object is to simplify the production of reports, statements, invoices and the like from computer files.

There are three divisions, input, calculation and output. The first lists the identities and field specifications of the input cards, the last controls the format of punched card or printed output, while the calculation division shows, two factors at a time, the operation to be performed and the result field.

Later versions have been developed as R.P.G.2 and R.P.G.3.

SPECIMEN EXAMINATION QUESTIONS

1. "COBOL programming is done in English, with a simplified vocabulary. This should make it easy for users to understand and perhaps to adapt COBOL programs."

"A business organisation using COBOL should recruit a staff of programmers with at least two years' experience." Discuss these apparently contradictory statements.

2. Discuss the advantages and disadvantages of high-level commercial languages such as COBOL.

3. Explain, with the aid of a specific example, the use of "levels" in describing the layout of a form in a COBOL data division.

4. Outline the purposes of the four divisions used in COBOL programming and briefly explain why they are not found in simpler languages such as BASIC.

5. List the information needed (*a*) to establish master files and (*b*) to update them, in connection with a computerised stock control system, of which you should also outline the main outputs.

6. In connection with COBOL programming explain the uses of: (*a*) PERFORM statements, (*b*) CLOSE statements, (*c*) program segmentation.

7. Explain how punched cards are used for COBOL programs and data and briefly discuss the effect this form of computer input has had on the language structure.

8. Distinguish between (*a*) key words, (*b*) optional words, (*c*) data names, (*d*) procedure names, (*e*) literals, in COBOL programs.

9. Discuss the thesis that the advent of computers provided an opportunity to use mathematical techniques in dealing with business data processing, while COBOL has prolonged the myth that business data processing is quite separate from other quantitative techniques.

Chapter 8

ORGANISATION OF A COMPUTER DEPARTMENT

PERSONNEL

The grouping of functions that contribute to electronic data processing results in a theoretical organisation chart along the lines of Fig. 61(a), with the data processing manager responsible, ultimately, for the systems analysis, programming and operating. Sometimes programming may be responsible to systems, resulting in a chart along the lines of Fig. 61(b). The reader should note that diagrams reflect the wide variety of terminology associated with computer work. The operations manager will probably have responsibility for editing, proving and preparation of data, to make it suited to computer input, as well as being concerned with planning and control of computer runs and the assembly of the output (*see* Fig 62); and the computer library may also be under him.

The degree of specialisation is determined by the size of the installation and the number of staff employed. Audit and security precautions will probably be a factor and may cut across the integration of jobs, these being spread to make collusion in fraud difficult.

In some cases a computer will be restricted to processing for one department only, in which case the manager of the user department may be in charge. This is likely to arise in the case of small computers, dedicated to a special purpose. Visible record computers have often been controlled on this basis. The growth of distributed processing, based on minis and microcomputers, has called in question the whole concept of centralised data processing and can be seen as a threat to the position of the data processing manager. However, it may be desirable for an organisation to follow a co-ordinated policy regarding the purchase of equipment and the systems to be run on it. Distributed processing can be integrated into a powerful data base. The departments using such equipment will, in any case, usually look to the computer department for advice on the purchase and running of their equipment and for help in the generation of software.

The success of a computer department may be closely linked

171

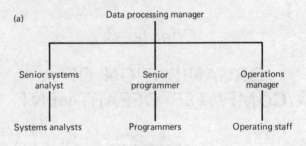

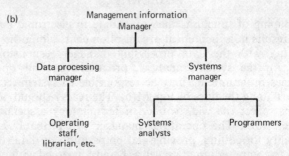

FIG. 61. Forms of data-processing organisation.

FIG. 62. Routine operations organisation.

with the qualities of the data processing manager. Such a job clearly requires a combination of managerial ability and technical knowledge. The manager will need to achieve results through his staff, to motivate them, to organise their work and to co-ordinate and control their activities. At the same time he must himself be an acceptable member of the management team, able to communicate with other managers, directors and staff. The special knowledge requirements involve an appreciation of the functions of and contributions to be expected from the different members of his staff and of the hardware and software, together with an appreciation of the general nature of the problems facing the user departments. The ability to keep abreast of developments in computing, both in hardware and software, and to estimate their possible relevance to his own department, is very important. In some cases the manager may initiate investigations into new approaches to data processing.

Systems analysts require data processing knowledge coupled with knowledge of commercial systems and organisation and methods techniques. Familiarity with the organisation and systems of their employer will make their work more effective, though imagination and creativity, which are essential characteristics, may be stultified by a slavish acceptance of existing methods. Ability to work methodically, to pay attention to detail and to observe everything that is relevant, to deal with work analytically and logically but with an enquiring approach, coupled with a personality that is acceptable and tactful, are desirable characteristics.

For programmers, the stress is more on logical thinking and commonsense, coupled with accuracy, a meticulous care for detail, considerable patience and a good memory. Social contacts will generally be more restricted than with systems analysts, but ability to work as a member of a team may be essential. Aptitude tests are available to assess the promise of aspiring programmers. With the introduction of high level languages programming has been made easier but there is still a need for intelligence and knowledge if efficient programs are to be written. A distinction is often made between systems programmers and applications programmers. The former help to maintain the general computer facility, while the latter program for specific uses.

Machine operators may be concerned with data preparation, such as punching, or with computer operating. Some of the work may involve a high degree of specialised skill, but computer operation itself is fairly easily learned. Ability to follow instructions and to produce accurate work, coupled with concentration and a placid temperament, are important ingredients.

In addition to these specialised computer staff a large computer department will also need clerks and typists. In planning the computer organisation attention will have to be paid to staff accommodation, which may involve a large floor area and will require furnishing at a cost extra to that strictly applicable to the data processing equipment itself.

With a new or expanding computer department problems of staff training, of transfer from other jobs, and of allocation of precise jobs in relation to the computer installation, will have to be considered. Where possible the development of the careers of individual workers should be facilitated, by encouraging attendance at courses, by allowing staff to expand their responsibilities and by planning for progression from, say, operator to programmer to systems analyst, if the worker is suitable and wishes to do this.

In some cases a special team of workers may be set up to cope with some major problem, which is systematically broken down into stages, with project leaders responsible for co-ordinating development at each stage. This may lead to a functional approach to computer staff organisation, where individuals or teams specialise in problems, perhaps of sales accounting or production control, closely related to specialised user functions.

PREPARING MANAGEMENT AND STAFF

Sociologists have stressed the need to pay attention to the impact of technical change on organisations and on the people who have roles in them. They have also lamented the scant acknowledgment of this by many managements, pointing out, however, that the introduction of computers may have such an impact on a company's information system as to force more attention to be paid to these aspects than might be the case with technical changes on the production side.

Managers and lower ranks tend to fear the implications of electronic data processing for their job security, professional standing and exercise of skills. To a certain extent new sets of disciplines cutting across the older specialist boundaries have emerged, and computing is relevant to them all. Examples are the development of management accounting, operational research and management information services. The computer man is at the same time a specialist and a generalist, in that he may be prepared to lump together as "data processing", in which he specialises, a wide variety of problems from different disciplines.

Much of the fear associated with systems' changes can probably be removed by sufficiently farsighted recruitment, training and personnel development programmes. If it is recognised that a major aspect of management is to initiate, respond to and plan for change then the revolutionary impact of such things as computers may be made easier. Continuous education for managers and their staff should be regarded as essential to business survival and progress. In this connection "crash" training programmes may be better than nothing but, ideally, the training should fit into the long-term planning of the company. With rapidly changing technology, as in the case of computing, a wide training, adaptable to changes and encouraging innovation, is probably best, but may be the most costly.

Computing has tended to be associated with centralisation of hardware, of information and of decision-making. Organisation will have to adapt to this, as will the job specifications of managers and other staff. It may be that fewer levels of management will be needed and that less responsibility will devolve on middle management. Possibly these tendencies have been over-stated, since computer technology has developed to provide multi-access facilities and small computers may increase the effectiveness of decentralised data processing.

Centralisation of decision-making will always be related to the efficiency with which managers can deal with increasing quantities of information. This may be aided by speedy computer processing if, for instance, operational research models are available. Programmable (routine) decisions will be more in evidence and standardisation will be applied to information systems of increasing size and complexity. The creative, dynamic drive needed at certain stages of business progress may, however, never be susceptible to such treatment.

The characteristics of bureaucratic management, which are related to large systems, may become more apparent, with the implications of danger for individuals, which is increased by the effectiveness with which possibly inaccurate information may be communicated. There may be a good case for providing each employee with a print-out of all the information relating to him that is stored in the computer system. This might reasonably be extended to information relating to any member of the community, at least in so far as it may be available to users of information services, such as relating to credit-worthiness. This topic is developed further in Chapter 11.

INSTALLATION OF HARDWARE AND SYSTEMS

Suitable accommodation for the computer hardware and operating staff, for data preparation, for the assembly and despatch of completed work, for storage of a library of tapes, etc., together with rooms for the data processing manager, systems analysts, programmers, chief operator and service engineer, must be available by the time the hardware is delivered. Additional room may be needed for an air conditioning plant.

The computer and its peripherals may have certain requirements relating to temperature, dust, etc., which may dictate that they be placed in an air-conditioned area, though some computers are designed to work under a wide range of normal office conditions. It may be desirable to avoid changes of temperature and humidity when items are drawn from the library for use with the computer. Such storage areas may best be located in the same controlled area as the computer, which will also reduce distances to be travelled.

The computer area will probably have to be specially constructed with a view to air conditioning, noise reduction, power supplies and accessibility for servicing, having a false floor and special ceiling, and the fire hazard must be recognised.

Obviously, with a new installation, considerable planning is required to provide these facilities, from decision on the site location, obtaining planning permission, seeking tenders and deciding between them, up to the final decoration of the computer room and ancillary rooms. If such work interferes with the normal operation of factory or office, temporary arrangements must be made. Sometimes the computer department may have a temporary home until a full-scale plan can be realised. In all cases the possibilities of expansion must be considered.

More planning will be involved in the ordering, delivery and installation of the computer, its peripheral equipment, computer furniture (such as cabinets for tape storage), tapes, etc., and also office furniture and stationery, among which may be coding sheets for programs and specially printed cards. With the delivery of the computer will go the engineers' acceptance test before final adjustments and handover.

Clearly all this involves a large number of jobs being organised and performed concurrently. At certain stages these different lines of development will link up, and delay in any one may delay all further developments. For this reason it is generally recommended that the installation and general organisation be planned as a network, using critical path techniques, as outlined in the next section.

With a new computing department, systems analysis and programming concerned with the work to be done by the installation may be organised well in advance of the delivery of the computer. This can considerably reduce the period when the computer is under-employed while waiting for work. These jobs can be included in the network scheduling. With an established installation the problems are less complex, but network planning is still useful, especially for large-scale development projects.

As far as system development is concerned there will have to be liaison both within the computer department (between analysts, programmers, operators, etc.) and also with the user departments and with senior management. The general sequence of events in the development of a new system will be:

1. feasibility study;
2. assignment of job application;
3. investigation;

4. development of system outline;
5. development of system details;
6. programming;
7. plan for changeover;
8. testing of system;
9. implementation of system;
10. parallel running, alongside the old system;
11. switchover to system.

The user department will be heavily involved in stages 1 and 2, and 7 to 11, while giving help where needed at the other stages, involving full facilities for investigation and willingness to discuss objectives, problems and constraints imposed by practical working conditions.

The development of systems has been considered in detail in Chapters 5 and 6 and will not now be further investigated. It must be remembered that time and facilities must be allocated for the setting up of the files that are to be the basis of the computer system.

NETWORK PLANNING

In the previous section the need to plan systematically for computer and systems installation was stressed. Networks, of which Fig. 63 is a condensed example, afford a satisfactory approach to a situation where a large number of activities, many concurrent, have to be planned to achieve final success. The present intention is to give the reader an appraisal of such techniques. He should appreciate that the specimen network is far simpler than would arise in practice and that it relates only to selected aspects of the planning problem. The data on which it is based (Fig. 64) is used as an an example of computer processing in Fig. 37.

A network consists of arrows and circles. The former are used to denote activities, that is jobs to be done, involving the expenditure of resources and time. They link together the circles, which represent events, which are distinct stages in the development of the project. Each circle is numbered and this numbering can be used to refer to activities, using the numbers at the tail and at the head of the appropriate arrow (*see* Figs. 63 and 64). The times for the activities are given alongside the arrows. It will be seen that two activities are referred to as dummy activities in the table. Such activities do not involve time or resources but are included for clarity and to enable the network to express correctly what is happening. Thus the activities of awaiting delivery of the computer (3–8) and of

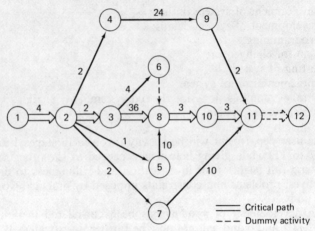

FIG. 63. Simplified portion of a planning network for critical path
analysis applied to computer installation.

planning for its installation (3–6) proceed concurrently and both
really link together events 3 and 8. If they were shown as two
arrows connecting 3 and 8, however, the two activities would have
the same number. To avoid this an event (6) signifying completion
of the planning, is introduced and linked with event 8 by a broken
arrow. The dummy 11–12 is an end tie, used to indicate clearly that
this is the final exit from the network. Though the arrows in a
network indicate a lapse of time they are not drawn to scale, which
would be impossible.

Networks are of use for clearly stating the planning, avoiding
pitfalls and indicating the dependence of events. Considerable

ACTIVITY DESCRIPTION	NUMBER	TIME (WEEKS)	CUMULATIVE TIME ON CRITICAL PATH
Agree on equipment	1–2	4	4
Order computer	2–3	2	6
Order peripherals	2–4	2	
Order computer furniture	2–5	1	
Order office furniture	2–7	2	
Plan for installation	3–6	4	
Await delivery of computer	3–8	36	42
Await delivery of peripherals	4–9	24	
Await delivery of comp. furniture	5–8	10	
Dummy	6–8	0	
Await delivery of office furniture	7–11	10	
Install computer	8–10	3	45
Install peripherals	9–11	2	
Acceptance tests	10–11	3	48
Dummy	11–12	0	48

FIG. 64. Data for network shown in Fig. 63.

work has been done on the mathematical treatment of networks. For present purposes it is sufficient to note that an event is not achieved until all the activities leading into it have been completed. Thus, event 8 is not completed until activities 3–6, 3–8 and 5–8 have all been accomplished, and activity 8–10 will await this. The longest path through the network, called the critical path, is what determines the over-all project time, and it is only by reducing the time taken for activities on this path that a reduction in this overall time can be achieved. Because of the importance of the critical path, network planning techniques are often referred to as C.P.M. (critical path method) or C.P.A. (critical path analysis), while the abbreviation PERT (project evaluation and review technique) is used where a more detailed statistical treatment is involved, taking account of the probabilities of the timing estimates.

ORGANISATION OF WORK

The organisation of work in a computer department presents problems similar to those faced by the management in charge of factory production or of conventional office work. Aids to scheduling (concerned with when work is done) and routing (concerned with how it is done), well developed in these other fields, may often be applied with only slight modification to data processing. Control problems, especially quality control, also arise, and again, statistical quality control techniques, of which there is considerable experience in these other fields, may be used.

The organisation of data processing work, from the point of view of routing, is shown in Fig. 65. The lower part of the diagram shows the flow of information from a user department. Documents received into the data processing department are assembled and checked prior to encoding in a form suited to computer input, such as punched cards. After punching and checking these cards are assembled, together with master files from the library and appropriate programs, and the required computer runs take place. The output is checked and assembled for the user department. This post-computer work may involve operations such as bursting (breaking at the perforations to separate one form from the next, when using continuous stationery), decollating (separating different copies and removing any carbon papers), edge-cutting (trimming off sprocket holes and any gummed strip used for attaching carbon papers) and batching and packing for despatch to user departments. The space occupied by documents and computer input and output media requires careful consideration and adequate assembly areas may greatly aid in efficient and accurate work.

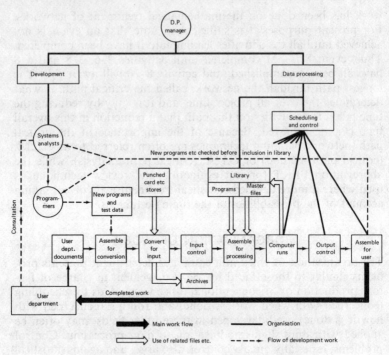

FIG. 65. Work organisation in computer department.

Figure 65 also attempts to show how systems development work fits in with routine processing. New programs and test data will be processed, interspersed with ordinary batch work. Print-outs will go back to systems analysts and programmers for checking. Satisfactory programs will eventually be stored in the program library.

Master files will have to be created, originally, by a sequence of activities similar to those shown for routine job processing. The sequence of operations in data processing generally affords little scope for flexibility and is fixed by the apparatus and systems available.

Scheduling of data processing work may present many problems. In Fig. 66 a simple bar chart form of scheduling is shown. Work may be planned on a weekly, calendar month or four-week month basis (of which there are thirteen in each year). Adequate scheduling requires that the period chosen should include all the demands on the computer. Some, such as preparation of the weekly payroll, will affect the working each week, while accounting operations such as updating sales ledgers may be on a monthly basis. Stock

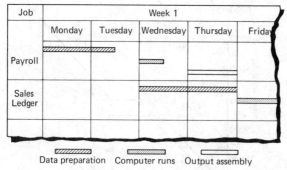

Data preparation   Computer runs   Output assembly

FIG. 66. Simple bar chart scheduling of computer work.

valuation and final accounting, if aping older systems, may be annual operations; with a reasonably complete management information system such information may be processed much more frequently.

The diagram breaks down the data processing work into preparation, computer runs and output assembly stages. Much more detailed scheduling can relate to each machine and worker involved. Staggering of work throughout the month, involving, perhaps, a different major accounting job each week, is an obvious way of avoiding bottlenecks. It is useful to reserve a period each day for work that cannot be precisely estimated and scheduled, such as development work or research programs. This time may be booked when the requirements crystallise.

The scheduling must allow for computer testing time, for regular maintenance and servicing, and also for down-time, when the computer or other equipment fails. Obviously this latter cannot be precisely scheduled but work loading, stretching well ahead, should be accepted at only a predetermined fraction of full capacity of the whole system.

Computers themselves tend to be grossly under-used but they are dependent on the rest of the system and on the flow of work from user departments and the deadlines of the latter for finished work. The satisfactory introduction of computing may sometimes imply that some of the user departments' needs, perhaps framed in terms of older equipment, should be reconsidered.

Timing and machine loading have been dealt with, briefly, in Chapter 6. Much routine work lends itself to estimation based on the number of transactions and the average detail in each. Special one-off jobs, such as program development and file creation, may have to be scheduled to be ready at specified target dates. Figure 67 gives an example of a scheduling chart with cumulative target

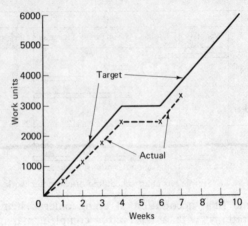

FIG. 67. Work control chart.

and actual output times, recorded week by week. Clearly, with the diagram as shown, the target date is not going to be met unless the rate of activity is speeded, perhaps by transferring extra staff to the operation. The "working units" shown might be based on visible record cards completed, program lines written and the like.

Control over the use of equipment may call for the equivalent of a job card, as is often used in factory production, though planning sheets on which are listed the jobs for the day and the times at which they are scheduled to run are perhaps more normal. The operator will probably be required to enter in a log book details of the jobs done, with times on and off, set-up time, down-time, etc. The computer itself may be equipped to provide automatically a log of the work it does, which can provide a useful check on time-estimates and costings, as well as discouraging misuse.

Computers often given rise to increased centralisation of data processing and organisational problems concerned with the transport of documents and cards may have to be faced. Alternatively, the data may be transmitted over telephone or other circuits.

REAL-TIME

The differences between batch processing and real-time working are discussed in Chapter 5. For the computer department organisational implications of real-time seem to be as follows.

1. Less data preparation is required, once the files have been established, and there will probably be fewer humanly-readable

print-outs. It must be recognised, however, that outsiders, such as customers, will require hard copy. Ultimately systems may extend to centralisation of the purchases and sales accounting of at least the major firms in an industry and reduce these needs. Hard copy records will normally be printed at intervals, at least of key data, for security and audit purposes (*see* Chapter 9) and because such records may be more convenient in some cases than terminal output.

2. More planning and programming will probably be involved initially and anything like a total system will require a degree of sophistication rarely required in batch processing.

3. Provision in the case of system failure will have to be carefully considered.

4. Movement of documents should be greatly reduced. This may be a big issue when processing for several departments or depots is centralised and access is through terminals. With batch processing it is, of course, possible to feed data, after suitable encoding, through a telephone circuit or special line (*see* Chapter 4).

5. There may be a subtle change in authority arising from the fact that the users are independent of the computer staff once the real-time systems have been established.

6. A record may be automatically kept by the computer of the times used on various jobs for different departments, which may be useful for checking costs and misuse.

LIBRARY ORGANISATION

The file librarian is responsible for the storage, issue, and receipt back after use, of all files of data required by the computer system. These may be maintained on media such as paper tape, punched cards, interchangeable disc packs and particularly on magnetic tape. Because of the importance of magnetic tape the term tape librarian is often used.

The term library is often applied to the standard programs available from the computer manufacturer for run-of-the-mill jobs. As is seen in Fig. 65 the librarian will be responsible for program storage as well as for data files, when such programs are on magnetic tape or other input media. On some computer systems, especially involving time-sharing, the program library may be on a disc backing system. The essentials of a good library, whether in the ordinary sense of books or in the computer sense are:

1. systematic storage, to ensure that any item may be located and retrieved with minimum delay. This implies careful coding and indexing;

2. protective storage, so that damage and deterioration do not occur. Appropriate storage racks, protective cassettes and the maintenance of satisfactory temperature, humidity and dust-free conditions can be important factors;

3. security of information against unauthorised access and alteration and also against loss. This involves a system for booking files in and out, the authorisation of substitute files, and a record of updated versions of programs, etc.

SPECIMEN EXAMINATION QUESTIONS

1. Describe the functional organisation of a large computer department offering comprehensive services within a large commercial company.

2. Discusss the possible effects of recent developments in hardware on the traditional organisation of computer services (a) within a user organisation and (b) in a bureau selling computer and ancillary services.

3. You have recently been seconded from your job of assistant accountant with a medium-sized group of companies to head a team responsible for introducing widespread computer services within the group. Outline the contents of a report to your directors on the timetabling of this project. State the assumption you make about the broad type of hardware to be used.

4. "A major cause of failure of computer systems is the lack of adequate pre-installation planning both of hardware and of software." Explain this statement and suggest how the major pitfalls may be avoided.

5. Describe the main problems likely to arise when purchases, sales and stock records are computerised, having previously been done manually and using book-keeping machines.

6. "Becoming computerised does not necessarily imply owning a computer nor even having one on the premises." Explain and comment on the merits and defects of the alternatives.

7. Describe some of the equipment, in addition to computers and input and output devices, which may be essential to running a computer system and give some details of one of the jobs concerned with handling some of this equipment.

8. As training officer of a company intending to introduce computing list the main points to which you would pay attention, giving an indication of the types of staff involved, the content and extent of their training, and the desirable timescale for the training.

9. An organisation has experienced a high rate of labour turn-

over with its computer operating staff. Suggest methods by which this might be reduced.

10. Discuss the different features which may be sought when selecting staff to fill four different jobs related to computing. Clearly state the four job designations you have in mind.

11. Explain how network planning may be desirable in the introduction of computing.

12. How may program and systems development work be done in a computer system already fairly heavily loaded with routine work?

13. Discuss the differences in the organisation of computer departments concerned with (a) batch working, (b) real-time working, (c) hybrid systems combining batch and real-time.

Chapter 9

SECURITY AND AUDIT

PHYSICAL PROTECTION

Realisation of the devastating consequences of business records being destroyed led to the use of safes and fire-proof cabinets in the days before computers. Possible causes of destruction or damage should be considered when equipment is being purchased and premises decided on, and the normal precautions of insurance and the use of fire detection systems should be taken, together with structural and storage devices, to minimise damage.

Some forms of computer record are especially vulnerable to incorrect storage (for example magnetic tape) while there is the additional hazard of records being destroyed or mutilated during the processing itself. Data loss on magnetic tape may occur because of drop-out due to edge crimping and impressed dust. Tape cleaning equipment is available to minimise this. The safest procedure is to maintain separate sets of records (it is easy to dump files on to magnetic tape) which are kept at different locations, so that the risk of both being destroyed is minimal.

The father and son technique is frequently used where the master file that has been updated (the "father" file) is retained after a computer run, so that the updated ("son") file may be reconstructed if anything goes wrong. The new file itself in turn becomes a father file, and so on. Sometimes three generations of files, of which the first is termed the "grandfather", are retained for additional security.

Security of random access files, such as magnetic disc files, usually involves keeping a copy on magnetic tape, or on another area of the disc. With real-time processing, after-state copying is often used, in which copies are kept of any buckets from which records have been updated. A copy of the main file is updated at intervals from these after-state records, which may require sorting if the processing is random or if several runs have been included. Several generations of the master file may be preserved. An alternative is partial copying, in which part of the file is copied each day, while after-state copies of the rest of the file are maintained. These methods have the merits of not disturbing the master file by frequent overwriting, and of enabling files to be recovered when movement data has not been preserved. It is a good principle to provide a print-out of all deleted records.

A major security risk, closely related to administrative controls (*see* later section in this chapter), may be that of the unauthorised tapping of computer files to acquire valuable information. The ease and speed at which this can be done on a large scale may call for stringent security against industrial espionage. Software, as well as file information, may be stolen, and have great value. Electronic methods of "bugging" computer systems, even from outside the building housing the computer, give rise to special problems which do not seem to have been adequately solved. There is also the risk of sabotage, ranging from wrecking the whole computer to destroying data files by magnets. The use of devices to prevent accidental overwriting of magnetic media is mentioned in Chapter 2.

PLACE OF THE AUDITOR

The responsibility of the directors of a company for the maintenance of adequate records is clear, as is that for the preparation of annual accounts to show a true and fair view of the business. The employment of computer service bureaux does not reduce the responsibilities of directors regarding adequate accounts. Neither can directors rely on the auditors, as such, to protect them against any failure in these duties, but auditors should be brought into contact with proposed systems and procedures in their planning stages.

Audit involves, among other things, a review of the system of book-keeping, accountancy and internal control. By internal control the accountant implies the following.

1. Internal check, which establishes routines for prevention or early detection of fraud. The division of work and authority among the staff, the proving of the work of individuals by that of others, the control of recording techniques and the use of check totals, are examples.

2. Internal audit, whereby the operations and records are reviewed by special members of the company's staff. Many businesses have no such audit while, in others, it may occupy a special staff and be done on a continuous basis.

3. Other controls aimed at securing accuracy and reliability of records.

Auditors rely heavily on the system of internal control and will be prepared to reduce the amount of checking to a small fraction of all transactions if they are satisfied as to its adequacy.

The idea of audit as being very much concerned with the soundness of a system is particularly relevant with computerised data processing, and special techniques have been established, such as audit programs and test packs, described at the end of this chapter. Auditors will rarely be experts at systems analysis, programming, etc., and will be more concerned with methods of controlling tasks rather than with the detail. An appreciation of the basic principles of computer operation and programming will be of considerable assistance to auditors, however, to enable them to understand the problems. The auditor knows what should be the results of certain data in a specified system. He is increasingly coming to regard the system as a link between data input and data output and demands that this should be satisfactory, while leaving the specialised systems planning, flow charting, programming, etc., to experts with whom he will consult on security aspects.

The present chapter attempts to keep in line with the advice on auditing provided by the major accounting bodies.

PECULIARITIES OF COMPUTER SYSTEMS

The reader of this book will be aware that the types and uses of computers and their associated apparatus can vary enormously between different electronic data processing systems. Computers are, however, usually associated with systems of greater complexity that take longer to design and get into working order and require more specialised skills than is the case with older methods. Underestimation of the initial problems and of the time and staff required is probably a major cause of unsatisfactory computer systems.

With batch operations the responsibility for processing data arising in a number of different user departments passes to the computer department. In the case of small computers this may not be so, while, with real-time terminals there may be a hybrid form of control, in which the computer department is responsible for maintaining the facilities but input and output equipment is installed in the user departments. It may be that the introduction of a separate computer department into the scheme of data processing, by removing some or all of the actual processing from the control of the user department, tends to make fraud less likely. On the other hand accountants and auditors may feel they are at the mercy of computer specialists, the details of whose work they are not equipped to investigate.

The fact that records, programs, etc., stored in the computer or on tapes and discs are not visible, requires differences in approach from those used where records can be visually checked, as can the successive stages of handling data, generally referred to as the audit trail, and regarded as vital in conventional audits. With such records copies may be obtained, possibly with tests spread over the year, or related only to current data, if there is a satisfactory continuous internal audit. Most computer systems (except visible record systems) eventually over-write the old records which are then no longer available, unless steps have been taken to obtain print-outs. Selective print-outs from files may be obtained by a suitable interrogation program, while some totals may be recreated clerically to check with the computer results.

ADMINISTRATIVE, DEVELOPMENT AND PROCEDURAL CONTROLS

The daily running of the computer system calls for strict administrative controls. The need for operating instructions and the use of manuals of standards and instructions, coupled with work scheduling, has been noted in previous chapters (especially Chapter 8). To these may be added precautions to prevent fraud such as:

1. never leaving only one operator in charge of equipment;
2. rotating the duties of operators;
3. programming so that all operator intervention is logged, generally by a console print-out;
4. division of responsibilities, so that one person does not have control over the whole sequence from original documents to final output. A simple example would be the separation of punching and verifying responsibilities;
5. restricting access to the computer room, the apparatus and the library to authorised persons at authorised times.

In addition the control of files and of library procedures, fire precautions and stand-by arrangements may be included under administrative controls.

Development controls are concerned with the initiation of new systems and the change of old ones. The stages have been dealt with in Chapters 5, 6 and 8. In the present context the emphasis rests on:

1. review at each stage of development to ensure that specified standards are being applied and that the user department's requirements are being met;
2. system and program testing, using test and actual (or live) data and pilot and parallel running where possible;

3. authorisation of changes and of further developments;

4. correct conversion of the files to be used in the system, generally checked by a complete print-out.

This leaves the procedural controls, applying to each separate computer application, and concerned with inputs, processing, outputs and control of master files. The first three of these are dealt with subsequently in separate sections. As far as master files are concerned amendments to these involve versions of the first three controls, while the state of standing data should be checked periodically by print-outs and the use of control totals, the latter being used also for checking transaction data on such files, with the addition of print-outs of individual balances.

CONTROL OF INPUTS

The accuracy of output from a computer system will obviously depend in the first place on the accuracy of the data that is fed in. The term "garbage in, garbage out", or some variation on this, is generally used to sum up this situation.

Input control implies that all input data should be authorised (having gone through an appropriate approval procedure) and that it should be correctly converted into computer readable form and processed only once. Control of punching and its verification are examples.

It is difficult to separate input involving peripherals from actual processing. In this section we shall consider "input" as indicating the reading of data by peripherals. Accountants often take the view that the input stage precedes the peripheral stage, which is regarded as part of processing.

Various computer input checks are recognised, of which the chief are as follows.

1. Reading checks, to guard against errors arising from the malfunctioning of peripheral equipment. With punched paper tape, for example, the code generally includes a parity check in which all binary coded characters are arranged to have an odd (or even) number of bits, by the addition of an extra bit if necessary. On reading, a test is applied, and characters containing an even (or odd) number of bits are rejected. A tear in paper tape, giving the semblance of an extra hole, would be detected by this means. Such checks can be applied at different stages of transfer of data (not restricted to paper tape) and will generally result in a halt in the processing (with a warning to the operator). In some cases the par-

ticular data may be automatically re-read and passed, and if it is then found to be correct, the fault may have been due to some transmission trouble. Some other purely mechanical checks may be conveniently included under this head, such as the double reading of input. The verification of punching of cards and tape has been mentioned in Chapter 2.

2. Check digits, to afford protection against the use of wrong reference and code numbers. All feasible numbers conform to some mathematical pattern, which is checked on read-in. Generally an extra digit is added to what would otherwise be the code number, to enable the pattern to be established. Patterns of varying complexity may be devised. The more involved the pattern the lengthier is the check but the less the likelihood of error.

As an example we may make the code exactly divisible by a prime number (such as 5, 7 or 11) by adding an extra digit. If the original code is 1234 and the prime number to be used is 7 then the final code will have five figures and be exactly divisible by 7. In this case the addition of 1 achieves this result (since $12341 \div 7 = 1763$ exactly.

A more complicated approach is to multiply each digit, depending on its position, by a decimal or binary number and then to add the products. This total has to be exactly divisible by a chosen prime number. The prime number selected should be as large as is convenient, 11 often being used.

If the original code is 9517 then multiplication of the digits from right to left by 1, 2, 3, 4, respectively, results in $1 \times 7 + 2 \times 1 + 3 \times 5 + 4 \times 9 = 60$, so that 6 must be added to make this divisible by 11, resulting in a code number 95176. With binary multipliers we should multiply by 1, 2, 4 and 8. If more than one digit (10) is required to be added the basic number may be discarded.

Check digit verification is useful to reduce errors arising from misreading of numbers and from the omission of digits or inclusion of extra digits.

A single check digit may be used to ensure that a feasible sequence of numbers is being handled. With an electronic accounting machine, for example, the keyboard may lock if the correct check digit is not typed when the account number and balance are picked up.

3. Format checks which verify, for example, that the correct characters, alphabetic, numeric or blank, appear in the correct fields of the data.

4. Limit checks, to ensure that data does not fall outside predetermined values. These are often built into programs to ensure

that ridiculous amounts do not appear as output in, say, bills or payrolls, but they may be usefully applied also as a check on input. Processing may continue with the offending data indicated in some way, or with a message printed at the console. When particular values cannot arise (for example odd numbers may be excluded from a coding system) a similar sort of check may be applied.

5. Consistency checks, comparing two items in a record (for example a child aged five could not be classified as married) or checking that the data shown is possible, may be devised as appropriate. These may be regarded as examples of validity checks, though the term is used with differing connotations.

6. Hash totals are nonsense totals of data such as account code numbers. The total after processing is compared with that obtained prior to processing, and should agree. If it does not there is a mistake in at least one of the codes processed.

7. Control totals are frequently used, with the total after a processing run compared to the total of a pre-list of the relevant data prepared before the run.

8. Counts of records are useful at the various stages of processing from the original documents onwards. It is good practice to divide work into artificial batches at some stages, to enable errors to be located. Item counts of records may be used when master files are updated to check that the new file is complete in this respect.

Processing the same item twice may be prevented by programming to keep track of each record as it is processed. The computer then tests each record for such a lock-out label before processing it.

9. Sequence checks can be applied to check the serial numbers of documents and can also be built into computer programs to ensure that records are in sequential order, which may be essential for the proper running of the program. In some processing, forms may be numbered sequentially before processing and the computer may be programmed to number each one separately, as it is used, starting at the same number as has been printed on the first form. The two numbers on each form should agree.

10. Logs of work done should be maintained. A manual log is not satisfactory and it is better that a print-out at the control keyboard should show programs used, volume of work done, control information and data input through the keyboard, and the times of the various activities. With real-time systems a log will be essential for restarting after failure.

11. Message acknowledgment is often incorporated in real-time systems so that a communication failure is made known to the

operator, who may have to rekey the transaction. Care must be taken that the same item is not entered twice.

12. Tape labels will be used both for visual and machine reading. A combination of good library control, carefully laid down procedures and identification within the tape by header and trailer labels is needed. This applies to data input, including master files, but the input of the correct programs must also be controlled.

Most of these checks may be equally regarded as processing tests. The name edit tests is sometimes used to denote these methods of comparing data with an appropriate standard. Rejections of data should be carefully controlled so that the items are investigated and corrections made, and so that they are eventually processed, if appropriate, and not lost to the system.

Many input tests will be applied before the computer-input or even the data-conversion stage. These are concerned with documents coming from the user departments for data processing and will follow the lines of normal accounting checks, including authorisation of input documents. The auditor will pay special attention to any changes consequent on going over to a computer.

CONTROL OF PROCESSING

Correct processing involves using correct input of data and of software, coupled with the correct operating procedures. We have already seen in the previous section that edit tests and control over rejections are often considered to be processing controls. This is the view taken by the Institute of Chartered Accountants.

Systems should be designed to be as foolproof as possible, with a log (preferably generated automatically) maintained of the jobs that have been done and of all operator intervention. The setting of switches by an operator may be checked by the program as it progresses through different stages, and error indications may be printed out at the console. The auditor will be interested to see that correct procedures are designed and are actually applied in operating conditions.

Programs may contain checks, perhaps arriving at results by two different methods and comparing them (sometimes called arithmetic proof), and also by crosscasting (adding across) appropriate columns and comparing the result with the sum of the total column (referred to as crossfooting) and an established method with pre-computer ledger posting equipment. Programs should also have routines built-in to test and deal with special situations such as overflow of data, when not enough space has been provided to accommodate all the digits.

When more than one run is involved in processing run to run controls are used, generally based on totals accumulated during each run, and aimed, primarily, at detecting loss of data at any stage. Any data that falls out of the system because it cannot be completely processed may be held on a suspense file, which may be directly printed out or held temporarily on backing store. In either case control should be exercised as over rejected data (see previous section).

CONTROL OF OUTPUTS

Controls after computer processing are concerned with verifying the output, disposing appropriately of it and ensuring that the correct procedures are adopted for dealing with exception reports.

Verification normally relies on clerical agreement of control totals and checks on selected items that have been processed. The accuracy of computer processing is likely to be very high, given adequately designed and tested software, and time may be best spent ensuring that a system gives the desired results before it is put into use. Faults in print units and the printing of nonsense from paper tapes that have been ripped or trapped may ruin work that has otherwise been perfectly processed by the computer. The loss of punched cards used for computer output should also be prevented.

Checks on the volume of output will probably be maintained throughout the computer runs, starting at the input stage, and despatch of the output to user departments will be recorded in a register.

Exception reports will cover items meriting attention when compared with standards specified in the programs. Examples might be variations from standard costs of more than a specified percentage, or exceptionally high gross pay. Such reports may indicate errors in processing or real deviations from standards. In either case prompt action is required by the computer department or by management in the user department.

With real-time systems arrangements are necessary to draw the management's attention to exceptional items. This may take the form of an immediate print back at the terminal. In the case of terminals, access to information on file must be restricted by use of codes, badge readers, etc., as mentioned in Chapters 2 and 4.

COMPUTER AUDIT PROGRAMS

Since computers can be very efficient tools for data processing it seems desirable to use their strengths to assist the auditor.

One approach is for the auditor to have his own programs to read a client's files and extract selected data from them and also to process such data. Generalised computer audit programs applicable to all clients would be ideal, but a difficulty arises from the variety of computer applications and data processing problems over the whole spectrum of business. Even when clerical procedures are the same, as between a number of firms in the same industry or offering the same professional service, problems arise from the use of different computers and configurations which may not be compatible. One procedure is to convert the client's files, or the data from them which will form the basis of the audit, into a standard format by means of an edit program. Such data is then processed by the auditor's computer or special programs may enable the client's equipment to be used. Alternatively, special purpose audit programs may be written for the auditor, or he may use suitable programs written by the client for internal control and analysis purposes and which have been tested by the auditor.

The use of specially written audit programs in final accounts and balance sheet verification may be particularly appropriate. Whether an audit program is primarily for this purpose or to provide a check on the internal control system there will be selection of items for further testing and the scrutiny of items to reveal exceptional data, perhaps involving a comparison of files.

Test packs

A solution to many of the problems posed by the use of audit programs is not to use such programs but to test the client's systems and programs thoroughly by using them to process data to which the solutions are already known. This enables the client's computer and operating staff to be used, under the supervision of the auditor.

The data so processed is called a test pack and may consist of data specially prepared by the auditor, or of client's data selected by the auditor, or used by the client's internal audit department, or devised for testing the client's system.

Such test packs are more suited to the testing of program controls than to checking final accounts and balance sheets. They should be devised to ensure that the program deals satisfactorily with normal data and also picks out invalid data which may be deliberately incorporated in the pack. There may be scheduling problems in processing test packs and costs and inconvenience may be high relative to the small amount of data that will be used. An alternative is for the auditor to set up data for test purposes on the client's master file and process this data along with the normal processing runs, taking care that such dummy data does not become confused with the clients' actual data.

STATISTICAL SAMPLING

A full treatment of this subject would be the province of specialist statistics books. However, auditors may find the following facts of use.

1. Sampling has long been the basis of accepted techniques for assessing the quality of industrial products and for controlling this within limits. Statistical quality control (S.Q.C.) has been established lished since the early 1930s and appropriate methods can be applied to office work.

2. Cheapness and speed are important attributes. The confidence in the result can be gauged beforehand if statistical sampling (as opposed to sampling by guess-work) is used. The accuracy of the information increases as the square root of the number of items in the sample. Costs tend to vary directly as the numbers of items used. The aim is to achieve a predetermined degree of accuracy with the smallest possible sample. Accuracy is bound up with the confidence level at which the auditor is prepared to work. For example he may decide that he is prepared to accept a possibility of one in a hundred or perhaps five in a hundred (the 99 per cent and 95 per cent confidence levels) that, if an error rate arises that varies by more than a pre-determined amount (the precision) from the standard, it will not be detected.

3. Sampling pays off best with large amounts of data. The reason is that the sample size to provide a given degree of confidence is not dependent on the size of the universe (or main body) of data from which the sample is drawn. This implies that a satisfactory size of sample drawn from a large universe will be a smaller percentage of that universe than with a small universe.

4. No sampling technique can guarantee to locate every error. Where such accuracy is required a 100 per cent check will be needed, but it should be recognised that such a check is itself liable to error.

5. As well as deciding on the number of items in the sample the method of selecting the actual items must be chosen. Sampling techniques fall roughly into two categories.

(a) Random sampling, in which each item of the universe has an equal chance of being chosen and bias is avoided. Random number tables or generators may be used in the computer to select sample items.

(b) Selective sampling, in which items are chosen according to the proportions in which characteristics occur in the universe, or systematically taking items at a chosen interval (which itself may vary randomly) from a random starting point.

SPECIMEN EXAMINATION QUESTIONS

1. "Precautions to prevent fraud were developed long before computers and they are largely still relevant." Explain this statement, giving at least four specific examples, and showing how they may be applied in computerised accounting.

2. Describe briefly the main areas of control which will need to be implemented in connection with commercial data processing.

3. Explain the use of: (a) reading checks, (b) check digits, (c) limit checks, (d) hash totals in connection with computer input.

4. Describe controls which may be desirable in connection with computer outputs.

5. Distinguish between development and procedural controls in connection with computer systems and give three examples of each.

6. Explain how computer logs can be used in connection with data processing controls.

7. "The auditor should take part in systems design from an early stage." Discuss the reasons for this statement and suggest methods for facilitating its implementation.

8. Explain the term "garbage in, garbage out" and show its relevance to business computing.

9. Discuss the use of alternatives to the "audit trail" approach, in which results are checked through several stages of documentation.

10. Explain the significance of internal check both in conventional audits, with an audit trail, and in systems where such trails are not used.

11. "Computing opens vistas of fraud on a scale previously impossible." Discuss this statement and comment on ways in which accountants may need to adapt their techniques.

12. "Auditing has become increasingly concerned with achieving a balance between attention paid to systems and that given to individual items." Comment, with examples.

Chapter 10

COMPUTER APPLICATIONS

DIVERSITY OF INFORMATION PROCESSING

It would probably be true to say that the information aspects of any process involved in business, manufacturing or science can be computerised. The applications of computers to standard situations involving masses of data are the most obvious. Processing the accounts and payrolls of large organisations were among the earliest uses of computers. A list of applications would be almost infinite. It would feature applications such as the development in medicine of diagnostic programs to aid the general practitioner, of body scanners to enable tumours to be assessed, and of systems to handle patients' records and to monitor their progress after operations. Computers may be used to control aircraft seat reservations, the flow of traffic on busy road networks and the operation of railways. Police can be aided by rapid access to central records ranging from criminal information and wanted and missing persons to motor vehicle details. The legal profession may come to accept terminals linked to legal data banks as a partial substitute for the volumes of statutes and case histories traditionally used. Atmospheric research is done on one of the world's largest computers. Some of the smallest computers are owned by individuals with uses ranging from playing games to planning family menus.

In the sections which follow some applications of interest to business men and managers are outlined.

ACCOUNTING APPLICATIONS

Such information as is available seems to show that the most popular uses of business computers are in connection with accounting, wages and cost control. This is not, perhaps, surprising in view of the bulk of data that falls under this heading and the comparative simplicity of the systems involved in handling it, while the hopes of eventual savings in staff employed and desire for speed and accuracy of processing must have been motivating forces. Typical commercial applications of computers are in connection with: invoicing, sales ledgers and statements; stock control and

198

evaluation; payroll, pay slips, end-of-year tax returns; purchase ledger; credit control; sales and purchase ledger analysis, remittance advices and cheques; budgetary control; cost accounting, job costs, standard costs, work in progress and labour analysis; assets registers; hire purchase records.

From the mid-1970s computers, especially minis, tended to displace other forms of accounting equipment. In many cases computer configurations were specifically designed for or adapted to accounting needs, which they could meet relatively cheaply and efficiently. Some organisations making the change found that they could not even give away their older equipment, though it was in perfect working order.

There has been a tendency for businesses to approach their data processing piecemeal, which is understandable when a firm is feeling its way and wishes to minimise risks. It would replace existing systems by computer systems which did little more than simulate the old procedures on the computer. Computers may offer opportunities, however, for integration of systems, which can only be realised if a broader view is taken of the objectives in the early stages of systems analysis. The older approach to integration assumed it to imply centralisation using a mainframe computer. Modern technology has also made available distributed systems, which can run independently or be linked to provide powerful but flexible processing and data bases. As computers become familiar objects in the office accountants and managers should increasingly come to regard them as adaptable machines capable of satisfying their needs for information.

As well as the accounting uses of computers in the private sector of industry the civil service, local authorities and nationalised industries have adopted them. To an extent their problems are similar to those of private enterprise, for example they have to prepare payrolls and bill customers for services such as gas, electricity and telephones. Even special activities, such as rate collection, may be regarded as a specialised form of billing.

WORD PROCESSING

The production of letters and similar documents has always been a major and costly office activity, while standards of accuracy and presentation are relevant to effective work and the image that a business projects. Electric typewriters helped with speed and consistency of results. A great deal of a typist's time is spent in making corrections and special keys were added so that a text, recorded in a memory unit, could be amended.

Word processing goes a stage further. Text is created by typing on a normal keyboard. It is displayed either as several lines on a visual display unit (V.D.U.)—like a television screen—or as a single line or thin window display. Additional keys enable the operator to amend the text, erasing or adding characters, words and lines, centring headings and moving groups of type about. The final text is then printed automatically, generally using a golf-ball or daisywheel printer. The former has characters covering its surface; the latter has them on upwards of ninety petals arranged in a circle. Both offer facilities for easy and rapid change of type face. Print-out at up to about fifty-five characters per second is possible, or, reckoning an average word to have five characters, the rate can be over six hundred words per minute. Special forms of apparatus, such as the ink-jet printer, can almost double this speed.

Word processing is really a special application of the editing facility available on computers which enables programs and data to be amended while they are held in the memory of the computer. Magnetic cards and tapes have been used to provide word processing memory but flexible or floppy discs became popular because of their considerable storage capacity. Such a disc, diameter 7 inches (175 mm), can store the equivalent of over 100 pages of A4 type, or about 250,000 characters.

Equipment can be of the stand-alone type, each typing station being self-contained, or of the shared-logic variety, in which several typing points share the same computer, usually a minicomputer, taking advantage of its storage and print facilities.

The techniques just described can be ideal for routine, repetitive correspondence, of which the bulk consists of standard sentences and paragraphs, assembled to suit particular circumstances and personalised with regard to name, address, etc. They are also suited to new drafts of letters and minutes, enabling corrections and adjustments to be readily made. The preliminary processes may be aided by electronic dictating machines and transcribing equipment on which the typist plays back the recording. Managers may dictate over telephone lines to recording apparatus in a central pool. Word processing stations may be linked to communicate between different departments or organisations.

BANKS AND FINANCIAL INSTITUTIONS

Banks, with over 10,000 branches between them in Britain, each branch potentially affecting the others, offer opportunities for advanced applications of computers, coupled with stringent security, that may profoundly alter our future economic system.

Electronic accounting machines tended to give way to computer batch processing of customers' accounts using terminals connected to regional centres and the development of real-time systems for interrogating accounts. Bankers Automated Clearing Services (BACS) provides an inter-bank computer bureau. The handling of cheques is speeded by the use of magnetic ink character recognition coupled with special encoding and sorting equipment.

Cheques, which have provided an effective substitute for cash, may give way to Electronic Funds Transfer (E.F.T.) in a cashless society. The customers of banks may find it convenient to obtain cash, make deposits, check details of their accounts and even pay bills directly (perhaps using a push-button telephone for encoding) without attending a branch which may be inconveniently situated or closed. Cash point facilities have spread, using magnetic cards together with a code which is keyed-in by the customer. Extensions to supermarket check-out points are possible. Developing these systems is expensive but banks expect big savings from reducing the costly business of handling cheques. Public acceptance is needed to produce the volume of transactions to make the newer methods viable as cost savers, however, and a long advertising process may be required to educate the public. Financial inducements may also be offered.

Among other banking applications is SWIFT, a network for the international transfer of funds.

The Stock Exchange has its own clearing problems arising out of the tens of thousands of daily transactions in stocks and shares. From 1972 to 1979 the TALISMAN system was developed and extended to cover all brokers and jobbers in the United Kingdom, with a data net operating through London and eight country offices. A system using minicomputers gives up-to-date share prices. Operating as TOPIC (Teletext Output of Price Information by Computer) it is based on the Prestel system of the Post Office. This replaces the old system (Market Price Display Service) used by the Stock Exchange to provide information through 2,000 terminals.

The Accepting Houses Committee developed a computerised share-dealing system known as ARIEL. It has been claimed that such a system makes unnecessary the physical existence of a Stock Exchange. Such exchanges originated as meeting places for individuals and firms engaged in particular activities. Lloyds, in insurance, and many of the London exchanges and markets which do not physically handle goods, have similar histories and strong traditions. Effective electronic communications may enable transactions to be conducted from the offices of individual firms, if the element of human contact can really be ignored.

Special databases have been set up relating to stocks and shares to help with day-by-day investment decisions or with financial research. DATASTREAM and EXTEL provide the former service, while the London Share Price Database has information relating to over 2,000 companies going back to 1955.

Building societies have problems similar to those of banking in that they operate through many branches and require up-to-date information on customers' accounts. Half-yearly statements, produced by computer, may be issued, though hand-written passbooks are general as well. Special passbook posting equipment has been produced but the on-line enquiry system is probably the key factor in operation.

With insurance companies and their agencies the use of time sharing systems has developed for calculations of premiums and special quotes, together with the valuation of pension funds.

DISTRIBUTION

Retail distribution forms a major sector of the economy and one which has seen many changes often aimed at improving efficiency in the face of fierce competition. Organisations and shops increase in size but the basic problem remains of satisfying the individual needs of millions of small purchasers while controlling the stock levels and purchasing and ensuring profitable over-all operation. The contribution which computing might make was recognised at an early stage in the development of business computers, especially in the U.S.A. where some very sophisticated experiments with automated shops were attempted and sometimes abandoned as too ambitious. Nowadays, equipment is available designed to link advanced computer technology with the peculiar needs of retailing.

The focus of attention tends to be the point-of-scale (POS) terminal with its associated devices. This is located at the check-out. It has rapidly developed from the electronic cash register (E.C.R.) equipped with magnetic tape cassette to record data for subsequent processing by computer. Modern units have logic and memory and may provide for data collection by a light-wand reader, scanning bar-coded tags (*see* Chapter 2) or using a magnetic wand to read information from tags which can be speedily encoded on a ticket unit. Codes which uniquely identify each product have been developed, and articles may bear the Universal Product Code (in the U.S.A.) or the Article Numbering Association symbols which are very similar (in Europe). Items can be priced and bills prepared automatically. Credit authorisation may be easily checked. All the information can also be recorded for stock control and financial purposes. The scanner can also be used in connection with stock control throughout the store. All these terminals can be controlled by a small store computer, which in turn may be linked over telephone or other lines (*see* Chapter 4) to the organisation's main computer. Stand-alone units with, say, 32K RAM capable of being supplemented are also available. Visual display units, which in this context may be called display stations, can be incorporated.

Looking into the future we may envisage a cashless payment system in which stores and banks are linked in one vast network, payments being made by direct debit from customer's bank accounts. The major banks are looking into this electronic transfer of funds but a workable system is not expected before the mid-1980s.

The systems outlined above are conceived chiefly for serve-yourself retail stores. Computers may also speed up service at garages selling manufacturers' parts and at other trade counters. Visual display units can be used to check items in stock and on order, together with their price location in the store. Invoices can be prepared automatically under computer control and the sales information may be used for stock control purposes.

PRODUCTION AND PROCESS CONTROL

Production management is concerned with setting realistic targets for production and with achieving these economically and within specified times. It must be recognised that "production" can range from building construction to producing patent medicines and from car production to pottery. No one blueprint will satisfy all conditions. The computer can assist in many ways.

In the early planning stages it may enable use to be made of operational research techniques so that, for example, movement may be minimised or an optimum product mix achieved. Critical path programs may be used to examine the timing of complex projects (*see* Fig. 37). More advanced programs deal with resource allocation and cost aspects.

Manufacturing conditions even in one industry such as engineering differ enormously from fully planned and integrated flow production to batch and one-off work. With the former a major aim is to keep the line moving and a computer monitoring the whole system can be very helpful. In the other case items may be made to order, when the time factor for delivery may be important and the main problem may be that of slotting the various jobs effectively into the available equipment.

Factory scheduling will involve the loading of departments,

equipment and individual workers or teams. This implies that the production times involved in the plan are related to the resources necessary to make it function. An aim is to reduce bottlenecks and idle resources. The computer can help by producing an accurate picture of current conditions and a forecast of the implications of future plans.

A breakdown of the orders scheduled for delivery, giving an analysis of component requirements split into bought-out and to-be-manufactured items is required first. The manufacturing requirements can then be further analysed on the basis of raw materials, components and assemblies. These requirements can be compared with stocks available and any necessary orders placed with the factory or outside. Effective stock control will ensure that requirements are met on time without incurring excessive costs of over-large stocks.

Implementation of the production plan will involve documents such as job cards, instructions and stock requisitions, and these form an obvious field for using the computer. Such documents can probably be produced more accurately from stored computer files than when written or typed out.

The final aspect, the control itself, implies that everything that happens is monitored, preferably continuously, and checked with the plan. Monitoring may be by print-out or on video screens or by other signalling systems, picking up from the workplace and displaying their findings to foremen, works managers, etc., in the most appropriate locations. Computer input devices may be strategically placed on the shop floor, in the stores, etc., and linked with the central processing unit. Ultimately, an aim of automatically signalling from the production and inspection equipment itself may be achieved. Devices to monitor machine performance and status automatically are available. In Britain there seems to have been a reluctance to accept them, on the basis that they are spies of management and interfere with the independence of workers.

Such production control systems may be linked with systems that enable vital factors such as cost estimates to be continuously updated if changes, such as material or labour cost increases, take place. Really effective systems will enable rescheduling to be done to achieve a new optimum in the light of the changed conditions. The use of interactive programs may enable managers to ask the computer the likely effect of any changes contemplated, and the computer may also be programmed to guide them in coming to the correct decision.

Production control is generally considered to relate to the operation of a factory or production department having processing facilities that are best used in a planned way. With some integrated plants, as may occur in chemical processing, or with special large-scale equipment such as rod rolling or producing steel strip, it may be worth while controlling the plant or the process itself by computer. The control may cover a variety of aspects of the work. For example it may direct the actual mechanics of operation, or may bring about adjustments to maintain quality, such as thickness in a strip mill, or it may be in the interests of the economic use of materials, slicing up the rods as they are made into lengths that will fit in with a demand pattern or adjusting the proportions in which different products are made in an oil refinery.

It was very expensive to tie up an old type of mainframe computer by dedicating it to the control of a process, especially as it would probably be grossly underutilised. The introduction of time-sharing and especially of small computers and microprocessors has made such control much cheaper. A good example is the numerical control of some machine tools by minis and by microcomputers.

There may well be a revolution in manufacturing based on micro-processors (*see* Chapter 11).

COMPUTER AIDED DESIGN

The use of computers to assist designers in the often complex calculations that arise is obvious. Even with computer batch processing, which usually involves delays, it may be worth while to do such computations, while, if terminals are available in a design office, appropriate programs may be called up and the designer has the benefit of an immediate answer.

Computer Aided Design (CAD), dating from about 1965, is generally considered to be concerned with more sophisticated systems, especially those involving the use of graphical displays on video units.

Extremely complicated software enables the designer to "sketch" with a light pen on the video unit screen and pull his design into shape, alter it and even rotate it, if it is in three dimensions, to see what it looks like from different angles. Stress calculations can be performed and, where the design is basically mathematical, as with aircraft wings, the effects of changes that take place due to, for example, deformation in flight, can be studied.

A good deal of design work involves the reproduction of standard shapes and these can be stored in the computer and called up when required. An interesting example is in the field of integrated circuit design, as used in computers, where a time of, perhaps, two months needed to produce the "artwork" can be reduced to days. Layout can be checked by the computer to ensure compliance with design specifications, errors can be corrected by a light pen and the layout can be output on to magnetic or paper tape which can be used to control an automatic drawing machine. Magnetic tape can be used to transmit design data between different centres. The computer can take over from the designer and perform the detail work, extending into the preparation of numerical control tapes for production and the design of inspection tools. The implications on employment for draughtsmen and other engineers are obvious.

Design in modern business conditions inevitably involves consultation between designers proper (who themselves may vary from technical designers to stylists) and production, development, marketing and estimating specialists. There seems to be evidence that the lengthy communications between these may be considerably reduced by a suitable computer system.

Much of the advanced work in computer aided design has been associated with large businesses, as in aircraft or car construction and the manufacturing of computers themselves. The development of time-sharing bureaux services has, however, placed many of these facilities within the reach of smaller businesses, who may find it profitable to have a contract with such a bureau and to use its packages as and when convenient.

The development of small, cheap, desk-top computers, with calculating facilities beyond those available with conventional calculating machines, has helped with smaller scale calculations. Microcomputers greatly extend the facilities available and, with colour displays, can cope dramatically with continuously changing graphic designs.

STATISTICAL AND OPERATIONAL RESEARCH APPLICATIONS

Business management is making increasing use of mathematical techniques to aid it in decision making. The term quantitative methods is often used to imply a range of such techniques embracing business mathematics, statistics and operational research.

Operational research (O.R.) developed during the 1940s, at first in connection with military operations, but later to be taken over by big business. The aim was to use scientific analysis to provide managers with a reasoned, quantitative basis on which they might make decisions. Major types of problem were swiftly recognised and techniques were evolved for dealing with them. The overall approach may be regarded as:

1. formulating the problem in consultation with management;
2. creating a "model" of the situation, which may consist of mathematical equations or be a simulation (*see* next section);

3. studying the effects on this of specified operations;

4. translating these effects back into practical management terms;

5. monitoring the subsequently evolving situation, after management has made the decisions.

Much of the work in operational research involves laborious calculations, which are not only time-consuming but have a high probability of error if done manually. The computer is ideal for much of this work. Some calculations would be completely impractical without its use. A feature of much operational research work is the use of iterative methods, implying that the same sequence of calculations is repeated over and over again, getting successively closer to a desired result.

Computer library programs are available for much of the work. Managers need to have an appreciation of the value of the various techniques and may themselves make use of some packages through desk terminals. More specialised studies will involve the employment of professional operational research workers, who themselves will wish to push the routine calculation on to the computer and also use it to help in developing new techniques.

This book is not concerned with the techniques in detail. A list would include topics such as mathematical programming, linear and non-linear programming, transportation and allocation, integer programming, parametric programming, queueing, stock-control, replacement, dynamic programming and probably also critical path techniques (*see* Fig. 37).

A good statistical basis is required for much O.R. work and computer packages are available for all the statistical applications likely to be of interest to managers and those advising them.

SIMULATION

Many of the simpler problems of operational research can be solved analytically. One or more equations may sum up the situation and their solution provides the answer.

Models of more complex situations, such as often arise in real-life management, cannot be dealt with so readily, often because the mathematical techniques do not exist or it may be too laborious to apply them. In such cases simulation may be used.

Simulation is especially useful for studying systems that are planned but do not yet exist (for example a new refinery) or for systems that exist but cannot be the subject of experiment directly (for example we might wish to study the effect of interest charges on the economic system).

The implication of simulation is that a model is devised having similar attributes to those of relevance in the real-life situation. Mechanical, electrical and electronic analogs may be set up. Analog computers work on this basis, often being specially designed for a restricted range of problems. Simulation in its most useful and powerful form sets up these models in a digital computer, for which the system must be described numerically.

Many processes in management are stochastic, i.e. the characteristics of the situation vary through chance causes. In these cases simulation may be used based on known or estimated factors in the situation. So-called "top-hat" or "Monte Carlo" techniques may be used to incorporate these chance elements, on the basis that any single event is as chancy as drawing a raffle number from a hat, but, in the long run, the average effect can be predetermined.

For example, if it is known that a particular event occurs once in five occasions on average, the hat might contain white and red counters in the ratio of 4 : 1. At each stage of the simulation when it is desired to incorporate this event a counter would be drawn, its colour noted, and, if red, taken to imply that the event had occurred. It would then be returned to the hat so as to leave the proportion of colours undisturbed.

A similar process may be performed on the computer by using random numbers, that is numbers between which there is no connection. One-fifth of these numbers would be assumed to indicate that the specified event has happened. The simulation program would be written to take the next random number, perhaps from a list of those read into store, and to test whether it fell within the range of these assigned numbers. The program would then proceed on the basis of this item of information. In practice pseudo-random numbers are usually generated by the computer, under the control of a special subroutine, so that lists do not have to be read in. Such numbers are not truly random, but, with ingeniously devised programs, may approach closely to the random state.

Such simulation enables complex interrelationships to be studied and results appear as they would in reality. The queue situation, referred to in the section of Chapter 8 dealing with real-time, is an example of a problem that can be handled in simple cases by the use of formulae but where simulation may be of great value in more complex situations. Such a situation could be the demand on lift facilities in a skyscraper block of offices. The effects of staggering working hours and running express lifts could be studied by simulation. A major benefit of simulation is that it can speed up the time process so that ten years' operation of a system could be simulated in a few hours or minutes.

So important is simulation that special computer programming languages have been devised to assist systems analysts, operational research workers and the like to convert their models into a form acceptable by a computer. Some such languages are based on existing language compilers; for example, GASP (**G**eneral **A**ctivity **S**imulation **P**rogram) is based on FORTRAN.

COMPUTER-ASSISTED LEARNING

Computer-assisted learning (CAL) or computer-aided instruction (CAI), to use an alternative description, is especially associated with time-sharing terminals accessing large mainframe computers. Minis and microcomputers are likely to play an increasing part. The target may be groups of pupils or individual students.

For groups, case analysis and group exercises may be used, while the computerised business game (*see* Fig. 68) may have advantages in speed and sophistication over games relying on tutors to provide information and to assess the outcome of decisions using key texts. There may also be a saving in the number of staff needed to run the game. The alternatives available as displays may be much wider, though much depends on the facilities available (size of memory, colour terminal etc.). A typical game divides the students into a number of small teams whose members may take on various management roles, and which, acting as different companies, compete in the manufacture and sale of a product in a simulated market. A team makes a decision which is fed into the computer, which then outputs the new position of that team. The time scale is contracted so that decisions made each half hour may represent periods of a month or longer. At the end of the training session one team is adjudged winner on some previously established basis. Fig. 68 shows parts of the terminal print-out of instructions for a game in international marketing originally developed by Leasco in conjunction with the Plessey Co. Ltd.

Terminals or microcomputers located in classrooms may also back up the teaching of subjects such as statistics, operational research and decision-making, especially for non-specialists studying business or management. It is possible for such students to work through simple examples to grasp the principles but to rely on a computer package, as would a business man, for the heavy, practical processing. Attention shifts from the mathematical theory to the practicalities of modelling and the input and output formats. Simple statistics may be coupled with the learning of elementary programming in a language such as BASIC. A problem with class teaching is that of making the display of a video unit, or the print-

```
OPTIONS ARE:
INS----TO OBTAIN INSTRUCTIONS FOR THE GAME
FOR----TO OBTAIN A TOTAL MARKET SALES FORECAST
RES----TO OBTAIN THE RESULTS OF THE LAST PERIOD
DEC----TO ENTER/ALTER YOUR DECISIONS FOR THE NEXT PERIOD
LIS----TO OBTAIN AN END-OF-GAME ANALYSIS
TIM----TO OBTAIN THE CURRENT TIME
END----TO END THIS SESSION


READY? INS


ABBREVIATED INSTRUCTIONS
------------------------

1.  OBJECTIVE - TO INCREASE ASSETS
2.  YOU ARE A FIRM SELLING UNITS TO EUROPE AND TO THE GOVT.
3.  THE GOVT ACCEPTS LOWEST TENDER/S, HAS DELIVERY PRIORITY
4.  THE GOVT PAYS CASH, EUROPE PAYS FOLLOWING PERIOD
5.  PRODUCTION BECOMES AVAILABLE FOLLOWING PERIOD (W-I-P)
6.  FACTORIES CANNOT BE CLOSED, THEY EACH PRODUCE UP TO 10000
    AND HAVE A FIXED COST OF $5000 PER PERIOD.
7.  MARKET IS ASSURED, YOUR SHARE DEPENDS UPON PRICE,
    MARKETING, COMMISSIONS PAID RELATIVE TO YOUR COMPETITORS
8.  MARKETING SPEND HAS STICKY EFFECT.
9.  EACH % COMMISSION OVER 10% INCREASES PENETRATION BY 2%
    UNSATISFIED ORDERS INVOKE COMMISSION AT HALF RATE
10. STOCK HOLDING COST $1 P.U., STOCK AND W-I-P VALUE=$5 P.U.
11. LOSSES ARE WRITTEN OFF AGAINST ANY ACCUMULATED TAX DUE
12. YOU DECIDE: NO. OF FACTORIES, QTY TO PRODUCE, PRICE/QTY
    TO GOVT.PRICE, COMMISSIONS, MARKETING TO EUROPE.
13. A STATEMENT OF THE PRESENT POSITION (PERIOD 0) CAN BE
    OBTAINED (BY TYPING 'RESULTS') FROM WHICH OTHER ASPECTS
    CAN BE DEDUCED.
14. AT THE END OF EACH RUN OF THE PROGRAM YOU WILL BE INFORMED
    OF THE NEXT DECISION DEADLINE TO BE MET.  IF THE DEADLINE
    IS NOT MET THE PREVIOUS PERIOD'S DECISIONS WILL BE ASSUMED
15. YOU ARE COMPETING AGAINST  4  OTHER COMPANIES OVER A
    PLANNING HORIZON OF 10  PERIODS.
```

FIG. 68. Rules for a business game obtained as terminal output.

out of a teletyper as it emerges visible to the bulk of students. A suitably located large screen television set, independently standing about a metre above normal desk or video level may supply an answer. One solution has been to use a special display panel like an electronic scoreboard.

Advocates of computer-assisted learning probably have individual students, rather than groups, chiefly in mind. The use of a terminal operating in conversational mode perhaps offers the best facilities. Readers who have access to a time-sharing terminal will appreciate the advantages of learning the BASIC programming language, using apparatus where their errors are almost instantaneously brought to their attention, and where the results of running the program appear quickly. Pupils may learn at their own speed, may catch up with topics missed through illness or other reasons, may repair defects in their background knowledge, may obtain an instant feedback and may have their weaknesses diagnosed and remedial reinforcement applied. These claims will be recognised as among those made for programmed learning many years ago. Programmed learning, first in book form and then aided by equipment using films, provided instruction incorporated with tests. These required "yes" or "no" answers or involved multiple choice. The correctness or otherwise of the answer decided which page (or section of film) was to be used next. Wrong answers might engender explanatory comment or force the student through a revision loop or new set of reinforcing instruction. There are various computer systems available which can be used by individuals each with a video terminal. One approach is for the teaching material to be prepared by a computer bureau offering a bank of educational courses. A popular alternative is for the computer manufacturer or bureau to supply a package which enables teachers easily to set up their own sequences of instructions, text, questions, branching and everything required. Teaching packages are also produced for use on minis and microcomputers, while special pocket calculators have been devised to help along the learning of subjects such as arithmetic.

Such systems are competing for educational finance with other equipment and traditional books and with more recent courses available on films and slides, some having sound accompaniment, and with recorded television material. There is a case for experimenting with the products of new technology, such as microcomputers, but in the end they must better serve the needs of the educational system if they are to be justified. A good library of well selected books to back up those bought by students is a basic educational resource without serious challenge except in-so-far as microfilmed versions may reduce storage space. The computer can, however, provide controlled and interactive learning, processing and text storage facilities, perhaps linked with microfilm as well as video displays. It can also be helpful in college library indexing, with the possibility of tracing data through specified links, for research and teaching purposes. National and international networks will grow in significance.

Colleges involved in computer training as such will probably have facilities which can be made available to students of business, management and related fields. The computer department may offer batch processing and/or time-sharing facilities with terminals located in other departments. There will probably be one or more teaching rooms equipped with several terminals so that one is available to each member of the class. Such a department can fulfil a useful role as a centre for information and inspiration on computer matters, not only within the college but also for smaller colleges in the area and local schools.

A report on *Computer Assisted Learning in Higher Education— The Next Ten Years* was issued in 1977 by the Council for Educational Technology. It concludes that, while not revolutionising teaching, CAL can usefully contribute to higher education, especially in teaching new topics untouched by traditional teaching methods. Funds, which are seen primarily as add-on costs, should be provided "to those practitioners who have gone beyond the initial try-out stage and have shown themselves capable of moving towards planned and regular use of computing within courses". The report comments that computers will gradually become assimilated into teaching technology though the distinctions between such instructional computing and uses for research and for administration will remain.

The term "computer managed learning" (C.M.L.) denotes the use of computers to keep student records, to mark tests and to progress students through courses. It is on the border between instruction and administration.

SPECIMEN EXAMINATION QUESTIONS

1. Explain what is meant by "word processing" and discuss its likely impact on office systems.

2. "Though computers can deal effectively with extremely complex and sophisticated problems their chief use has been in connection with routine processing of bulk business data." Comment on the reasons for this state of affairs and discuss its future relevance.

3. Discuss the view that computerisation is bound to lead to greater centralisation both of data processing and of management decision-making.

4. Give an account of present and possible future applications of computing in connection with banks and financial institutions.

5. Discuss the extent to which computers may revolutionise aspects of retail distribution.

6. Outline three applications of computers of interest to business men but not directly concerned with the processing of accounting data.

7. Explain how computers may assist in (*a*) production control and (*b*) process control.

8. Discuss the impact of computer aided design on drawing office methods and organisation.

9. "Computers are particularly suited to processing statistical and operational research calculations and may afford the only practical way of arriving at a solution." Explain this and comment on the use managers may make of appropriate computer "packages" to solve some of their problems.

10. Discuss the role of computer-assisted learning in connection with management training.

Chapter 11

SOME WIDER IMPLICATIONS

EFFECTS ON MANAGEMENT AND WORKERS

By the early 1970s business data processing had been revolutionised by the computer. In this change a new technology had taken over the role once filled by punched card equipment and electromechanical accounting machines. Business men and the man in the street came to accept the computer as something operating in the background, rather mysteriously, but said to be doing a good job and benefiting society. Claims that it should drastically reduce paper work and office jobs did not seem to be borne out. The providers of stationery did not go into decline nor did office workers feel the pinch, though they had often to adapt to changed procedures. On balance, computers appeared to provide jobs, not only for the new ranks of systems analysts, programmers and operators but also for workers involved in the conversion of data for computer input. The information industry expanded rapidly and was hailed as the future economic heart of advanced nations—a position currently occupied by the automobile and its related industries, such as oil and steel. Organisations had tended to increase in size and centralisation and merging of business interests were thought, in the 1960s, to be keys to better performance, growth and stability.

The large, mainframe type of computer seemed ideally suited to the information processing needs of these developments. True, such systems might be highly impersonal, with remote and inflexible information stores, which came to be called data banks or data bases. Managers and ordinary private individuals would also become very dependent on the satisfactory functioning of equipment over which they had no real ultimate control. It was located in a new department, run by people trained in strange new skills and representing a threat to the existing organisational power structure. Batch processing could involve several stages of data preparation, the transport of punched cards to a computer site, the waiting until processed results became available, and the frustrations arising from not having access to updated information between computer runs. The newer terminals could effectively manage a massive computer many miles away. But what if the computer broke down, or its backing store became damaged, or the telephone line developed peculiarities, or operators went on strike, or too many other people were trying to access the same computer at the same time? There were horror tales of computing systems which had gone wrong or never even started. It was said that an organisation was sending out accounting statements to its customers with a computer produced slip asking them to "ignore the attached statement". Pensioners were frightened by bills for millions of pounds, while others were pursued with demands for less than a penny. The Swansea Driver and Vehicle Licensing Centre became a focus of critical attention and it was rumoured that the Government would develop no further plans for similar centralised systems.

The idea of the total computerised systems approach for business was pursued, but never really caught. The time spans and costs involved in realising such aspirations seemed to rule them out for practical business purposes, while they could also be viewed as contrary to the more adaptive management philosophies which emphasised the importance of individual and group contributions, and flexibility in the face of a changing environment. At higher levels of management, concerned with policy, decisions and appraisal of the future, disappointment seems to have hinged not so much on computer deficiencies in operating models but on the inadequacies of the models themselves, or perhaps from the exaggerated claims made for some of them. A dubious forecasting technique, for example, is not improved because we can apply it quickly and without arithmetic error. The most spectacular success was probably in the control of moon rocket projects, but here the objective was clear and the funds astronomical, though there was criticism that they might be better employed elsewhere. The technical spin-off from such projects could also be considerable, however, while human progress seems linked to inquisitiveness and ingenuity in developing what may at first glance appear as solutions to intractable problems. There seems little doubt that many early (and perhaps more recent) computer installations have resulted from such motivation and faith on the part of management, which has thus gained experience in using new tools. In spite of problems computing grew and flourished and the evidence was that it could provide a satisfactory service if managers and others made reasonable demands on it and learned to adapt.

As the 1970s unfolded changes became apparent in computing and in the economic and social systems in which computer systems operated. Remote terminal access to large computers was successful. Small and fairly cheap but increasing powerful minis and microcomputers emerged. In offices they threatened not only electro-mechanical equipment but also the older mainframe computers. Microprocessors began to be produced very cheaply and could be used not only as parts of office equipment but also to control factory processes and individual machines, while their incorporation in the products of industry, such as motor cars, could radically affect design and the demand for traditional manufacturing skills. By 1978 the microprocessor or silicon chip "revolution" had become of major general concern. The Government prepared plans to pump funds through the National Enterprise Board into a new company (INMOS) with the object of securing the British manufacturing base for very large scale integration (V.L.S.I.) chip production. The Advisory Committee on Applied Research and Development advocated a policy to make British industry aware of the significance of microprocessors and to design products using them. Study and training programmes for managers and designers were sponsored. The British Robot Association was formed with promises of Government help.

The economic and social impact could be serious. If we look back on the Industrial Revolution of the eighteenth and nineteenth centuries we see a picture of short-term social devastation following technical change. Perhaps we can learn something. The silicon revolution may reduce the amount of work in offices and factories. Along with a reduction in paper work there would almost inevitably be a falling demand for clerks. Typists may see threats to their jobs in word processing equipment. One effect of the increased mechanisation of offices is that they are no longer chiefly the abodes of "pen-pushers" but rather of machine minders who process data as factories process materials. Equipment may also be used intensively on a two or three shift system. Possible developments of the electronic business office are the subject of the section that follows. As far as computer personnel are concerned the prospects in the transitional stages look good, though there may be a reduced need for workers in conventional areas of data capture, such as punched cards. There is likely to be a heavy demand for systems analysts and programmers to help launch the new technology. The very success, however, of the new systems could have the, at first glance, peculiar effect of reducing the need for such specialists. Programming may be developed to the stage where the office worker and manager can easily cope with it, drawing up a tabulation on the computer system as easily as they can now sketch it out using pencil and paper. The extreme cheapness of producing pre-programmed chip memories, if they can be sold in large quantities, may also reduce the demand for special software. Standardisation as between systems could accelerate this progress, but this is a path business management has been reluctant to follow. It has always, theoretically, been possible to reduce the amount of *ad hoc* programming by encouraging organisations to adopt a common policy with regard to their data needs, format and processing.

From the organisational and administrative point of view developments in minis and in microcomputers tend to be associated with decentralisation of equipment, of staff and of decision-making. This is consistent with management thinking which advocates the inculcation of responsible attitudes and the making of decisions at as low a level as possible. The electronics industry itself has had to learn how to adapt management structures in the face of rapid technological change. It has been an area of opportunity in which some able people have been able rapidly to develop from scratch businesses which have challenged some of the international giants. As for managers, they will increasingly have to show that the decisions they make are ultimately not programmable (so that a computer could take over) and that the discretionary content of their jobs is substantial.

Production work may progress to automation, implying that human control can, to an increasing extent, be replaced by systems which go beyond the automatic and adjust themselves to take account of the variability in the situation they are handling or in the component they are processing. Work in factories will become more capital intensive (using more equipment and less labour). These ideas are not new. They were being propounded long before silicon chip microprocessors had been invented. Some of the early hopes came to nothing and Britain increasingly lagged behind its competitors in the acceptance of earlier forms of automation. The microprocessor may offer the means by which such a revolution can really come about and presents a challenge to many established social concepts. The fears of workers and of the union leaders who represent their interests can be readily understood. High technology, functioning properly, however, has the economic implications of high wages, shorter working hours, earlier retirement, more leisure and higher living standards. People have to adjust to change but like to feel they are benefiting from it and have some say in the pattern that eventually emerges. Perhaps the most unfortunate factors relating to the beginnings of the microprocessor age are that it coincided with a period of reduced economic prospects. The expansion and complacency of the 1960s gave way, after 1973, to recession, stagnation or very slow growth, to uncertainty, and to much higher levels of unemployment than had applied for the previous quarter century.

THE ELECTRONIC BUSINESS OFFICE

In the previous edition of this book an attempt was made to survey "conventional data processing equipment", implying equipment still being used which could not be classified under the heading of "computers". The trend has been for much of this equipment to give way either to machines of considerably more sophisticated design (often based on electronics) or to fully fledged computers which are available in bewildering variety of size, price, speed of operation and suitability for particular types of work. The term automatic data processing (A.D.P.) covers all mechanical and electronic methods of data handling, while electronic data processing (E.D.P.) is used to imply that the heart of the system uses electronics, as with computers. Some of the older equipment, such as that associated with punched cards, survives largely because it has traditionally been linked with computers to provide them with input or output.

Larger organisations tended to be the first users of computers. This was chiefly because early computers were very expensive and could only be employed effectively in handling large amounts of data. During the 1970s, however, equipment became available priced to appeal to much smaller organisations and designed to cope effectively with their reduced scale of operations. Such equipment was also of interest to large organisations who saw it as offering an escape from the centralisation demanded by large, mainframe computers. Processing could be dispersed or distributed between many centres. This change was aided not only by the development of small computers but also by offering terminal facilities on big computers so that they could be effectively used by managers in their own departments.

The automation of office functions seems likely to proceed alongside that of production and to face similar problems, such as those associated with displacement of workers and the need for retraining. Automation really implies that some, if not all, of the controls involving human judgment and expertise will be taken over by equipment. The term electronic business office (EBO) sums up this situation in which traditional office desks with their in and out trays or their typewriters may be replaced by "work stations" designed to link into a communication system. Filing cabinets may largely give way to electronically stored archives or data banks. Word processors can cope with much of the repetitive element in correspondence and text processors enable large volumes of text to be manipulated. Much of the routine associated with feeding data into the system, such as by punching cards or preparing tapes, may be eliminated by equipment which can recognise characters of the alphabet or numeric digits which have meaning to human beings. Networks for electronic communication will be expanded both within and beyond individual organisations. It may become as natural to transmit a letter electronically as it has been to use the telephone. Within such systems there can be a place for more humble techniques. It is perhaps easier to jot down a telephone number with a pencil ("graphite chip technology"?) on a piece of paper than to use a pocket electronic calculator with a memo device for this purpose. It is also easy for the eye to scan a sheet of such numbers. If, however, we wish them to be assembled in a particular order, or associated with other data, an integrated electronic system may be better.

The first impact of computers on business and its managers was chiefly in relation to data processing in the sense of dealing with numbers and the calculations involved with them. Alphabetic data and text tended to be subsidiary to this main function and were largely included to make data more comprehensible to human beings. This coincided with an emphasis on the need for numeracy, implying the ability to think and communicate in quantitative terms. Much of office work cannot be so expressed, however. Communications, whether verbal or using written, typewritten or printed media, including diagrams and other pictorial forms, constitute a very important aspect. It is this area that began to receive serious attention as the 1970s progressed, giving rise to the probability of an information processing revolution. Equipment became available which was relatively cheap, very effective, capable of being run as a decentralised system (distributed processing) and offering a serious challenge to increasingly expensive clerical and typing services. There were threats to long established divisions of work, such as between typing and typesetting, which had already become blurred by copying processes such as offset-litho. Single keystroking (implying that journalists can set up their own copy through terminals) became an issue. Mixed media systems seem likely to spread, in which computers are linked not only with terminals and visual displays but also with microfilm and other storage systems, and with reprographic equipment, facsimile transmission and voice communication networks. There seems evidence that the computer industry is realigning to reap the harvest of this integrated market.

COMPUTERS AND PRIVACY

Concern has been felt about dangers to private persons and businesses arising from the storage and possible availability of confidential information relating to them. Both the private and public sectors of the economy were the subject of reports in the 1970s.

The Younger Committee Report (1972), dealing with the private sector, could not conclude on the available evidence that the computer constituted a threat to privacy but saw the possibility of its being so in the future. It recognised the immense gains to human welfare which computers could bring. The following principles were advocated for computer information.

1. Information should not be used for purposes other than those for which it is specifically held.

2. Access should be restricted to those authorised to have it, for the purposes for which it was supplied.

3. Only the minimum necessary information to achieve a specific purpose should be collected and held.

4. With statistical data identities should be separated from the rest of the data.

5. Arrangements should exist so that the subject can be told about the information held concerning him.

6. The user should specify in advance the level of security to be achieved, which should include precautions against deliberate abuse or misuse of the information.

7. Monitoring should be provided to aid the detection of any violation of security.

8. A period should be set beyond which the data will not be retained.

9. Data held should be accurate and the system should provide for correction and updating.

10. The coding of value judgments (such as "fair" being replaced by a number) should be handled carefully.

The setting up of a Standing Commission, with members from within computing and from outside, was advocated, to keep developments under review and to make recommendations.

A White Paper on *Computers and Privacy* (1975) together with *Computers: Safeguards for Privacy*, dealt with the public sector. It claimed that no evidence was disclosed "to suggest that fears about the improper use of computers in the public sector are justified by present practice" and that substantial safeguards are provided by administrative rules and procedures. However the Government concluded that "there is need for legislation to be introduced to set up machinery, not only to keep the situation under review, but also to seek to secure that all existing and future computer systems in which personal information is held, in both the private and public sectors, are operated with appropriate safeguards for the privacy of the subject of that information". The principal potential dangers to privacy were seen to stem from three sources.

1. Inaccurate, incomplete or irrelevant information.
2. The possibility of access to information by people who should not or need not have it.
3. The use of information in a context or for a purpose other than that for which it was collected.

A Data Protection Authority (D.P.A.) was proposed with powers either to issue licences, subject to prescribed standards being met, or to investigate complaints, publish findings and make recommendations.

The Committee on Data Protection (chaired by Sir Norman Lindop) reported towards the end of 1978. It advised that a Data Protection Authority be established to safeguard individual privacy by vetting both private and public sector computer systems. A maximum of twelve board members, supported by forty executives, would prepare over fifty codes of practice, which would lay down detailed rules to cover any system for collecting, processing or storing personal information, where any part of the system is automatic. Such systems would have to be registered with the Authority, which would have power to refuse registration for applicants from the private sector. There would be powers of inspection. Failure to register and breaches of the codes would constitute criminal offences. It was recommended that certain criminal and national security records should be excluded. The general recommendation followed the well-established pattern that details stored should be "accurate, complete, relevant, up to date and no more extensive than necessary for the purposes for which they are used".

At the time of publication the Government announced that it did not propose to introduce legislation immediately as further time was needed for consultation with parties concerned.

Fears have been expressed from members of the computer industry that the wrong controls would impede technical progress and social acceptance of computers and that routine commerical data processing might be saddled with expensive registration fees and complex rules. Sensitive areas such as medical records, police files, credit ratings and national security systems might be selected for early treatment. An interesting clash developed between the Ethical Committee of the British Medical Association and the Department of Health over the latter's proposals to encourage the computerisation of medical and social information relating to young children.

The Council of Europe recommends that the following principles should be observed in the public sector.

1. As a general rule the public should be kept regularly informed about the establishment, operation and development of electronic data banks in the public sector.

2. The information stored should be:

(*a*) obtained by lawful and fair means;

(*b*) accurate and kept up to date;

(*c*) appropriate and relevant to the purpose for which it has been stored.

Every care should be taken to correct inaccurate information and to erase inappropriate, irrelevant or obsolete information.

3. Especially when electronic data banks process information relating to the intimate private life of individuals or when the processing of information might lead to unfair discrimination:

(*a*) their existence must have been provided for by law, or by special regulation or have been made public in a statement or document, in accordance with the legal system of each member state;

(*b*) such law, regulation, statement or document must clearly state the purpose of storage and use of such information, as well as the conditions under which it may be communicated either within the public administration or to private persons or bodies;

(*c*) the data stored must not be used for purposes other than those which have been defined unless exception is explicitly permitted by law, is granted by a competent authority or the rules for the use of the electronic data bank are amended.

4. Rules should be laid down to specify the time limits beyond which certain categories of information may not be kept or used.

However, exceptions from this principle are acceptable if the use of the information for statistical, scientific or historical purposes requires its conservation for an indefinite duration. In that case, precautions should be taken to ensure that the privacy of the individuals concerned will not be prejudiced.

5. Every individual should have the right to know the information stored about him.

Any exception to this principle or limitation to the exercise of this right should be strictly regulated.

6. Precautions should be taken against any abuse or misuse of information. For this reason:

(*a*) everyone concerned with the operation of the electronic data processing should be bound by rules of conduct aimed at preventing the misuse of data and in particular by a duty to observe secrecy;

(b) electronic data banks should be equipped with security systems which bar access to the data held by them to persons not entitled to obtain such information and which provide for the detection of misdirections of information, whether intentional or not.

7. Access to information that may not be freely communicated to the public should be confined to the persons whose functions entitle them to take cognisance of it in order to carry out their duties.

8. When information is used for statistical purposes it should be released only in such a way that it is impossible to link information to a particular person.

(Based on Table 9, Cmnd. 6354)

SPECIMEN EXAMINATION QUESTIONS

1. "The computer caused an upheaval in data processing but had little significant over-all effect until it was given a real competitive edge by developments in microprocessing." Critically discuss this statement.

2. Analyse the likely effects of recent developments in computer technology on business organisation.

3. Distinguish between "automatic" and "automated" and examine the role of computers and microprocessors in connection with each.

4. "You can't eat silicon chips." Comment on this statement as a summary of Britain's future employment problems.

5. The electronic business office—fact or science fiction? Discuss.

6. Assess the extent to which computers have tended to eliminate the differences between staff and manual workers and attempt a forecast of the future situation.

7. Discuss the present and possible future role of government in relation to microprocessor development.

8. Discuss the dangers inherent in storing personal data in computer systems and outline proposals for regulating such systems.

APPENDIX

AIMS

The following sections contain information not called for by some syllabuses but which may be regarded as background knowledge, helping the reader to feel more at home in a world of new and often puzzling terms.

BRIEF HISTORY OF DATA PROCESSING

A very early aid to calculating was the abacus, invented in India and named from the Greek equivalent of "dust", since early versions seem to have consisted of a dust-covered board on which columns and figures could be traced, and pebbles probably used for markers. The design of the modern abacus varies. The Russian abacus has, basically, ten beads for each rod. In this simple decimal form of abacus one rod would represent units, the next tens, etc. The first number is set up by moving the equivalent beads on each rod and the number to be added is then merged by moving the necessary number of remaining beads on each rod, shifting the whole line back when there are insufficient and moving one bead from the next higher line. The Chinese version consists of a number of parallel rods on each of which seven beads are threaded, five on one side of a dividing bar and two on the other. The Japanese version is the most economical of beads. Each rod has four and one, this latter counting as five, so that numbers up to nine can be coped with on each rod.

Early in the seventeenth century John Napier designed rods or bones to help with multiplication. Each reproduced, from top to bottom, one of the multiplication tables from 1 to 9. When arranged in the order of the multiplicand these enabled the user to read across at the appropriate multiplier values, shown in the rows, the values to be added into the total. Napier's development of logarithms, which enabled numbers to be multiplied by an addition process, is certainly more memorable. Though associated with the use of tables logarithms formed the basis of operation of the slide rule, where the numbers are placed along the scales at distances proportional to their logarithms.

224

The first mechanical calculator, laying the foundations of all later developments, was devised in 1642 by Blaise Pascal. This adding machine consisted of a number of wheels, each with ten segments, and connected so that a complete revolution of a wheel turned the wheel to its left through one segment. Another seventeenth-century machine was devised by Samuel Morland and consisted of wheels which were turned by a stylus inserted into appropriately numbered holes. This had no carry-forward mechanism. He also devised a "multiplying instrument" of sorts.

Towards the end of the seventeenth century Leibnitz produced an ingenious machine based on a number of drums to represent decimal place positions and with carry-over between adjacent drums. On each drum teeth were mounted, the number varying from nine at one end, reducing by one for each tenth of the drum's length, to give none at the other. A gear wheel mounted on a shaft parallel to the drum could be moved opposite any of these sets of teeth. Each revolution of this wheel would multiply by the equivalent of the number of teeth on the drum in that position. From these beginnings can be traced calculating machines, those of Thomas Colmar in 1820 and of Odhner, using wheels instead of drums, in the 1870s. An alternative approach, using a key for every value in every position, resulted in the William Seward Burroughs equipment, first exhibited in 1884 and popularised some years later.

Charles Babbage worked for ten years in the early nineteenth century on what he called an "engine of differences", considered to be the forerunner of modern computers. A small working model was produced but his designs for large machines were beyond the production techniques of his time and never went beyond the drawing-board stage. He envisaged the use of punched cards, as already employed in silk-weaving by Jacquard, for the input of data, and even his first model could print data.

It was left to Dr. Herman Hollerith to adapt the punched card principle to data processing. He was head of the American Bureau of Census and designed a calculating machine to speed up the work in 1890. From these beginnings developed the punched card industry, representing the most advanced form of business data processing before the advent of computers. The use of punched cards for computer input and output gave companies such as Hollerith and Powers-Samas an important stake in this new industry. James Powers was Dr. Hollerith's successor at the Bureau of Census. His company in the U.S. was acquired by Remington Rand Corporation, while Dr. Hollerith's Tabulating Machine Company became the International Business Machines Company (I.B.M.).

In Britain the British Tabulating Machine Company merged with Powers-Samas to become International Computers and Tabulators (I.C.T.) and, eventually, with further mergers, International Computers Ltd. (I.C.L.).

The first computer is generally considered to have been conceived in 1937 by Howard Aiken and produced with the co-operation of an I.B.M. team as the Harvard Mark I computer in 1944. Its full title was Automatic Sequence Controlled Calculator. Using electro-mechanical techniques it performed calculations at the rate of a third of a second for each addition.

The first electronic computer was produced in 1946 at the University of Pennsylvania and rejoiced in the name of ENIAC (Electronic Numerical Integrator and Calculator). Its prime purpose was to solve military problems in ballistics and aeronautics but it was bulky and not very adaptable, though it survived in operation until 1955, having been converted from panel-board control to stored-program control in 1947. This represented a major breakthrough in design, as modern computers all rely on the principle of the control being within the computer itself. This concept is generally associated with the name of Dr. John von Neumann, who worked with a team from the same university to produce a more versatile computer called EDVAC (Electronic Discrete Variable Automatic Computer), completed in 1950. Manchester University had developed a stored-program computer by 1948, under T. Kilburn and F. Williams.

A similar approach was used at Cambridge University by a team led by Dr. M. V. Wilkes, resulting in EDSAC (Electronic Delay Storage Automatic Computer) produced in 1949. This team, in association with J. Lyons and Co. Ltd. produced the first British commercial computer, LEO (Lyons Electronic Office) in 1951.

From 1948 general purpose computers were being produced in the United States by I.B.M. The UNIVAC (Universal Automatic Computer) in the early 1950s became the name of computers of the Sperry Rand Corporation, the result of collaboration between designers Mauchly and Eckert, who had been associated with ENIAC.

Computers became accepted for business data processing in the mid-1950s, a period during which a large number of computers were developed by universities and business firms. With earlier computers the tradition of devising names was followed, examples being MADAM, DEUCE, ACE, PEGASUS, HEC and MERCURY. This gave way in the mid-1960s to the use of series numbers, with series such as the I.B.M. 360 and I.C.L. 1900 becoming very well known, numbers or letters being added to indicate different models, speeds, storage capacities, etc., such as 1903A. Ranges of machines all became compatible within a series, and configurations could be suited to the particular requirements of users by provision of alternative forms of input, output and storage devices. Expansion of systems on a modular basis was offered.

The early valve machines (now referred to as "first generation computers") began to be replaced by computers using transistors in the late 1950s and early 1960s (termed "second generation computers"). Transistors resulted in the size of computers being reduced, as were the problems associated with the heating of valves (ENIAC had 18,000). Solid-state technology (based, for example, on transistors) can also result in reduced maintenance.

Printed circuits simplified the problems of wiring and microminiaturisation was developed to achieve high component density in what are known as integrated circuits. Film circuits used layers of conducting and insulating materials deposited on a carrier or substrate, while even greater component density could be achieved by semi-conductor circuits formed within single pieces of silicon. This is dealt with in the following section. Integrated or monolithic circuits, developing from the mid-1960s, gave rise to smaller and more reliable "third generation" machines. By the early 1970s minicomputers were becoming popular while microprocessors began to achieve real significance by the mid-1970s. At about the same time the typical form of storage was moving from core store to silicon chip semi-conductor store and the costs of producing the new circuitry dropped very rapidly. An early effect observed by the man in the street was in the great cheapening of pocket calculators, which also become much more sophisticated.

One of the most significant developments associated with improved computer technology has been the increase in speed of operations. From speeds of fractions of seconds with the earliest computers it has been necessary to quote in terms of milliseconds (thousandths), microseconds (millionths), nanoseconds (thousand millionths or 10^{-9} seconds) and picoseconds (trillionths of a second). The term "gigaflop" implies a thousand million floating point operations per second.

Considerable contributions are expected from bubble memories and from memory systems using lasers. An interesting development is based on holographic optical recording. Holography is a three-dimensional photographic technique. The holograph containing digital information may be stored on thermoplastics. Human and machine readable microfilm may be used. The technique employs lasers and offers great possibilities for data compression and speed of operation. Cryogenic, superconductive technology, operating at very low temperatures by immersion in liquid helium, may hold the key to a future revolution in computer design. Liquid nitrogen has been used to increase the operating speeds of silicon chips by several multiples.

SILICON CHIP TECHNOLOGY

The introduction of transistors towards the end of the 1940s was followed in the late 1950s by the very rapid development of an entirely new technology, in which transistors, resistors and capacitors, and their associated circuits, can be photolithographed into very small chips of silicon. These became the large scale integrated circuits (L.S.I.) and the very large scale integrated circuits (V.L.S.I.) that form the basis of the silicon chip revolution, when designed as microprocessors. The basic process involves heating silicon and adding controlled amounts of impurities or dopants (generally phosphorus or boron). The latter give n-type and p-type semiconductor characteristics respectively. From the molten silicon is grown a crystal, about 100 mm (4 inches) in diameter and a few metres long. This is ground into a cylinder and then sliced into wafers about 0·5 mm thick. A film of silicon dioxide (an insulator) is formed on this by heating in oxygen or water vapour. Another coat of light sensitive material is then applied, ready for exposure through a mask or by projection. The mask contains the circuit diagram of electronic devices together with their links. Where the light penetrates the coating becomes insoluble but the rest can be dissolved in hydrofluoric acid along with the underlying layer of oxide. More advanced techniques enable substances to be diffused and implanted at different depths in the silicon to build up a three-dimensional structure. Hundreds of circuits can be placed, by photographic reduction, on each wafer, and a batch of, say, a hundred wafers may be processed together. After processing, the individual circuits are tested by a probe. Faulty ones are rejected and the rest, when separated, form the dice or silicon chips which provide the memories, logic and arithmetic units, etc. of microcomputers. The chips have to be provided with electrodes to enable connections to be made. This can be done by fixing them to metal stampings, connecting the necessary leads, covering with plastic and separating into individual components. One version deposits them on Super 8 film from which they can be cut by users. The technology develops rapidly.

The design process involves deciding the architecture of the chip and converting from a logic diagram to its electronic equivalent. A large master drawing, which can be produced largely under the control of a computer and is at a magnification of several hundreds, is used to produce the mask.

It is no part of the aim of this book to convert business men and managers into computer designers. However, some terms occur frequently in the literature and may be conveniently mentioned. The basic abbreviation is MOS (metal oxide semiconductor). This is extended to n-MOS and p-MOS transistors and also CMOS (complementary MOS) devices which include both of these in the same unit. The latter require low power and are suited to portable devices. A technique using silicon on sapphire has been applied to their production. Transistors are of two basic types, Bipolar and MOSFET (field effect transistors). Speed of operation, packing density, costs and power consumption tend to determine which is used. Integrated-injection logic (I^2L) has been developed to give low power consumption coupled with a fair speed of operation and a high packing density.

BINARY ARITHMETIC

Most schools now introduce their pupils to this form of arithmetic. Readers who are unfamiliar with this mathematical basis of most computing should find this section answers their queries.

Various systems for recording numbers have been developed, such as lines and symbols. A favourite was the use of words, which became shortened to the first letter of the word, as in the Greek system, which the Romans copied. Our present number system seems to be derived from the Hindus, through the Arabs, and has the important characteristic of place value, so that the same symbol, say 6, means six or sixty or six hundred, depending on the position. The binary system, so important in computing, couples simplicity of characters (only 1 or 0) with place value.

The radix, or base, for counting has varied. The decimal base of ten has been the most popular, perhaps related originally to the number of fingers. Some units relate to the Babylonian system, using a radix of sixty, examples being minutes and seconds, while the use of twelve for fractional parts seems to derive from the Romans, and gave rise to dozens and inches. The use of the radix two (as well as eight and sixteen) is dealt with in what follows.

The binary form of coding data has been referred to briefly in Chapter 1. Binary arithmetic will now be dealt with more fully, though it should be emphasised that it is not necessary for the computer user to be able to handle binary calculations. These are suited to computers, the operation of which depends on high speed repetition of very simple calculating routines. For human calculations the decimal (or denary) system, involving characters from 0 to 9 and the memorising of tables, is much more satisfactory.

In the decimal system the value of a number is denoted by the character used (0 to 9) and its position relative to other characters. Each shift of position to the left multiplies the value of the character by 10.

In binary arithmetic there are just two characters, 0 and 1, the former implying that a position is not filled while the latter mean that it is. The position farthest to the right represents 1 and each shift to the left results in a doubling of the value. Numbers are built up as follows.

Binary values	16	8	4	2	1	Decimal equivalent
					1	1
				1	0	2
			1	0	1	5
		1	0	1	0	10
	1	0	1	0	0	20

It will be seen that the binary equivalent of 5 (101) when moved one place to the left gives binary ten (1010), and a further move represents 20 (10100). Each move doubles the previous value.

The addition of binary numbers recognises that $0 + 0 = 0$, $1 + 0 = 1$ and $1 + 1 = 10$ (which is "nought carry one"). The addition of 7 and 13 would be as follows:

```
 7 =        1  1  1
13 =     1  1  0  1
    _____
20 = 1  0  1  0  0
```

Subtraction may be performed as with decimal numbers, so that 20 minus 7 gives:

```
20 = 1  0  1  0  0
 -  7 =        1  1  1
    _____
13        1  1  0  1
```

in which, working from the right, 1 from 0 is 1, borrow 1 from the position on the left, in which $1 + 1$ from 0 is 0, borrow one from the next position on the left, and so on. Computers generally subtract by using the complement of the number being subtracted and adding this.

The complement form of a number is the number subtracted from some other number which (with decimals) is usually the power of ten just in excess of the number of digits being used (to give the tens complement form) or one having all the digits as 9's (giving the 9's complement form).

With decimal numbering, using two digits, 7 would have the 10's complement form of $100 - 7 = 93$ while the 9's complement form would be $99 - 7 = 92$. The calculation of $20 - 7$ would involve the addition of 20 to the complement of 7, giving $20 + 93 = 113$ or $20 + 92 = 112$, respectively. Since only two digits are available the hundreds figure is eliminated in each case, giving 13 (the correct answer) or 12, to which 1 must be added to give the required 13. The addition of 1 when the 9's complement form is used, is termed the "end around carry" method.

In binary arithmetic the same principle is employed. The 2's complement form may be used in which the complement is the number subtracted from the next highest binary number in excess of the allowed number of digits. In the case of 7, and using five binary digits (00111), we have 100000 (6 digits) minus 00111, resulting in a complement of (0)11001. Added to 10100 (binary 20) this gives (1)01101, which, ignoring the sixth position from the right, is binary 13.

A simple rule for finding the 2's binary complement of a number is to start at the right and keep the digits the same up to and including the first 1. All other digits are reversed, replacing 0 by 1 and vice versa.

The alternative complement form of a binary number is achieved by "bit reversal", replacing 0 by 1 and 1 by 0. Thus, using five bit numbers, the complement of 00111 (binary 7) is 11000, which, added to 10100 (binary 20) results in 101100, from which the 1 on the extreme left (involving six digits) is taken and added to the right (the "end around carry"), resulting in 01101, which is binary 13. Bit reversal is the equivalent of subtracting the number from one less than in the case of 2's complement form and is called 1's complement form. This may seem rather involved but it enables a computer to use its adding capabilities directly for subtraction.

Binary multiplication involves shifting the binary version of one number an appropriate number of places to the left, according to the position of the 1's in the multiplier. The results are added to give the product. Thus 20×7 involves multiplying 10100 by 111, resulting in

```
   10100    (no shift—multiplied by 1)
  101000    (one shift—multiplied by 10)
 1010000    (two shifts—multiplied by 100)
---------
10001100           (multiplied by 111)
```

It will be seen that 10001100 is the binary equivalent of decimal 140.

Binary division involves the reverse process. The divisor is placed as far to the left as is possible, without exceeding the number to be divided, and subtracted. This is repeated until there is no remainder, the number of shifts being counted, and giving the quotient when converted into their equivalent value. The division of 140 by 7 is performed as follows:

```
140 = 1 0 0 0 1 1 0 0
          1 1 1            4 binary shifts left = 16
      ─────────────────
      0 0 0 1 1 1 0 0
              1 1 1        2 binary shifts left =  4
      ─────────────────
          0 0 0 0 0  6 total shifts      = 20 (quotient)
```

So far only whole numbers have been considered. If a point is placed after the unit position then places to the right of this will represent, successively, values of $\frac{1}{2}$, $\frac{1}{4}$, $\frac{1}{8}$, $\frac{1}{16}$ etc. Thus 2·75 will be represented by 10·11 or $2 + 0 + \frac{1}{2} + \frac{1}{4} = 2\frac{3}{4}$.

The manual conversion from decimal to binary form can be performed by successive divisions by 2, when the final quotient and the remainders, read in reverse order, give the binary number. For example the conversion of 29, results in the binary form of 11101, as follows:

```
2 )29
   ──
2 )14 rem 1
   ──
2 ) 7 rem 0
   ──
2 ) 3 rem 1
   ──
    1 rem 1
```

The reason for this is that a remainder at the first stage indicates an odd number. At the second stage it indicates the presence of a single 2, at the third of a single 4, and so on. Conversion from binary to denary is by taking each 1 at its place value. Thus 11101 converts to $16 + 8 + 4 + 0 + 1 = 29$.

COMPUTER STORAGE AND CODING

This section (and the following two sections) develop certain aspects of data storage beyond the level of the earlier chapters and may be considered as additional reading.

The storage of numbers and characters has been briefly mentioned in Chapter 1. If a computer has words consisting of twenty-four bits then it can cope with integer values up to just over 8,000,000. With real numbers, which may have decimal parts, storage is normally in two parts. There is a mantissa (M), which is usually less than 1, and an exponent or power (P). A number is regarded as $M \times 2^P$, where M determines the digits in the number and P determines the value of these in terms of shifts to the left (P positive) or to the right (P negative). If two words are used to store a real number this makes forty-eight bits available, of which nine may be reserved for the exponent, leaving thirty-nine bits to cope with the mantissa and to indicate the sign of the number. The nine bits for the exponent (P) enable a power up to 111111111 (binary) or 511 denary to be coped with. Negative as well as positive exponents are really required (from -256 to $+255$) but these are all stored as positive by adding 256 to each.

The sign bit of the mantissa is generally 0 for positive and 1 for negative numbers, in the first position on the left. The apparatus used for the input of computer data will, in conjunction with the computer, provide automatically for conversion from normal decimal numbers to the binary form.

A popular system, referred to as binary coded decimal (B.C.D. or bini-ten), encodes each separate digit in binary form. As successive digits are read in those previously read are multiplied by ten, each time, and added to give the pure binary form of the number. This goes on until the end of the number is indicated by a space or perhaps a comma. As an example the B.C.D. form of 327 (using four bits) is 0011 0010 0111. The three would be read in first. When the two is read it is added to three multiplied by ten, $(0011 \times 1010 = 11110)$ giving 100000 (32). This is further multiplied by ten $(100000 \times 1010 = 101000000)$ and seven is added, resulting in 101000111, which is the pure binary form of 327.

Because of the lateral spread of binary numbers octal coding is sometimes used. The binary number is broken into groups of three bits, starting from the right, and each group is referred to by its decimal equivalent, which may be from 0 up to 7 (with binary 111). The number 327 would be split into 101 000 111, giving an octal coding of 5 0 7. Another way of looking at this is that it uses 8 as the basis instead of 2. Each shift leftward is the same as multiplying by 8. For example, $5 \times 64 + 0 \times 8 + 7 \times 1 = 327$. A hexadecimal (based on 16) form is sometimes used, where four bits are combined. In this form 327 becomes 0001 0100 0111, which is $1 \times 256 + 4 \times 16 + 7 \times 1 = 327$.

Many other coding systems have been devised. In the case of excess-three (XS3) coding, binary 3 is added to each number so that zero becomes 0011, one becomes 0100 etc. This has the effect of making the 9's complement of a decimal digit the same as the 1's complement of four binary digits but gives rise to other complications.

Codes must generally cope with alphabetic characters, punctuation and instructions such as "carriage return/line feed", in addition to the purely numeric values. The use of one extra digit to give a parity check on the correctness of punching has been dealt with in Chapters 2 and 9.

In connection with computer storage and operation, the terms parallel and serial may be noted. In the former case several bits are accessed at the same time, so that a whole unit of information is moved at one time, while in serial operation, which is slower, bits are moved one at a time.

ARITHMETIC AND LOGIC

This summary attempts briefly to show how computer circuits can achieve the results described earlier in the book. The terms used occur frequently when computers are being discussed and some acquaintance with them is desirable.

An essential function of central processing units is the handling of information available in immediate access store. This involves logical and arithmetical operations, which will now be briefly considered and which the computer simulates by electronic devices.

Boolean algebra (named after the mathematician G. S. Boole) is

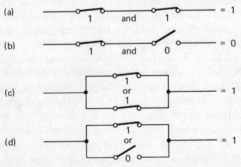

FIG. 69. Electrical switches simulating Boolean algebra (1 indicates current flow).

isomorphic with certain electrical circuits; that is, the statements contained in it represent symbolically what is occurring in the circuits (*see* Fig. 69).

Truth tables show the effects of the truth or falseness of two statements (or more with larger tables) when both apply (called the conjunction or "and") or when either apply (called the disjunction or "or"). The two statements, referred to as **p** and **q** may be combined in four ways, as shown in the following table, where T = true and F = false:

p	**q**	**p** and **q**	**p** or **q**
T	T	T	T
T	F	F	T
F	T	F	T
F	F	F	F

Obviously, the third column is true only when both **p** and **q** are true, while the fourth column is true if either **p** or **q** are true. Boolean algebra replaces T by 1 and F by 0 and uses symbols . for "and" and + for "or". The above table then converts to:

$$
\begin{array}{ll}
\text{AND} & \text{OR} \\
1 . 1 = 1 & 1 + 1 = 1 \\
1 . 0 = 0 & 1 + 0 = 1 \\
0 . 1 = 0 & 0 + 1 = 1 \\
0 . 0 = 0 & 0 + 0 = 0
\end{array}
$$

Switches may be used in electric circuits to give the same effects, if it is assumed that a switch allowing current to flow represents 1, while a switch that is open or off represents 0. The AND table is equivalent to having switches in series, when both have to permit the passage of current for the circuit to be complete. The OR table is equivalent to switches in parallel, where the circuit is complete if only one switch passes current, and the closing of the other does not affect this. These effects are illustrated in Fig. 69, where **a** and **b** are circuits in series and **c** and **d** are in parallel.

In computer circuits electronic devices replace the switches or gates as they are usually termed. Early computers used valves which tended to be replaced by transistors. The use of separate components in turn gave way to silicon monolithic integrated circuits, which could be mass-produced cheaply. Such circuits are produced on very small chips of silicon. Silicon chip technology is so important that it has already been described in a separate section.

The appropriate gates are assembled to give the logic and arithmetic results required by the computer designer. An AND gate reproduces the logical AND operation, its single output wire giving a signal only if the two or more input wires themselves are simultaneously activated. The OR gate gives an output signal if any input wire receives a signal.

The EXCLUSIVE-OR circuit produces an output signal if a signal exists at one, but not at more than one input. This is referred to logically as disjunction.

The NOR (Not **OR**) gate produces zero output when any input is present and a positive output voltage if all inputs are zero. If zero voltage represents 0 and a positive voltage denotes 1, then the effect is that inputs of 1 and 0 result in output of 0, while inputs of 0 and 0 give output of 1, etc. This can be called the INCLUSIVE-OR operation. If the interpretation is reversed, so that zero denotes 1 and positive voltage represents 0, the gate has become a NAND (**Not AND**) gate, resulting in 0 and 1 giving 1 and 1 and 1 giving 0 etc. The process of converting OR to NOR and AND to NAND is termed inversion (or logical NOT) and is performed by an electronic gate known as an inverter or negater.

The association of a positive voltage with 1 is termed positive logic while the converse, where a positive voltage is associated with 0, is termed negative logic. The term fan-in denotes the number of inputs to a single gate while fan-out is used for its output capability.

Logic requires bistable storage (sometimes called a binary, flip-flop or toggle) as well as a simple gate system. This is referred to in Chapter 1. Gates themselves may be interconnected in large scale integrated circuits to form memories.

The use of monolithic systems technology (M.S.T.) for main store as well as for logical and arithmetical circuitry gives a saving of space as well as a claimed inherent reliability and economy.

The application of circuitry to the simple problems of binary addition involves number and carry inputs and sum and carry outputs, if a full-adder is required. (A half-adder does not provide for carry-in, and two half-adders may be combined for binary addition.) Thus addition involves three inputs, the two bits being added and any carry-in from the addition of other bits to the right, while there are two outputs, the sum and any carry-out. For example addition of binary 101 and 111 will involve, working from the right:

$$1 + 1 + 0 \text{ carry-in} = 0 + 1 \text{ carry-out}$$
$$0 + 1 + 1 \text{ carry-in} = 0 + 1 \text{ carry-out}$$
$$1 + 1 + 1 \text{ carry-in} = 1 + 1 \text{ carry-out}$$

resulting in 1100. The appropriate logical gates discussed above are connected to inputs and outputs to give the correct result for particular combinations of input.

Computer design becomes very largely a matter of linking the logical building bricks provided by electronics manufacturers in a way to achieve required results economically.

There are two approaches to the handling of numbers in arithmetic. Fixed-point arithmetic involves the numbers as they would normally appear with the decimal point in its appropriate position, or scaled by moving the point a predetermined distance to left or right, whereas, in floating-point arithmetic, only the significant digits are recorded together with a power of the base of the number system. Thus, using decimal notation, the number 527·65 could appear as just printed in the fixed-point version, or as, say, 0·052765 when scaled four place to the left, whereas the floating-point version might be 0·52765 + 3 or 0·52765 E3. In floating-point arithmetic the numbers are standardised, often in a form so that the first significant digit comes after the decimal point and the power of ten by which this must be multiplied is shown as, say, +3 or E3. Negative values of this exponent enable small decimal numbers to be handled; thus 0·62 − 5 is the floating-point equivalent of $0·62 \times 10^{-5} = 0·0000062$. This system has a merit in that the register capacity of the computer does not become overloaded as it might by multiplying fixed-point numbers. Binary numbers may be similarly treated.

ADDRESSING

The particular part of the storage in which data is held is called its address. With high level languages, such as have been used for programming in this book, the problem of addressing is taken over by the compiler and the programmer knows that, when he uses a data name, such as A or X or STOCK, storage space will be allocated into which values may be placed or from which they may be withdrawn.

With lower level languages the actual location in the storage will have to be specified according to a code provided by the computer manufacturer. When the actual code number of the address is given directly (such as 7320) it is often called a specific or absolute address. Sometimes it is more convenient to identify the storage area relative to a base address or reference address from which a number of addresses may start. This is useful where the same set of instructions in a program are to be used on different sets of data, as with loops, or in the case of time-sharing or multiprogramming where the absolute addresses will vary according to the particular use of the computer at any time. To the base address is added an address modifier to give an actual address in a form such as

7000 + N. A more general form would be START + N, where the position of START would depend on what else was being stored in the memory.

MERGING AND SORTING ON TAPES AND DISCS

Magnetic tape sorting

Internal sorting (*see* Chapter 3) sets an obvious limit to the volume of data that can be so handled and rules out the method for use in many practical applications.

Probably the most important sorting situation arising with commercial data is when data is unsorted on *magnetic tape* or is in a different order from that needed and it is required to reproduce this data on magnetic tape in a predetermined order. This is often required prior to an updating run.

A standard approach to this problem is to write a program that will merge ordered data from two tapes and output the result, in order, on to a third tape. This program is quite simple to produce, involving reading a number from each tape, printing out the smaller, reading the next number on the tape from which the smaller number was derived, and so on. The reader should attempt a flow chart, remembering to cope with the situation where both numbers currently in store are the same.

This merge program cannot be used directly with the unsorted data. It is first necessary to read these in, dealing with one item at a time, and splitting the data between two output tapes, so that each contains groups of numbers in order, each group having an end marker. As each number is read it is output on to one of the two tapes as long as it is the same as or greater than the number previously read. When a smaller number arises an end marker is placed on the first tape, and the output switches to the other tape, on which it continues as long as the numbers are the same or rising. A smaller number results in an end marker being placed on the second tape and output switches again to the the first tape. This is repeated until all the numbers have been dealt with.

The merge program is then applied to the two tapes, merging the first groups on each tape, then the second groups, and so on. The results can be output on to two other tapes, which are themselves merged, the output going on to the first two tapes (overwriting them), and so on. Each run results in about half the previous number of groups on each tape, each group containing more numbers than previously. Finally all the numbers end up in order on one tape.

The process is illustrated below, using the data on page 75, shown

as on tape A, and ending, sorted, on tape D. Here E is used to indicate the end markers, and the order of numbers is from left to right.

1. Tape A	4, 1, 3, 2, 9, 8, 7	
2. Tape B	4, E,2, 9, E, 7, E	
Tape C	1, 3, E, 8, E	
3. Tape D	1, 3, 4, E, 7, E	
Tape A	2, 8, 9, E	
4. Tape B	1, 2, 3, 4, 8, 9, E	
Tape C	7, E	
5. Tape D	1, 2, 3, 4, 7, 8, 9, E	

It will be seen that this process involves four magnetic tape
decks, though it can be done, at greater length, with only three, if
the merged groups, at each stage, are first output on to one tape,
later to be split between two tapes.

Such sorting is a lengthy business, though the time depends on
the disarray of the data to start with. The time may greatly exceed
that involved in a computer updating run once the data has been
pulled into order.

Random access file sorting

The method of sorting disc files maintained on random access can
now be readily understood. Unless the whole file of data can be
handled in the immediate access store of the computer at one time
it must be dealt with piecemeal, dividing it into segments, each of
which is sorted internally and then written back to the random
access device. Repeated merging is then used until all the data is in
sequence. This is very similar to the process of sorting on magnetic
tape. It is, however, possible to use just the key numbers of the
records and a tag giving the record location. After this sorting the
full records are put in sequence.

SORTING WITH PUNCHED CARDS

Punched cards continue to be used extensively in connection with
computers. The following account of sorting independently of a
computer may still be of interest.

Cards are placed in the feed of the sorter and the column selector is set for the column on which sorting is to take place. Only one
column can be handled at a time. A field of several columns is
sorted one column at a time, starting with the least significant
(right-hand) digit. The cards each drop into one of thirteen pockets
or stackers (one for each of the twelve punch positions with one
extra for specially selected or unpunched cards).

With numeric sorting there is one pass for each column of the selected field. The first pass places, say, the cards with similar units-column figures in appropriate pockets from zero to nine. These are taken out in the stacking order and the cards are placed in the feed hopper and sorted on the tens column, and so on. A simple example with six cards having a three-column field is given, brackets showing cards in the same pocket.

Unsorted		Sorted on	
	Units	Tens	Hundreds
367	367	367	731
435	435	435⎤	621
621	422	731⎬	435⎤
422	621⎤	430⎦	430⎬
731	731⎦	422⎤	422⎦
430 first card	430	621⎦	367

Alphabetic sorting presents more difficulties. A digit selector can be set to ignore the eleven and twelve zone positions and the column is sorted as though it contained numbers. The same column is then sorted on the zones, resulting in alphabetic order. This is done for each column of the field, progressing backwards.

This standard method of sorting requires all cards in a batch to have been so processed before they can be passed on for subsequent processing. Waiting time can be reduced by sorting first on the left-hand or highest column in the field, setting aside all but the "zero" stack of cards, which are then sorted in the normal way, and passed on. The batch of cards from the "one" stack is then sorted normally, and so on. Obviously the "zero" batch will be at the start of the entire file, followed by the "one" batch, etc. This is known as block sorting.

The sorter can be used to select cards with a particular hole punched in one column. Special facilities may be available to extend this selection to up to eight columns at a time. This could be used with a deck of material issue cards to pick out all the cards relating to the issue of a particular material to a selected department. This is called group selection.

A card counting attachment, linked with each pocket, enables a count to be kept of all possible punching positions.

ACCOUNTING MACHINES

These machines go back to the days before computers. They were designed to cope with repetitive office tasks, such as sales and purchase ledger posting (with associated documents such as statements), updating stock record cards, payroll preparation (with payslips and tax records), building society and hire purchase accounts, etc.

The tendency is for them to be replaced by computers or for them increasingly to incorporate computer features. Readers may still find the following account of interest.

The book-keeping machine is a combination of adding machine and typewriter, generally automatically controlled as to the sequence of steps required for the type of posting run being performed. Jobs are usually done on a batch system; that is, similar jobs are accumulated until, say, the work for a week or month can be conveniently performed at one time. Such book-keeping involves:

1. picking up a previous balance (if any);
2. posting a debit or credit;
3. calculating a new balance from (1) and (2), involving addition or subtraction;
4. printing additional information such as date, type of transaction and reference numbers.

For convenience of operation the old debit page and credit page concept traditionally used with handwritten ledgers was amended to give adjacent debit, credit and balance columns. One posting is made on each line and the balance after each posting is calculated and printed by the machine.

A feature of such machines is the summary sheet (or proof-sheet or journal sheet) inserted in the rear feed of the machine. This moves on a line at a time, recording everything that has been entered during the posting run.

The accounting documents are generally inserted in a front feed of the ledger posting machine. With some models a wrap-round document, such as a statement, is lined up with its ledger account card and both are simultaneously produced, using carbon or no-carbon-required forms. In other models the statement and ledger card (backed by the proof sheet) are side by side; each has original printing by means of a repeat-printing operation (or a simultaneous print with dual print heads) which is automatically controlled. Statements, etc., will be headed prior to the posting run, perhaps using address plates. Continuous stationery may be used, with perforations along each edge, which are engaged by the pins of the feed wheel.

Dating devices may be constant, to print the same date automatically as required, or variable, keyset by the operator, to correspond with invoice dates, etc. Descriptive keys, usually giving three letter abbreviations such as CSH (cash) may be available as may full alphabetic keyboards; some machines are purely numeric.

Adding registers facilitate checks on postings done during a particular run. A pre-list is usually prepared from the source documents; this is a list of the amounts to be posted and is totalled. This may be directly compared with the register total for the debits (or credits) actually posted on the machine. An extension of this method accumulates the totals of the old and new balances, before and after posting; the difference should equal the pre-list total. This is suitable for low activity accounts, where by no means all the accounts have to be updated at each run. With high activity accounts the pre-list total may be added to the total of all old balances (where they are to be updated or not) and the result should agree with a proof-list total of new balances of active accounts, to which inactive balances have been added. Crossfooting is the term generally used to refer to double checking by accumulating column totals for calculations that are performed horizontally, line by line, and performing the same calculations with these column totals.

Checks are applied to test the accuracy of the pick-up of balances, perhaps involving a second reading of the old balance which clears the appropriate register. Verification of the account number may also be provided for.

The time wasted in picking up balances and verifying them can be reduced by using magnetic stripe ledger cards. These have one or more vertical stripes, similar to magnetic recording tape, on which information, such as balances, may be recorded electronically and picked up automatically. They can provide sophisticated calculating, information storage and print-positioning facilities, under control of a program read into the machine's memory, and are really similar to small computers.

Speed of operation is an important factor in deciding on equipment. Comparisons may be made on the basis of print speeds, including the speed at which skipping and column and line positioning can take place. However the hourly throughput of the types of documents for which the machine is to be used, together with the typical quantity of information to each document, is more relevant. With invoicing, for example, information as to, say, the number of four-line invoices that can be handled each hour may be available. The ease of loading documents and positioning them and also of

operating the keyboards, together with the presence of locking devices to prevent the wrong sequence being input by the operator, or
invalid code numbers, or impossibly large amounts, should also be
examined.

Index

Some of the chief words in BASIC and COBOL programming are shown in capitals.

245

Details of some other Macdonald & Evans publications on related subjects can be found on the following pages.

For a full list of titles and prices write for the FREE Macdonald & Evans Business Studies catalogue and/or complete M & E Handbook list, available from Department BP1, Macdonald & Evans Ltd., Estover Road, Plymouth PL6 7PZ

Basic Computer Science
J. K. ATKIN

This HANDBOOK is intended to provide an introduction to computer science, emphasis being placed on fundamental principles rather than specific details of particular machines and programming languages. The text is suitable for use at "A" Level, at colleges of further education and on first-year introductory courses at polytechnics and universities.
Illustrated

Case Studies in Systems Design
R. G. ANDERSON

This HANDBOOK aims to give students and general readers an insight into practical everyday problems confronting businesses with regard to the design of business systems. It is also intended to prepare students for the examinations of various professional bodies, Higher National Certificate and Diploma, and degree courses in business systems and systems design. The case studies used in the book represent a cross-section of typical systems currently employed in a wide variety of industries.

Data Processing and Management Information Systems
R. G. ANDERSON

This HANDBOOK, winner of the Annual Textbook Award of the S.C.C.A., provides a comprehensive study of the field of data processing, embracing manual, electro-mechanical and electronic systems and covering such topics as data transmission, systems analysis and computer programming. It is designed to fulfil the needs of students preparing for

examinations, including those of BEC, in data processing and computer applications and "... will also be valuable to those no longer concerned with examinations who require an understanding of the method and techniques available for the processing of data for management". *The Commercial Accountant*
Illustrated

Elementary ALGOL
ALAN BRUNDRITT
This book explains concisely the principles of the computer language ALGOL, and equips the reader to write simple scientific and mathematical programs. Students embarking on computer studies, in science, engineering and mathematical courses, will find it a most helpful introduction to the subject.
Illustrated

Elementary FORTRAN
T. M. H. PETERSEN
This book introduces the student to the FORTRAN computer language, gradually building up his knowledge and his ability to use it in solving problems with a computer. Several chapters deal in detail with the specific numerical methods necessary for writing simple but comprehensive computer programs. These numerical techniques are introduced progressively and demonstrate the principles and use of particular features of the FORTRAN language discussed.
Illustrated